Real
Port Talbot

Other Titles in the Series:

Real
Port Talbot

Lynne Rees

SERIES EDITOR: PETER FINCH

SEREN

Seren is the book imprint of
Poetry Wales Press Ltd.
Suite 6, 4 Derwen Road, Bridgend, Wales, CF31 1LH

www.serenbooks.com
facebook.com/SerenBooks
Twitter: @SerenBooks

ISBN 978-1-78172-652-5

A CIP record for this title is available from
the British Library

The publisher works with the financial assistance
of the Welsh Books Council

Printed by 4Edge Ltd, Hockley

CONTENTS

SOUTH

EAST

AFTERWORD

ADDENDUM 2021

THE POEMS AND THE PROSE

SERIES EDITOR'S INTRODUCTION

You could argue that if the industrial revolution still spins anywhere in Wales then it does so at Port Talbot. The town has a reputation as a place hazy with steam, smoke and smog, jammed between the railway and the sea. The motorway, on stilts, snakes right through its centre. The Inuit have eighty-four words for snow while in Port Talbot they have the same number for dust, or they did, before Tata modernised the steelworks. The town has a past vibrant enough to be celebrated in world histories but a future secure only so long as the demand for well-made Welsh steel continues. In this town you'd expect to find dark depression and blighted lives and perhaps, in the grimy horny-handed past, you once could have but not today. Today it's hard hats, hi-vis vests and clean air, apartments on the sea front you wouldn't mind living in and a beach with a golden mile, if you forgive the weather, to rival Marbella.

As you stand there facing the sea, taking care not to look left to the three graces and the great industrial shambles of port and blast furnace that run south east almost right back to Porthcawl, you could be on Gower. In fact you almost are – Mumbles is visible across the bay with its lighthouse and its pier, its pubs and its restaurants. And we envy them, a bit, but we stick to what we have, the two mile prom that is Aberavon, one of the great unrecognised joys of coastal Wales.

If that industrial revolution that still hangs in Port Talbot's air had never occurred then this place would have remained a market town on the Severn shore – Aberavon – a settlement addled by sand at the mouth of the Afan. But C.R.M. Talbot put an end to all that. It was he, Christopher Rice Mansel, along with his daughter Emily, who opened the first ironworks, brought the railway, developed the docks and encouraged other industry to cluster. Coal went out to the world from here. The Talbots made the port and they named the land. Aberavon, Taibach and Baglan may be well known names locally but in the wider world it's Port Talbot that sticks.

Currently Port Talbot, like most of once industrial Wales, is in decline. The steel they make at what was once British Steel, briefly Corus, and is now Tata, remains the town's sulphur-odorous backbone. Without the sprawling Margam plant there'd be nothing. BP Chemicals have come and gone. The docks have the largest turnover of any of ABP's south Wales operations. They service the steel works with bulk imports of iron ore and coal. They bring more stuff in than they take out, and by a considerable margin.

There's talk of change and of a new future. New power stations will be built. The Baglan Energy Park will enlarge. If the barrage gets built, slicing the estuary from Lavernock to Brean Down, then the port at Talbot will be well placed to capitalise. With its deep water, good transport links, and with some enlargement and a little investment it would be perfect to take the new generation of ultra large container vessels (ULCV). Those giant super whales won't fit at Barry nor at Cardiff. We'd only have to lose half of the Sandfields Estate to accommodate. But think of the jobs.

For a conurbation of less than fifty thousand inhabitants the town has produced more than its share of the well-known: Rob Bryden, Anthony Hopkins, Clive Jenkins, Andrew Vicari, Sir Geoffrey Howe, George Thomas, Ivor Emmanuel, Paul Potts, Michael Sheen. All men, you'll notice. There's more fame here per street than in Cardiff and Swansea combined.

In the list of Britain's crap towns Port Talbot makes no appearance although some wag has suggested that apart from Ron Evans' pies the best thing about the town is its close proximity to the M4. She's unclear if this is so you can arrive or leave.

That wag was certainly not the author of the book you now hold. Lynne Rees, who is, tells me that if you've left because you could no longer face the smog and the smells then now, as everything has been improved, is the obvious time to return. We're on a sort of Port Talbot odyssey – a walk from the east to the west, or is that the south to the north, from Margam to Baglan. It's a return home for her and a familiarisation for me. The sun is shining.

Lynne is a native. You can tell from her accent. She's a novelist, poet and haiku writer of some distinction. She's the author of the latest Real title. What you need for these alternative guides, psycho-geographies and off-piste handbooks is an irreverent but informed attitude, a zest for place, and the ability to delve. You need to look where you are not supposed to, know the difference between information and entertainment, and manage both. Lynne is an expert.

She originally left Port Talbot to work for the Midland Bank in Jersey. She got into writing as a fulfilment activity, sold a story to *People's Friend* and never looked back. Food is her big thing. She writes a weekly blog, The Hungry Writer, which mixes food and authorship in equal portion. "Are there any good restaurants in Port Talbot," I ask?

"You'd be surprised. I was. La Memo and Giovanni's in town are outstanding. And the Aberavon Beach Hotel does a mean Welsh rib-eye even if the dining room is more tundra with seating than intimate dining experience."

The circumnavigation starts at the far southern end of the Borough. Port Talbot begins down there in the SSSI wastelands where the Afon Cynffig dribbles its way through the Kenfig Burrows to reach the sea at Margam Moors. On the map it looks clean white. On the ground it's gasp and dust. These southern reaches of a four-mile stretch of heavy industrial smog land are cluttered with ash tip, coke waste, conveyor belts, smoke stacks, coal mounds, crushers, tanks and pipes. You can't imagine dowsers walking here and if there were leys once then by now they will have fused right into the ground.

If you are a local then access, disputed by the steel company, is down Longlands Lane behind Margam Crematorium. This is the only house of the dead with its own signposted exit from a major motorway. Tata Steel bought the plant from Corus and have plans for expansion, the building of new power stations and other facilities to further enlarge their already much diversified industrial empire. Despite considerable investment only the failing economy is now holding them back.

The way ahead may well look unwelcoming but we walk on. The path hugs the coast running along the stacked stone of the sea defence. To the east is the steelworks' Haul Road, a service road along which blackened trucks the size of moon launchers roll with abandon. To the immediate west is the sea. We are separated from it by a beach that most resorts would die for. Yellow, unblemished sand running flat for miles. Not a single person present. No-one with a dog. No-one digging for lugworm. No-one with a rod. We're below the Morfa coke ovens now. Rushes of smoke and fire emerging. Morfa colliery, the pit that was once worked here, may open again. Seams abandoned as uneconomic have become economic again. Tata have identified them, stretching out inland under Mynydd Margam.

As we approach the arms of the tidal harbour that grasp at the sea beyond the entrance to ABP's Port Talbot comes into view. The roads of the steelworks bend inland to pass mixed stacks of ash and waste metal. Beyond are the blast furnaces. Signs designate the Blender Plant, the Sinter Plant and the Burdening Department. The furnace mists drift. The singe of hot metal is in the air.

And then we are stuffed. A white pick-up with roof-mounted hazard lamps pulls over in a cloud of roadway dust. "You are on private land, do you know that? Can I ask what you are doing here?" I give him the full story, book, walk, research, which is undoubtedly reasonable. But it's clear that the camera is the real problem. With my bulky Nikon D90 and its long lens hung around my neck I can hardly claim to be just taking snaps. And with security there's the ever-present threat that they'll demand your memory card and trash it right in front of you. Yet Roger Maher couldn't be nicer. I get his name from the calls he makes reporting our capture to base. He offers to drive us on rather than back and takes us through the dirt-ridden and pipe-crossed roadways that riddle the works' centre. We are dropped above the Port on the safe public highway of Dock Road just south of the main railway station. En route Roger acts as an impromptu guide. He talks of hot slab-steel moving through the plant on carriers and of the blast furnaces being refurbished. He points out the site for a future wood-burning power station. He shows us the sand wharf and the control centre for port movements. Finally there's the demolition in progress for the building of Port Talbot's transportation future, the new five kilometre road link between the M4 and the docks. That deal is financed by Europe. Sometimes it pays to be in an area of comparative deprivation.

On foot again going down the north side of the Afan river there are brown tourist road signs directing visitors to somewhere called Hollywood Park. I've seen these signs elsewhere in the town. The array of symbols – crossed knives and forks, theatrical mask, cup, beach, historic building – make this destination look quite something. I ask Lynne what they mean but all she does is smile. "Best not to ask," she says.

Aberavon north of the river is in complete contrast to the smog belts we've just come through. What were once sand dunes that ran all the way to the River Neath have been levelled and transformed into a unique experiment in social housing. This is now a council estate of three thousand uniform brick and rendered dwellings. It was built after the War complete with lido and funfair and is fronted by a mile and a quarter strip of golden sands straight out of the brochure. At the height of Port Talbot's industrial fortunes, in the early Seventies, when the docks were new and the steelworks booming, the place was nick-named 'treasure island'. In the centre was once the Afan Lido but that was destroyed by fire in 2009. At the north end, unexpectedly for a holiday destination serving a local population of industrial workers and a hinterland of mining valleys, have sprung up an old people's home and a mental hospital.

The present centrepiece is just beyond the 1980s painted concrete whale and somewhat before you come to the million pound grass-covered mound known as the Telly Tubbies Toilet (a set of new millennium facilities complete with motion operated hand dryers that don't work in the Gents and ones with a sign that reads Do Not Dry Your Feet Here in the Ladies). It's the much-vaunted Hollywood Park. It's the 3-D Apollo Cinema, a boarded-up burger bar, a never-opened bowling alley and the Afan Lido reborn but now flattened Aquadome. Some grass. No one on it.

The front does possess two splendid pieces of public art. Both are by Andrew Rowe and reach for the sky as once did the steeples of churches. They stand as symbols of what could be if the future brightens.

At the northern end where the prom runs out are what remain of the Baglan Burrows. Beyond them Witford Point and the estuary of the River Neath. Here the town's industrial brackets close – the once sprawling BP chemical plant might have gone but its ghost hangs on. The area has been renamed Baglan Energy Park. It has a bright new gas-fired power station as its centrepiece. Full ground work remediation is in progress. A rush of Super Cannes-styled soft-shoed light industry replacements are already in place. But it's the size that stuns. 1500 acres of rusted railtrack and empty hard core. Fenced, double fenced, crossed by pipeline and rabbit warren. Waiting. Other than the family I momentarily glimpse in the distant bushes, blackberrying, there's no one about. Our route is a half official, half fence ducking, rail-track leaping and bramble dodging haul which emerges onto the brand new Central Avenue. This is where Baglan Bay, residential population zero, runs out. The end of the town.

But stay with it. *Real Port Talbot* which covers the whole enlarged conurbation is full of gems. Lynne Rees reports on the lost and the found, the past and the present, and puts the whole of Port Talbot into its glorious human context. It's an engaging read from a first rate writer. Read on.

Peter Finch

INTRODUCTION

Easter 2011. I'm in France watching a video-link of a scene unfolding on Aberafan Beach, a scene that alarms, intrigues and moves me. It's the first day of *The Passion*, Michael Sheen's seventy-two hour continuous-action secular passion play, backed by the National Theatre of Wales and a cast of thousands.

In one of his many interviews at the time[1], Sheen said: "Port Talbot has always been the butt of the joke. It is bypassed and overlooked by the M4. In this town you wake up every day and you have the message reinforced that there's nothing worth stopping here for. The chance for this town to get a fresh look at itself is really important."

That chance arrived when the play erupted across Port Talbot's housing estates, beach and mountains, attracting the attention of the national and international media, drawing thousands of people into the town to watch the live performances, and a worldwide audience for the online coverage. The play spawned a script, novella, documentary, feature film, an anniversary event – The Passion: Memory – in 2012, and a deliberation of Facebook groups. It ignited the enthusiasm and pride of a town and its people, reawakened a passion for accountability and change.

This positive and artistic attention was refreshing. In the sixteenth century, the agrarian village of Aberafan (part of contemporary Port Talbot's town centre), didn't score any brownie points with the historian John Leland (1503-1552) when he passed through on his great tour of England and Wales[2]. "A poor village," he said. "The ground about it is barren and sour."[3] The first sparks of the iron industry were struck in the area at the beginning of eighteenth century, with copper on its heels, but it was the building of the largest steelworks in Europe, between 1947 and 1953, that made Port Talbot synonymous with steel. And still today, despite the intervening sixty years and the plant's workforce hacked from 18,000 to 3,000, Port Talbot generally only tends to hit national headlines with announcements about the steel industry.

With industry came the need for housing: the sprawling Sandfields Estate was built along the coast in the 1950s, flattening a dune system that would, today, have been one of the UK and Europe's largest. This was where I was born and grew up in the booming 1960s: plenty of work around, the town's pubs and clubs shrieking at full capacity and the beach packed with locals and day-trippers during the summer. The subsequent decades delivered a different reality: strikes, industrial decline, unemployment, beach-front attractions left to crumble, and the estate censured more than once by the Crown Court for levels of vandalism, burglary and car thefts.

In 1978 Midland Bank offered me a job in their Jersey offices and I ran for the plane, delighted to be leaving, like a lot of young people from Port Talbot in the late 1970s and early 1980s. Three decades later I am running in the opposite direction, a combination of serendipity and the emotional legacy of age, to write about the place I have always called home. And it's not the place I left.

The summit of Mynydd Dinas, the most westerly of Port Talbot's three main mountains, is a good vantage point from which to observe Port Talbot. It still has one of the original triangulation pillars, or trig points: concrete pillars around four feet high constructed for the Ordnance Survey mapping of Great Britain that began in 1936[4]. From east to west, steelworks, docks and harbour, a welter of housing and roadways ensnaring a few pockets of green, industrial sheds and towers, all set against the sandy belt and grey-glimmering expanse of Swansea Bay. Today, the local authority's visitor website[5] actively promotes outdoor attractions:

Aberafan Beach, a recycled paragon of its coal dust and scum days, walking and cycling trails in the mountainous backdrop where industry scarred slopes have been restored through a combination of both natural and human intervention. But my candid observations of Port Talbot have also taken place at more urban levels: in streets and underpasses, village halls and chapel pews, amongst the rubble of brownfield sites awaiting development and in the face of new technology that is revolutionising Port Talbot's, and the UK's, energy consuming and producing industries. And in a proliferation of cafés, of which there are no shortage in Port Talbot, where I've drunk some of the best coffee in my life. And not a single Costa or Starbucks in sight.

Real Port Talbot is a record of the town I have met for a second time, a bit like a date with an ex-boyfriend: we're both older, a different shape and less worried about impressing each other. I've been surprised, angry, bewildered, humbled and convulsed with laughter by a cornucopia of stories. "Everything that made us, everything that made the town more than just bricks and glass and concrete."[6] More than the town's industrial heritage of copper, iron and steel, and much more than the M4's metaphor of indifference.

Lynne Rees, February 2013

notes

1. *The Telegraph Online* 20.4.11 http://tiny.cc/3n9crw.
2. http://en.wikipedia.org/wiki/John_Leland_(antiquary)#Itineraries.2C_ca._1538-43
3. Roberts Jones, *History of Port Talbot*, p.31
4. Davies, John, *Primary Trigs in Wales*, privately published ebook 2012. Amazon: http://tiny.cc/r1lzrw
5. http://www.visitnpt.co.uk/
6. Sheers, Owen, *The Gospel of Us*, Book Three: Sunday, National Theatre of Wales 2011

CENTRAL

ABERAFAN

Blanco's[1], where I'm staying, might be listed as a Port Talbot hotel but it's really in Aberafan – on the north bank of the River Afan within the arterial clasp of the M4 and the A4241 Afan Way. There's been some kind of settlement here since before the Romans tramped past on the Via Julia Maritima and dropped their loose change: roman coins were found during the ninteenth century excavations for the docks and on several occasions during the twentieth on Morfa Beach[2]. Port Talbot (pronounced Port Tall-but not Port Albert) was the name given to the new docks that opened in 1837[3] but the name was popularly used to encompass land on both sides of the river and the new borough of Port Talbot – which included the villages and parishes of Aberafan, Baglan, Bryn, Cwmafan, Margam, Oakwood and Taibach – came into existence in 1921[4]. The mongrelised Welsh/English Aberavon was retained as the name of the local parliamentary constituency.

Today's Aberafan is an eclectic conurbation of the good, the bad and the ugly. And the bewildering. Take Neath Port Talbot Hospital in the west: one of the biggest of all Wales' Private Finance Initiative (PFI) schemes at a build cost of £66 million. PFI schemes employ private contractors, to undertake projects essential to an area's infra-structure like schools, hospitals and roads, who are then paid back over decades by public authorities. They've been supported by successive governments since 1992 often with the argument that the private sector was more efficient at delivering services than the public sector. But private contractors are always going to have profit, rather than social benefit, as their primary goal and these contracts have created huge financial burdens for local authorities and ultimately the taxpayer.

The Welsh Assembly Government ruled out PFI in the healthcare system back in 2007[5]; too late for Neath Port Talbot Hospital whose repayment costs are estimated at over £300 million[6]. That figure might not be quite as alarming if, ten years later, the promised 270-bed hospital for acute medical emergency admissions, elective surgery, a 24-hour local accident centre, outpatient and children's services, rehabilitation and diagnostic facilities[7] was living up to promises. But after a decade of downgrades and cutbacks there's no A&E, no acute medical admissions and no doctors. That's right: no doctors. It's a hospital, Jim, but not as we know it.

THE GOOD, THE BAD AND THE UGLY

There's a five minute walk between sipping cappuccino in Blanco's glass and leather lounge and side-stepping the largest collective amount of dog-shit I've ever encountered at the end of Glyn Street in White City. That's not a name you'll see on any map: it's the south-east corner of Aberafan below Ysguthan Road where it curves around to meet Water Street. Why White City? A number of theories. *Because no white person would go there – it was a black ghetto. Because all the cottages were lime-washed many years ago. Because the whole place was filthy.* The ghetto theory is a ridiculous invention; the lime-wash theory carries the most weight. Though the ironic use of 'white' also rings true given the clank and smoke of tin-works, chemical works and gas works in this area in the nineteenth and twentieth centuries. And the dog-shit doesn't help either.

There were high hopes for the disused lot on the corner of Water Street – Farm Foods, the frozen food retailers, received planning approval back in 2005 – but there's been very little activity since and the place looks as derelict as ever. The local grape vine reports rumours about land contamination and a dispute over who's responsible. The idea of contamination is believable as this used to be the site of the Aberavon Burrows Tinplate Works which closed in 1953 after developments at the Steel Company of Wales made their work redundant[8]. The site was later used by the borough council as an engineers' yard and confusion over its name, Burrow/Borough, has reigned since, and maybe even before. Borough Street was built back in the time of the tinplate works.

It's in an alley behind Borough Street that I find the stump of an old gas lamppost but any excitement over uncovering this relic is soon wiped out by the contemporary reality of fly-tipping: car parts, ragged carpet, split bin bags, an old sofa and some stuff I decide not to look at too closely.

The back alleys are a legacy of late nineteenth and early twenti-eth century house building and in other parts of Aberafan they've been equipped with gates to prevent tipping and keep out trouble-makers[9]. The first alley gates were installed in 2008, with fifteen more in 2012: seven foot high, green metal, with keys for residents and emergency services, they've been successful in reducing house burglaries and general criminal damage. But problems with back alley vandals apart I reckon the earlier terraced streets of dressed

stone and brick, with a few boarded up exceptions and those suffering from tired pebbledash makeovers, are standing the test of time
a lot more attractively than the later 1950s builds to the west.

A couple of streets here – Fairfield, Fairview – remember the
twice yearly fair held under the old Charter of Aberafan. Others
take their names from builders and landowners, from the Aberavon
Harlequins RFC ground[10], and from the Welsh for rushes (Brwyna
Avenue), a memory of the moorland that once covered this spot. A
clutch of international reputations are honoured in Newton, Nobel,
Rhodes and Lister Avenues. When it came to naming a new enclave
of housing a decade ago, at the far end of Nobel, could there have
been a better choice than Blair Way? Answers on a postcard, please.
Read Arthur Rees's *Some Street and Place Names of the Port Talbot
District* for lots more stories.

Two contemporary monuments at either end of Castle Street
commemorate Aberafan Castle which Caradoc, one of the Welsh
Lords of Afan, had built by the twelfth century, probably of wood
if historical accounts of it being burned down are correct. His son
Morgan rebuilt it in stone[11] and it was one of their descendants,
Leisan ap Morgan Fychan, who, in 1304, issued a charter, the first
official record of the borough of Aberafan. Or, as he'd chosen to call
it, Avene, a name he also took for himself – Sir Leisan d'Avene –
which his English friends could have pronounced without spitting

at him. There's a Bailey Street nearby too, possibly another echo of the early fortification.

Local industrialist, Sir Arthur Pendarves Vivian[12], has a personal walk of fame in Aberafan (and elsewhere in Port Talbot) with himself and various members of his family immortalized in Vivian, Pendarvis[13], Dunraven, Adare, Gerald, Lilian, Lady Jane, Stair and Dalrymple. And then there's Rees Street[14]. In my dreams.

Back at Blanco's the quest for immortality continues. The lounge and bar are packed out: there are auditions for extras with Mad Dog Casting Ltd[15] in the Michael Sheen Suite upstairs. A new film, *One Chance*[16], based on the life of Paul Potts[17], the Port Talbot based tenor who won the first series of *Britain's Got Talent* in 2007 is being shot on location in Port Talbot in 2012 with a release scheduled for 2013. James Corden (Smithy from *Gavin and Stacey*) plays Potts; Julie Walters stars as his mother; and Jessie J. and Simon Cowell interject some celebrity glitz. Another agency, The Casting Network, offered the following encouragement on their website:

...we usually restrict some applications by size/build/hair length etc. This does NOT apply to South Wales Applicants. For South Wales we are looking for all shapes, sizes and ages – so don't be shy.

I suppose it can only be an improvement on *The Valleys*[18], MTV's reality TV show, that installed a group of libidinous, surgically enhanced, desperate-for-fame late teens and twenty-somethings from some distinctly valley-less parts of South Wales in a house in Cardiff. In the first series, Lateysha Grace from Port Talbot who's, like, 'fun and flirtatious, golden delicious,' did us, like, proud in her interview, like.

> happy hour
> her breasts the most
> upright part of her

Potts appears on Blanco's tribute mural in the hotel foyer. I also recognise Michael Sheen, Anthony Hopkins, Rob Brydon, Rebecca Evans the soprano from Pontrhydyfen, a quadrilateral-looking James Hook[19], and, by virtue of his autograph underneath, John Collins[20] in his Welsh International cap. As John himself might quip, 'It was painted when I was older.' If Blanco's owner, Clive Hopkins, who's been catering in Port Talbot since 1962, ever decides on a past celebrities board I hope he'll include the following two Aberafan men.

Ossie Morris[21] was born in Water Street, the same street as Blanco's, in 1906. He went to Sandfields School on Pendarvis

Terrace and by the age of ten had developed an impressive talent for whistling and mimicry. He began performing at the Liberal Club on Ysguthan Road and before long was earning as much in a night at local clubs than he did in a week at the Burrows Tinplate Works. In 1949 his performance on Hughie Green's *Opportunity Knocks* attracted national attention and he was invited to appear in the popular radio show *Welsh Rarebit*[22]. After only nine appearances he was appointed resident comedian, launching his professional career, and in the following years he topped the bill in variety shows all over Britain. When he was home, at 20 Gladys Street, he made sure not to forget his local audiences: for twenty-one years he gave shows for patients at Port Talbot & District General Hospital.[23]

He was only 58 when he collapsed after a show from a heart attack which was followed by further attacks he never recovered from. He died at the hospital where he'd performed so often on 7th April 1968, mourned by a generation of variety stars including Stan Stennet, Dorothy Squires and Harry Secombe.

Colin Spong Jones's biography of Percy Hunt is an entertaining and moving elegy for a man who espoused training and fitness, from his private gym at 15 St Mary's Street, half a century before 'work-out' entered everyday language. Hunt was born on 5th August 1891 and his diminutive stature – 4ft 11in – and his childhood brush with TB may well have been the catalysts in his quest for fitness. He joined the Health & Strength League[24] in 1907 and was an early supporter of 'Maxalding', a technique of muscle control and development created by German strong men and physical culturists Max Sick and Monte Saldo around 1909.[25] In 1914 he was awarded a Gold Medal for Physical Development in London just before volunteering for World War I. But his fame in South Wales arose from his stage athlete performances as The Great Mavello, a name adapted from 'marvellous' but deliberately misspelled to avoid confusion, and possibly any copyright problems, with 'Marvello' a popular analgesic ointment of the day.

He opened his Health & Strength gym in 1920 and continued to consolidate his stage persona with shows in workmen's halls, YMCAs, miners' institutes, welfare clubs and variety theatres. His act consisted of 21 feats including, 'A 12 Stone Man Jumping off a Chair onto My Stomach' and 'Showing Winston Churchill's Face in My Abdominal Muscles'[26]. In true Variety spirit he closed with a tenor solo.

In 1936 he won Health & Strength's competition for Best

Developed Man in Great Britain over forty. Twenty years later he was voted the Fittest Old Age Pensioner in Wales by the Welsh National Physical Culture Association.

Spong Jones knew Percy Hunt. His book opens with an evocative account of his first visit to the gym as a sixteen-year-old in 1953 and this intimacy deepens the pathos of the closing sections. In 1962 Hunt was 71. His 1920s' Health & Strength ideals were looking outmoded in the light of modern fitness ideas and new sporting premises. But given the contribution he'd made to health and fitness in the town, and in Wales, many people expected to see the veteran athlete on the guest list for the star-studded charity event, Cavalcade of Sport and Midnight Cabaret, at the steelworks in January 1963. Percy reminded one of the masters of ceremonies, D. Bryn Thomas, a Port Talbot business man and local celebrity in his own right[27], of the support he'd previously shown for Percy in his weekly newspaper column, lamenting the fact that "great men are rarely recognised in their own countries"[28]. But here he was not even being recognised in his own town. Thomas's excuse was said to have been that Percy didn't easily fit any specific sporting category. Fifty years later the excuse still sounds hollow and the *Port Talbot Guardian* came to Percy's defence with their headline, 'No Invitation for 'Grand Old Man''[29].

When Mr & Mrs Great Britain was held at the Afan Lido in October 1971, a show whose star attraction was Mr Universe 1970, Arnold (soon to be Schwarzenegger) Strong, Percy felt sure he'd be admitted if he turned up at the venue, despite not having received an official invitation. But the compere, one of his former students, tried and failed to find him a complimentary ticket. An inexcusable 'lack of grace'[30] from the organisers.

Percy died in 1977 and was buried at Holy Cross churchyard, Taibach.

I walk past 15 St Mary's Street and along the alley at the back. It's an ordinary house, an ordinary alley. But it wouldn't be too late to change that with some small plaque celebrating an extraordinary man who was a trail-blazer for health and fitness in our town. Would it?

I don't think many people stay at Blanco's for the view: a car park on two sides and hugging the perimeter of the town's by-pass roads. But they do come here for a comfortable night's sleep, free wi-fi and the breakfasts, in particular the Eggs Benedict with Welsh bacon.

The yolk of a freshly poached egg bursting into a velvety hollandaise is a thing of beauty. Less beautiful, in my opinion, is the 24hr McDonald's just up the road.

Big Mac, Large Fries, Full Bean Freshly Ground Coffee, Breakfast Wrap, Galaxy Caramel McFlurry. I'm not pondering the menu; I'm reading the litter blown along Green Park[31], the road that runs from the rear of Blanco's, along the side of the Craddock Arms[32] to McDonald's at the other end of Water Street. The McDonald's site and immediate surroundings are squeaky clean but I still hold them responsible for putting disposable packaging in the hands of wandering egits. It wasn't a litter protest, however, that made a Port Talbot man ram his car into McDonald's in 2011[33]. He was annoyed because they wouldn't serve him at the drive-thru hatch even though he was on foot. Why didn't he take his car into the drive-thru? The eight pints of lager probably had something to do with it. When staff told him to order in the restaurant he went to get his car, parked it on the kerb and walked back to the drive-thru hatch (you can't fix stupid) to make another fuss at which point they, understandably, refused to serve him anywhere.

"You'd better move yourself, I am coming in. Even if I've got to ram these doors down, I am coming in." That's the voice of a man desperate for a McDonald's.

What a lot of people chowing down on their burgers here don't realise is that McDonald's is built on the site of the old town abattoir. The delivery of animals became more circumspect in later years but older people still remember herds of cows being driven down Water Street, the lowing and clatter of hooves, the smell of piss and fear rising into the air from their hides. Would you like fries with that?

THE CHURCH OF ST MARY

It's a pretty Victorian church[34] but you're best viewing it up-close because from a distance, in nearly every direction, it's mauled by the Heilbronn Way[35] flyover. Lorna Beckett, Church Warden at St. Mary's, part of the Benefice of Aberavon,[36] gives me an enthusiastic welcome to the surprisingly light-filled interior. Jackie Radford, from Cefn Cribbwr, is also there researching for her book on the impressively industrious Marmaduke Tenant (1837-1915), Town Clerk, JP, Clerk to the Magistrate, Town Solicitor, Church Warden and serving Grand Master for 38 years. It was his Freemasonry brethren who installed a showy brass plaque in his honour in 1916, beneath one of the stained glass windows.

Lorna also points out the hidden compartment in a wooden sill on the south wall of the sanctuary containing a twelfth century *piscina*[37] (which looks irreverently like a commode when you lift the wooden lid) and points out the Calvary[38] and Floriated[39] Cross headstones in the entrance, evidence of a church on this site since at least 1199 when a chaplain is mentioned in the Margam Abbey Deeds.[40]

St Mary's churchyard cemetery had hit full capacity for burials by 1870 and the church's patron, Griffith Llewellyn of Baglan Hall, donated land for a second burial ground between it and St. Joseph's Catholic Church. If you look above the entrance gate you'll see the dedication to him engraved in the cast iron archway and the empty hexagonal bracket that used to hold a coal gas lamp. Emily Talbot, of Margam Castle, gifted a further three quarters of an acre to the site in 1906.

The churchyard cemetery was officially closed in October 1871 and the first body interred in the new graveyard on November 6th was Emily Schreiber, age 3. Six weeks earlier the Burial Register had recorded the burial of Balbina Schreiber, age 26 and new born,

William, whose recorded lifespan of a quarter hour snaps at the breath in your throat.[41]

There's a Celtic stone cross, not far from the church door, where you'll occasionally see a small wreath or wilting posy. This is the memorial gravestone of Richard Lewis, more familiar as Dic Penderyn. Lewis, who was born in Aberafan in 1808 in a thatched cottage called Penderyn[42], moved to Merthyr, the principal iron manufacturing centre of the Industrial Revolution, with his family when he was eleven years old.

By 1831 he was working as a miner, the year of the Merthyr Rising[43], an iconic event in Welsh industrial history. For six days in June 1831 thousands of protesters, calling for reform, higher wages and better standards of living, took to the streets of Merthyr, ransacked public buildings and besieged magistrates and local industrialists in the Castle Hotel. On 3rd June soldiers were sent in and by the time the authorities had regained control at least 24 members of the public had been shot dead and 16 soldiers injured.

Private Donald Black was one of those soldiers, stabbed in the leg with a bayonet, and Dic and Lewis Lewis, the main leader of the revolt, were accused of the attack. Black's injuries weren't fatal, he couldn't identify his attacker and there was no evidence that Dic had played any significant role in the riot yet both men were sentenced to death. The people of Merthyr signed an 11,000 strong petition and along with the *Cambrian* newspaper demanded his release. Joseph Tregelles Price, the Quaker ironmaster from Neath, tried to intervene on Dic's behalf but it seems the home secretary at the time, Lord Melbourne, wanted a scapegoat and a deterrent against further unrest. Twenty-three year old Dic Penderyn was hanged at Cardiff on 13th August 1831 and brought back to Aberafan to be buried.

Lewis Lewis had his sentence commuted to transportation thanks to the testimony of a special constable who Lewis had shielded during the riot. In 1874 a Cwmafan man, Ieuan Parker, admitted to stabbing Black and fleeing to America[44].

It's alleged that Dic's last words were, "Oh Arglwydd, dyma gamwedd/ Oh Lord, this is iniquity" and his martyrdom and that passionate exhortation have inspired authors and songwriters, among them the novelist Alexander Cordell[45] and Welsh singer/songwriter Martyn Joseph[46] whose lyrical ballad haunts you long after the last bars.

ABERAFAN SHOPPING CENTRE

I'm buying Welsh cheese, Perl Wen[47] from a stall on the ground floor of the shopping centre, in between Barista's café and the kiosks for The Fragrance Shop and Go Mobile. There's not a lot of room here and this is a small 'circle the wagons' kind of set up: the sellers bounded on all sides by trestle tables. I'd like to call it a market but I don't think four stallholders constitute one. And anyway, any mention of 'market' in Port Talbot tends to raise the hackles of people over the age of fifty, mine included.

The shopping centre, a giant concrete rubric rectangle belonging to the neo-brutalism school of architecture, is named after the old town. There's virtually nothing left of that since town planners wiped out a century of architectural, social and retail history in the 1960s and early 1970s, including the Municipal Buildings that housed a shopping arcade, town clock and the old covered market building, built in 1908.

My memories of Aberafan post-1971 are vague even though I didn't move away until 1978. When I think back it's always this area of town that comes to mind: the arcade and market, Woolworths to one side, the Prince of Wales Hotel opposite, Oliver's shoe-shop in Water Street where my mother took me to buy my school shoes, the short cut past the back of the Walnut Tree Hotel, with its smoky glass windows engraved with a tree in full leaf, to the corner of David Evans on the High Street. And that's just a handful of buildings imprinted on my mind: the full list of casualties would fill a page and some.

The loss of the old market building feels particularly sad, perhaps because an appreciation of markets and farmers' markets has been growing in recent years. And for the atmosphere these old markets seem to retain: a kind of stillness that exists above the bustle and noise of crowds, something in the air that might even transcend time.

> market stall
> buying the smell
> of tomatoes

There was a market on both floors of the shopping centre when it first opened but the stalls were small and cramped. The market subsequently moved to a purpose built annexe near the bus station, now B&M Stores, but most traders had difficulty meeting the rents. Port Talbot Library is now installed on the shopping centre's upper floor after being a serial squatter in its own town for years. The old Aberafan Library, as you might have guessed, was pulled down with High Street in its entirety.

Don't get me wrong: I'm not against modernisation, just against modernisation that dismisses and obliterates a community's heritage. It's true that the traffic congestion on the A48 through the town, considered to be one of the worst bottlenecks in the country, and exacerbated by the Rhondda and Swansea Bay Railway level crossing on the south side of Aberafan Bridge, had to be resolved somehow but both reason and emotion tell me it wasn't necessary to destroy so much of the old.

There's a popular refrain to be heard on the streets of Port Talbot, and I've sung it myself: "There's not a single decent shop. You can't buy anything here". Then one day last Spring I arrived at the shopping centre with a list and managed to tick off all ten items within forty-five minutes: a laundry bag, a small rucksack, a no-frills mobile phone, 7 pink balloons, wool to knit a mouse's tail, a make-up mirror, a cushion for lumbar support in the passenger seat of mam and dad's car, some black high-heeled shoes to wear with trousers, £50 cash and a good coffee. I'll admit to the list's original-ity but it struck me over my café latte in Barista's that I'd just been repeating what I thought I believed.

When people complain about the impoverished shopping what they really mean is there's no Marks & Spencer, no Next or Debenhams, no Monsoon or Gap. But they're the kind of shops I hit like the SAS: in and out as quickly, and with as little collateral damage to my patience, as possible. So Aberafan Shopping Centre, on the inside at least, is my kind of mall. Yes, a lot of the shops cater for the cheaper end of the retail market: Wilkinsons, B&M Stores, New Look and Argos but everyone likes a bargain, don't they? When a new 99p shop opened last year, in competition with Poundland, someone on Facebook wisecracked: "I'm going to save myself a fortune!"

Ever since my successful shopping spree I've become more attached to the Centre, something that Kay Rees, the Centre's Promotions Manager, is pleased to hear as she works hard to make it a part of the community. Fashion and dance shows, circus and craft workshops all pop up here during the year. Lower Dyffryn

School, Margam, celebrated their centenary with a display of pupils' artwork in July 2012. The following September local artist Bert Evans[48], whose paintings inspired by *The Passion* led to Michael Sheen becoming one of his collectors, had an exhibition of his oils and watercolours. The ground floor was where the flayed and ridiculed Sheen, as The Teacher in *The Passion*, was tended by the town's women in 2011. On its anniversary, Easter 2012, the upper floor was transformed into a gallery of artwork and memories while Sheen spoke to the BBC below about how *The Passion* and its effect on the town was, "incredibly moving... a community remembering itself."[49]

Kay's always happy to listen to local people's ideas and requests. She listened to mine and then sent me off with Lee Rogers, the Deputy Manager.

I don't imagine that the unprepossessing doorway opposite Argos in the West Mall gets paid a lot of attention but this door unlocked evenings of delicious sophistication in the late 1970s: this was the entrance to the Troûbadour nightclub. It reinvented itself over the years, as Raffles and Wall Street, but has fallen on less glamorous times and is currently used as a storage area for cleaning equipment and the centre's Christmas decorations.

The red staircase still engenders a frisson of excitement as I follow Lee down into the club but as much as I want to re-experience those heady nights of crème de menthe and lemonade and Thelma Houston singing 'Don't Leave Me This Way' neither the club or I are able to resurrect even a faint echo of times past. I'm tempted to head for the Ladies to see if a whisper of Charlie perfume remains in the air but there's only so much disappointment a girl can take. Was it always this small?

THE CIVIC CENTRE

Princess Anne, who officially opened the shopping centre in 1976, returned for a repeat performance at the Civic Centre in 1989. The Princess Royal Theatre takes up the right wing while in the left you can query your housing benefit and council tax, get your taxi re-licensed or, if you're stuck for something to do on a Tuesday afternoon, earwig on the Council's planning meetings in the upstairs chamber. It's also where disabled drivers or passengers can apply for their Blue Badge, a process I am intimately familiar with because in 2012 the interviews took place in reception, the acoustics of which generously share information about permanent limps, numbness and medication with anyone else sitting there. If there was ever an opportunity to shout 'Get a room' at a council employee this would be it.

I was unwillingly eavesdropping on the lives of the disabled while I waited for my appointment with The Leader. It was delayed by the local elections but The Leader was re-elected and The Leader had now agreed to see me. It could be just me but I started to wonder if the town was in the grip of a North Korean dictatorship rather than a Representative Democracy.

The Leader is Cllr. Ali Thomas, veteran of local politics, ex-miner, Welsh speaker and occasional Father Christmas. He's one of 52 Labour councillors, out of 64 in total, at Neath Port Talbot County Borough Council, formerly Port Talbot Borough Council, formerly The Borough of Afan, formerly the Borough of Port Talbot. Glamorgan and West Glamorgan County Councils squeezed in there too. Local government does like its reorganisation.

Ali Thomas is a man of presence: forty years working on the coal face must contribute to your strength of character as does a quadruple heart by-pass and still working a nine hour day at the Civic Centre. When I ask him what qualities a good councillor needs, he says, "Listening. And being broad-minded. Avoid parochialism." Which, on the face of it, are admirable assets. But when I ask about the council's decision to demolish the Port Talbot Railway and Docks Company building on Talbot Road and he says it was part of cleaning up the town I decide that an element of parochialism would have been a good thing in that case. Cllr. Thomas is the candidate for the electoral ward of Onllwyn which, in the Neath Port Talbot constituency, is about as far away as you can get from Port Talbot town.

The application for affordable housing on this site, submitted by Coastal Housing, that wove its way through Planning between 2009 and 2011 was discreetly entitled 'Former Royal Buildings, Talbot Road' and concerned three buildings near the railway station between Eagle Street and Beverley Street: the Port Talbot Railway & Docks Company offices built in 1897, Custom House built in 1903, and Royal Buildings that popped up sometime in between. The red brick and neo-classical decorations of Royal Buildings were, at least superficially, in a state of disrepair, and the merits of refurbishment might have been open to debate, but the dressed

stone of the PTR&D Company building and Custom House, fronting Eagle Street, was a testament to the quality of their design and construction. Both these buildings, arguably the most important remaining fragments of Port Talbot's industrial heritage, were funded largely by Emily Talbot of Margam Castle after the passing of the Port Talbot Railway & Docks Act 1894. The Act led to the expansion of the docks her father had built in 1837, and the construction of railway links between them and the South Wales valleys' collieries transformed Port Talbot into a major coal exporter of national importance.

Campaigner Ian Shakeshaft championed the retention of these buildings for over two years. In 2011 he questioned the council's claim that they'd fully consulted Cadw who could only find an enquiry about Royal Buildings. After a further consultation Cadw declared they were still unable to list the buildings but confirmed they "contribute greatly to the appearance of the area and they are locally important for how they help to define the distinctiveness and historic character of the Talbot Road"[50]. Ian also contacted Huw Lewis, Welsh Assembly Government Minister for Housing, Regeneration and Heritage, who said he recognised the contribution the buildings made to the historic character of Port Talbot but couldn't intervene in a local matter. Bethan Jenkins, Plaid Cymru

AM for South Wales West also made several passionate pleas to Mr
Lewis at the Senedd but he still refused to get involved.

The argument to, at least, retain the dressed stone façade was
also dismissed: Coastal Housing had already done their maths
around earlier talks with the council who were always supportive of
demolition. Councillors on the planning committee were also
categorically informed that if Coastal didn't get the planning
permission then Welsh Assembly Government funding would be
reallocated, not ring-fenced for Neath Port Talbot who could lose
out on a significant regeneration project: £5.8 million with a grant
value of £2.7 million[51]. Well, if you put it like that...

And my point about parochialism? Sometimes limiting your view
to the local area highlights what's irreplaceably important to that
community. Only two councillors, out of around forty who
attended the Planning & Development Control Committee
Meeting in February 2011, replied to my email asking what pressing issues, for them, over-rode the buildings' historical significance.
It seems they were the only two who opposed the application.[52]

So despite the Local Development Plan's aims "to build communities that are sensitive to the cultural and historic environment, the
distinct identity and character of communities"[53] by the end of 2012
we were looking at a building site and by the time you read this
there'll be a "vibrant and quality redevelopment" with "positive
impact upon the street scene"[54]. No need to worry that there'll only
be 27 off-street parking spaces when current parking standards
require 55[55]: there's a "robust travel plan"[56] in place. But doesn't the
LDP[57] say that vehicle ownership is increasing in Neath Port Talbot?
What's that smell? For once it isn't the sulphur from the steelworks.

The clearance on this site was only a fraction of the area of
Aberafan cleared for the shopping centre over forty years ago and
it was this blitzkrieg approach to rebuilding and modernisation that
Bob Dumbleton explored in *The Second Blitz*. The damage to the
town's historical heritage was an obvious effect but before reading
his book I hadn't properly considered the social damage to people
who lost their community – their homes, pubs, cafes, churches,
shops and clubs – and who were subsequently locked out of their
replacement town when the centre closed at night. *Dyma gamwedd*,
as Dic Penderyn said.

A more insidious by-product of the town centre development
project was the "gloomy and seedy story of corruption"[58] that

followed. In 1980, two former Mayors and magistrates were given suspended sentences of 15 and nine months for conspiring to commit corruption[59]. Andrew Scott (Civil Engineers) Ltd were fined £250,000 and a quantity surveyor, retained by Scott and the council, was fined £4000 and given a six month suspended sentence. These were the last in a series of corruption charges to be brought in a police investigation that started in 1974. One other key figure in the investigation, a Port Talbot architect, managed to avoid the police by fleeing to Majorca.

Bob Dumbleton's book, despite being written in the late 1970s, highlighted an aspect of town planning that's still relevant today: how major projects, by virtue of the huge investments and grants involved, funds that local authorities generally don't possess, can so often be developer driven. Councils "get used to the definition of progress and prosperity that the developers have touted."[60] Port Talbot is facing another major redevelopment programme on its disused dockland and other brownfield sites. Current plans indicate significant consideration for local people: new schools, colleges and sports venues form part of the package as well as other improvements to the existing town centre.

There's some interesting artwork in the Civic Centre: watercolours of local scenes by historian A. Leslie Evans[61], some signed prints by Andrew Vicari[62] and a painting by the Welsh artist David Carpanini among them. And there's a plaque donated in 1998 by the family of Owen Baker from Velindre, a community north-east of Port Talbot town centre.

Twenty-year-old Baker was serving as a sick-bay attendant aboard *HMS Amethyst* in 1949 when it sailed up the River Yangste to Nanking, China, likely to be needed to help evacuate British nationals from the area after heavy fighting had broken out between the Communists, under Mao Zedong, and the Nationalists under Chiang Kai-shek. The captain had ordered large Union Jacks to be painted on either side of the ship so no-one would mistake her for an enemy vessel but the Communist forces fired on her in the early hours of April 20th and Baker was one of seventeen crew members killed. The memorial plaque was originally hung in the Royal Naval Hospital in Hong Kong but after its closure and in light of the pending handover of Hong Kong to China, Baker's brother enlisted the help of MPs John Morris and Michael Portillo, former Conservative Defence Minister, to retrieve it.

Unfortunately neither the art nor the plaque is accessible to the public without an appointment to access the inner sanctum corridors. With all the new town developments in the pipeline a small building, or even a couple of rooms in one, for a local history museum and visitors' centre shouldn't be that difficult to organise.

If you walk past reception on the ground floor you can get to see the old stone Aberavon Borough plaque, thoughtfully rescued from the façade of the Municipal Buildings, and, in glass display cabinets, a big wooden chopping block and a stuffed fish.

The chopping block claims to be the hiding place used by a portreeve of Aberafan when Oliver Cromwell's heavies arrived in the seventeenth century and demanded, unsuccessfully, the town's charter – proof of its independence, protection for traders and the rights of the town to charge tolls – possibly in punishment for their royalist sympathies[63].

The fish was the first salmon caught in the River Afan[64] for 150 years, by Colin Walton on 4th September 1988, after decades of environmental work by the Afan Valley Angling Club that rescued the river from a "rat infested liquid tip"[65]. There's also a note about the Legend of the Sacred Salmon: one that used to appear under Aberafan Bridge on Christmas mornings, tame enough for people to stroke. "Let us hope that one Christmas morning we might yet see the legendary Sacred Salmon", the card reads. I'm not sure if stuffing one of its descendants is going to encourage a return visit any day soon.

PORT TALBOT TOWN CENTRE

If you threaded a piece of elastic through the M4 from Junction 40 in the west to Junction 41 in the east, and then pulled both ends towards the sea you'd gather up the town centre. Even without the elastic if you walk through the back streets – Edward Street, Glyndwr Street, King Street, Evans Street and Pont Street – you still feel the tension where the motorway flyover crowds up to and over the houses there.

The Port Talbot By-pass Special Roads (Improvement) Order 1961[66] identifies, with the impersonal language of progress that holds messy human emotional experience at bay, 'highways to be re-aligned and regraded' and 'highways to be stopped up'. Nothing about having one half of your street demolished or chopped off or next-door reduced to rubble. There's a strange mix of noise and

silence around here: the overhead drone of traffic and the truncated dead-end streets plugged with the motorway's flat walls of concrete. I suppose most people who live here now haven't known the town any other way. And, if my all-time favourite (chalked) graffiti of 'Sheep in The Dark' in Pont Street (probably long-washed away by rain) is anything to go by, the kids seem happy enough too.

Some of the encircled streets betray their Edwardian gentility and origins with beech trees planted along the pavements and coal holes, mostly bricked in, along the back alley walls. The architecture here, apart from the occasional modern interruption, is solid: good brick, dressed stone, sprinklings of stone bay windows, miniature first floor balconies, shared arches of porches set back into the walls of flat fronted but roomy terraced houses. Steady, reliable. These are the words that come to mind from a time before 1914 when trust in humanity and the progress of society was shattered.

The Aberavon RFC, or The Wizards[67], rugby ground is at Manor Street and Dan y Bryn Road, the team to whom Richard Burton pledged allegiance, until death. Aberafan rugby on the Port Talbot side of the River Afan, and Port Talbot Town Football Club on the Aberafan side: teams that play away even when they play at home.

The rugby club's origins can be traced back to 1876 when they did play on several grounds in Aberafan[68] but from 1879 they bounced around a number of temporary pitches and fields across the river, at the docks and on land subsequently acquired by the Port Talbot Steelworks (1901), before touching down at their current ground, the Talbot Athletic Ground. It was used as allotments during World War I but officially re-opened in 1921.

In old aerial photos you can see a railway circling the Athletic Ground. This was the Port Talbot Railway & Docks line running from Port Talbot Central Station, one of four stations located in an area of around a square mile. Port Talbot Central, at the back of Plaza cinema, closed to passenger traffic in the 1930s and to goods traffic in 1960. The line branched east to Taibach and west around the rugby ground towards Aberafan Town Station where Tesco's car park is today. The up-gradient run meant that a stone viaduct had to be built to carry the rails and you can check out some disconnected sections of it, virtually running parallel with the M4 flyover, on Dan y Bryn Road and Glyndwr Street.

Aberafan Town Station and Aberafan Seaside Station, over the river at the top of Victoria Road[69] were part of the Rhondda & Swansea Bay line. They closed in 1962 leaving Great Western's Port

Talbot General Station to reinvent itself as Port Talbot Parkway, the station we all know and don't love.

I became particularly hostile towards it when I was travelling between the South of France and South Wales in 2010 and 2011, flying into Heathrow and then catching the Intercity train from Paddington. The station has an island platform between its east and westbound tracks so no matter what direction you're heading in you have to confront the steep stairs on either side of the footbridge. And I have cursed every one of them while grasping the handrail in one hand and a 22 kg suitcase with the other. Once, when I was carrying two suitcases, I persuaded (actually I begged) a guard to open the gate at the far end of the platform, so I could exit over the level crossing, but on a dozen other occasions I had to battle the ascent and descent. Heading back to London, in the triumph of hope over experience, I'd ask at the ticket office if someone could open the gate for me. 'Sorry love, I'm here on my own,' was their mantra. What about disabled people travelling from here? How do they manage? There's a number you can call, 24 hours in advance. Bureaucracy: the enemy of spontaneity.

But there's good news on the horizon: a £9.5 million facelift using steel produced by Tata Steel's Port Talbot works. There'll be a café and shop and lifts[70] – yay! Too late for me but the other 499,999 people who use the station can stop worrying about hernias.

The station improvements are part of the major regeneration programme that includes 140 hectares of brownfield site to the south of the railway line: the old docklands and the former Port Talbot Industrial Estate. It's easy to forget, or not even realise, how close you are to deep water and the local authority's master plan[71] evidently hopes to imitate other dockland regeneration projects around the UK that have transformed redundant land into desirable waterfront zones with the usual residential, hotel, office, retail and leisure trimmings. Twenty-first century town centres. The plan also includes a new college campus and a research and development village that Tata Steel and TWI[72], one of the world's foremost independent research and technology organisations, have already signed up for.

One new building has been occupied. The Justice Centre, which opened in July 2011, has a functional, square Lego-look about it, in vivid contrast to the listed Neo-Georgian Magistrates Court[73] it replaced, currently empty at the back of the station. Colin and Ralph, the two security guards on duty, tell me the new centre doesn't handle criminal matters anymore; it's for tribunals, family and coroner's court cases as well as housing the fines, warrants and enforcements department where 80 people are busy calculating the cost of our sins and blunders. Apparently, we send our criminals to Neath now. They also tell me that no photographs are allowed, not even of the outside of the building. It's HMCS[74] property, they say.

I wasn't keen on a trip to Neath so I didn't admit to taking a photo of the heraldic Royal Coat of Arms, and its motto *Honi Soit Qui Mal Y Pense*, carved into the wooden shiplap outside the main entrance. The motto, which appears on the front cover of every British passport, has made me giggle ever since Del Boy, in an early episode of *Only Fools and Horses*, claimed he could speak French with a flourish of "onny swacky mally ponce". Although the origin of the phrase does have a fourteenth century sit-com flavour to it. Edward III was dancing with his daughter-in-law when her garter slipped down to her ankle and the courtiers started sniggering. He strapped it to his own leg and warned them in French: "Shame on him who thinks ill of it"[75]. You didn't disagree with kings in those days.

PLAZA

The grimy and neglected Plaza cinema, opposite the railway station, is marked on the Harbourside plan as a key building for enhancement. Plaza became a focal point in Port Talbot during the weeks leading up to Michael Sheen's Passion play when it was painted with The Teacher's image and 'IT HAS BEGUN...' along a side wall, so it was appropriate that a campaign by Port Talbot residents to save the cinema, which had been empty since 1999, began the following month. The campaign's Facebook page, Plaza for the People and the Arts, currently has nearly 1,000 members and its steering group, which includes Sheen's father, Meyrick, has been meeting regularly with Gareth Nutt, Head of Property and Regeneration at Neath Port Talbot Council to talk about possible future community uses. The most the near future is likely to see though is some stop-gap repairs to prevent the building falling into even more disrepair and some cosmetic prettying up around the front entrance.

Plaza is Grade II listed[76] and must be one of Wales' last remaining Modernist cinemas of the 1930s. Despite its grungy appearance you can still appreciate the rise of cream faience tiles on the front wall and the curve of the Art-Deco semi-circular shop-fronts on either side of the main doors. It was built in 1939 to replace a smaller cinema, The Empire[77] further along Talbot Road, which had, ironically, burned down the week it was showing *The Firefly*[78] but the beginning of World War II delayed Plaza's opening until

1940. At this time it was one of five cinemas[79] in and around Port Talbot, along with The Majestic (later Odeon) in Forge Road, The Grand in the High Street, The Regent in Taibach and The Taibach Picture Palace.[80] The first film to be shown at Plaza was *Babes in Arms*[81] with Mickey Rooney and Judy Garland.

I saw *Love Story*[82] here in 1971, wearing too much make-up in a successful attempt to look old enough for the film's rating. I looked more or less like every other woman and girl in there by the end, stumbling down the terrazzo steps of the lobby, my eyes swollen with tears and face smeared with block mascara. I sneaked in again, under the rating radar, with my parents to see *The Godfather*[83] the following year. There's an 'up-against-a-door' sex scene shortly after the film opens that no fourteen year old wants to witness while sitting next to her father. I imagine fathers might feel the same way.

The refurbishment of Plaza will be of particular interest to Alex Jones, child prodigy cinema manager, if there is such a thing. If there isn't there should be because Alex was running a paying film club in his bedroom at the age of eleven with a Super 8 projector his dad had given him and worked as a projectionist at The Windsor Cinema in Neath from the age of fourteen. After he left school, although still employed as projectionist, he became, to all intents and purposes, the cinema's manager, responsible for advertisements, film programming and staff. In 1985, at the age of 20, he re-opened Plaza, which had wobbled through the early 1980s as a combined cinema and bingo hall but had been used exclusively for bingo since 1983.

Perhaps Alex was lucky in that 1985 was British Film Year, a project launched by distributors and exhibitors to fight a dramatic decline in cinema attendance as a result of the ever-growing video market. But Plaza would never have achieved the success it did over the following fourteen years without his own brand of creative energy. It became a fulltime independent cinema with films running three times a day, seven days a week. He increased seating capacity, installed a high-tech sound system, introduced a kids' Saturday Club with its very own pie-throwing Phantom of the Plaza and converted the stalls to a multi-screen venue. There were some financial hiccups along the way but Plaza kept going, and on a couple of occasions, for the showing of *Batman* and *Indiana Jones and The Last Crusade*, pulled in over 5,000 people in a day.

In the early 1990s Plaza was able to capitalise on being the only cinema between Cardiff and Swansea but as the decade marched on announcements of multiplexes at Bridgend and Port Talbot were threatening its ability to compete for audiences and film distribution. The closure of the Swansea Odeon in 1997 gave a brief reprieve but following the opening of the multiplex, just off the M4 on the outskirts of Bridgend in late 1998, and the imminent opening of the Apollo at the presumptuously fêted Hollywood Park[84] on Aberafan Beach, the final curtain was quivering.

Plaza officially closed at the end of October 1998 but with a Swansonesque[85] flourish Alex re-opened it for a farewell six week programme until the credits rolled for the very last time in January 1999.

Alex joined Rank Odeon cinemas and rose to General Manager designate of the Rank Groups but his heart remained in independent cinema which he returned to in 2012 as General Manager of Phoenix in Falmouth. He remains connected to Plaza as Information Officer[86] on the Steering Group. I asked him which one of his bottomless repository of film quotes he'd add to his and Plaza's journey and he gave the last word to Miss Swanson. "This is my life. There's nothing else, just the cameras, and those wonderful people out there in the dark".[87]

Apart from Michael Sheen's attentions, Plaza has also been remembered by Sir Anthony Hopkins in *Composer*, an album of his own classical music compositions released by Decca in 2012. Philip Anthony Hopkins was born in Margam on 31st December 1937, the son of a Taibach baker. He started piano lessons when he was six, practising "those terrible scales, those tortuous finger exercises, with such verve, such unbridled passion"[88], qualities that millions of people now associate with his on-screen appearances. The track 'Plaza' recalls his childhood visits to the cinema where he revelled in the racy action of black and white films filled with cigarette smoke and American gangsters or the glamour of MGM's Technicolor extravaganzas. The young Tony Hopkins' life changed for good after he won a scholarship to Cardiff's Welsh College of Music and Drama in 1955. After National Service and a period in repertory theatre he auditioned for RADA, becoming the star student of his generation. He's been a patron of the YMCA in Port Talbot[89] since 1985, appropriately so as this was where his own acting career began. His father, fed up of him hanging around the house, told him to go to the YMCA in Talbot Road and learn to play snooker. Instead he joined in the rehearsal for a play.[90]

Hopkins, Burton and Sheen: Port Talbot's most obvious connections with Hollywood. The chances of anyone suggesting, 'Entwistle' are slight.

Peg Entwistle[91] was born Millicent Lilian Entwistle on February 5th, 1908 at 5 Broad Street, Port Talbot, the home of her maternal aunt, two blocks away from where Plaza would be built 30 years later. She grew up in London and moved to the United States with her actor father around 1913. Between 1926 and 1932 she was living and working in New York, appearing in a number of Broadway shows. In May 1932 she starred in a Los Angeles production of *The Mad Hopes*, alongside another minor actor at the time, Humphrey Bogart. In June that year she signed a contract with Radio Pictures, later RKO Studios, to play one of the women in David O. Selznick's *Thirteen Women*[92]. The film's test screenings were poor and scenes that Peg had starred in were cut to reduce its running time. On or around September 16th 1932 she walked up to the Hollywoodland (as it was then) sign[93], climbed a workman's ladder to the top of the H and threw herself off.

There's a photo-montage of Peg Entwistle's life on You Tube[94], made by James Zeruk Jr., author of *Peg Entwistle: The Girl on the Hollywood Sign*. He says that it wasn't RKO's scene deletions that led her to take her own life, "there were a number of rungs on her fateful ladder". (An unfortunate turn of phrase given the circumstances of her death.) "These are detailed in the book, but the deleted scenes are a fascinating subject unto themselves." *The Los Angeles Herald Express*[95] suggested the number 13 figured in her death: she was the thirteenth person to be cast for *Thirteen Women*; the thirteenth person to commit suicide in Los Angeles County in a 24 hour period. But we'll probably never know the full story as Zeruk's Hollywood Sign Girl website is defunct and there's no trace of the book either.

FORGE ROAD

I am sitting on her lap in the dark, the rubber studs on her suspender belt pressing into the backs of my legs, my knees grazing the velvet seat in front. When the heavy curtains slide open, the light is almost too bright for my eyes. The usherette in a pink and white uniform walks back up the aisle with her tray of ice-creams, trailed by the scent of perfume and cigarette smoke. The swing doors softly bump against each other as they close. On the screen a man with an oiled chest strikes a big brass gong.

This is one of my early memories: watching *The Three Lives of Thomasina*[96] with my mother at the Odeon in Forge Road. The Odeon was also the venue for the Saturday Morning Club for Boys and Girls and if you're of a certain age you'll appreciate the 1960s You Tube rendition of the welcome song[97]. We might have been 'Greet-ing ev-'ry-body with a smile' but I doubt we had any notion of being 'Cham-pions of the Free' unless that meant free hot-dogs from the stall in the foyer.

Forge Road was named after the Afan Forge, set up by Lord Mansel of Margam in 1717, where Forge Road meets Ynys Street today, for the smelting of local iron ore[98]. The Forge created the first sparks of industrial iron production in the area but the most heat I ever experienced here was in 1973 at Hair by Walter, now Madcaps, when the tonsorially dedicated Mr Walter bleached the upper half of my curly brown hair platinum blonde for the South Wales round of a national hairdressing contest at the Top Rank Suite in Swansea. I was fifteen, had persuaded my parents to let me be one of his models and set their expectations at a few red lowlights. But Mr Walter was otherwise inspired, an inspiration that led a couple of lads from Sandfields Comp to comment that I looked like a glass of Guinness.

The lower half of Forge Road was pedestrianized in 1987. The Odeon and the shops on either side of it, from the junction with Station Road all the way along to the little bit of Ancient Greece in Port Talbot that is the Masonic Temple, were (it's a familiar refrain by now…) demolished. The Afan Masonic Temple[99] and Tabernacl Newydd[100], a couple of doors along, both built in 1909, escaped the cull. Emily Talbot funded the building of the Temple; her late brother, Theodore (1839-1876), had set up the first Aberafan Lodge in 1860, on the other side of the river, in the old Walnut Tree Hotel. Take a look at the temple's gable-end façade and you'll see what I mean about Ancient Greece: tapering Ionic pilasters set into the red brickwork on the top storey, three oculi with moulded stone surrounds, and three framed square stone tablets. The masonic symbol of Square and Compasses is also set in stone under the classically angled roof.

Her generosity towards the chapel-goers was more restrained, after all the Talbots were Anglo-Catholics. She donated the land but

added a condition that the front of the chapel should look like a church, so it has a tower on the right hand side of the main door although the spire that once crowned it has since been removed.

With the Temple and Tabernacl in front of me, Bethany Chapel[101] to my left on the corner of Station Road, St. Agnes's Church to my right on the corner of Prior Street, and the Romanesque Ebenezer Chapel[102], just a Baptist minister's exhortation away in front of the Civic Centre. I could be drowning in devotion and good works but fortunately, or unfortunately, both Tabernacl and Bethany are locked up, not in service so to speak.

Bethany was up for sale in 2012 at £80,000, not a bad price for over 8,000 square feet of space but as it's Grade II listed there are restrictions on what you can and can't do and there aren't a lot of business ventures that can usefully incorporate a pipe organ, wooden pews and a gallery seating area into their daily function. It is joyfully and expansively lovely inside though, as long as you don't let yourself dwell on heating bills. Or parking – it's bang in the middle of a pedestrianized precinct with no land of its own. I'm

thinking market premises in the chapel and local history museum and visitor's centre in the basement school room, one of the town library's temporary homes until it found sanctuary in the Aberafan Shopping Centre. I can't think of a better place for a local history museum. In 1879 when the chapel's foundation stone was laid by H.H. Vivian[103] there were only fields here. There are few older witnesses to the birth, expansion, falls from grace and resurrections of Port Talbot than Bethany.

I like a nice chapel but given a choice between checking out rock-faced stone and hoodmoulds or sipping a glass of chilled Pinot Grigio as I contemplate a king prawn risotto singing with notes of chilli, ginger and thyme then the latter is always going to win. Luckily, I can do both at La Memo[104], the restaurant opposite Tabernacl, where everything from the service to the food and the presentation is deserving of high praise. The owners are Turkish but the menu swings through mainland Europe with an enjoyable stopover in Britain for Sunday lunch. I have decided that the risotto will be my last meal of choice if Fate ever hurls me into an American penitentiary. *Afiyet olsun.*[105]

STATION ROAD

You'll never starve around here: in Forge Road and Station Road alone I counted 25 eateries that range from class (Trellis Patisserie, La Memo, Giovanni's[106]) and quality (Coffee Bound[107] – in a 'homeward' sense, I believe, rather than an 'egg' sense – and Shah[108]) to café/takeaway cheerfulness (Jenkins, Gregg's – I'm a big fan of a Gregg's custard slice, or custard hunk as I prefer to call it) through to a range of fast food trougheries (Istanbul Kebabs, Pizza Pizza – so good they named it twice?). And that's not including the half a dozen pubs, bars and clubs. Are we abnormally hungry in Port Talbot? I don't think so: the high street in the small town where I live in Kent has a similar number of chow-houses, if a little lighter on the takeaway joints. Regardless of the economy people will always eat. And die. And I'd rather see a surge of cafés and restaurants than funeral directors. How hairdressers, who also seem to be breeding at a spectacular rate in most town centres, fit into that theory I'm not sure.

It's Station Road all the way south to The Grand Hotel and, predictably, the train station but when these buildings were first erected (mainly between the 1890s and 1914) most of the western side, from the junction with Forge Road, was made up of two storey terraced houses – Plough Terrace and Courtland Terrace – complete with front gardens and railings. Look up, above the modern shop fronts and fasciae, above the weather canopy, and you'll recognise the rooflines and chimneys that could only belong to residential property. In fact looking up is often the best way to view Station Road, particularly once you pass Courtland Place, to the late Victorian and Edwardian three, and occasionally four, storey facades on both sides of the road that speak of the town's original elegance and early prosperity, before the pointing started to crumble and buddleia took root in the cracks. Some of these top storeys housed shipbrokers and colliery agents after the expansion of the docks at the end of the nineteenth century increased exports from 235,000 tons of coal, coke, patent fuel, tinplate and steel in 1899 to over 2.5 million in 1913[109]. There were upper-storey hotels for the travelling man, and clubs, and at street level a bustle of commercial activity that's significantly absent amongst the colony of estate agents and fast food premises that have since encamped here.

There were two bookshops at this southern end a hundred years ago. Look above Shah Indian Restaurant and you'll see the W.H. Smith[110] (WHS) logo under the small gable roof and, to the left of the restaurant's sign, a section of the original bullion glass window frame that owner, Sayeed Rahman, recently discovered during refurbishment.

Edward E. Day, a former manager at Smith's, opened his own bookshop directly opposite after a difference of opinion with his employer. He advertised himself as a Stationer but sold souvenirs and fancy goods too as the stamp on the bottom of the Arcadian china salt and pepper pots I picked up on EBay confirm. *Ymgyfoda Ac Ymddisgleiria* they formally announce on a banner unfurling beneath a coat of arms, belying the informal translation of 'Rise and Shine'[111].

The Golden Wand Magic Shop, which adds a pleasing anachronistic touch to the brash shop fronts along so much of Station Road, was a restaurant at that time – H.B. Comley & Sons Ltd, Caterers & Confectioners – and The Ruskin Circle, a local literary society, met in an upstairs room there every week[112]. While the town might not have produced a literary equivalent of Burton or Hopkins, its writerly associations are richer than I realised. Bards, hymn-writers, historians, poets, novelists, critics: there are sixty-seven of them listed in Sally Roberts Jones's *Writers of the Afan District*[113]. These men and women span seven centuries, from Llewellyn Y Glyn, or Lewis Glyn Cothi[114] (1447-1486), who wrote in praise of Margam Abbey, right up to the poet and academic,

Gwyn Williams[115], and popular novelist Elaine Crowley (1927-
2011). Crowley came from Ireland but moved to Port Talbot with
her locally born husband in 1962. She had six children and was in
her fifties when she started to write but achieved instant success
with her first novel, *Dream of Other Days* (1984). This and her
subsequent novels drew on her memories and knowledge of Ireland
and its history as did her first volume of autobiography, *Cowslips
and Chainies* (1996)[116], a memoir of Dublin in the 1930s.

A poet of national importance, who wasn't born in Port Talbot
but spent her formative years here, was Ruth Bidgood (b.1922)[117]
who grew up and went to school in Port Talbot while her father was
vicar at St Mary's in Aberafan between 1929 and 1945. In 1933
Bidgood joined the town's grammar school, Port Talbot Secondary,
where Philip Burton (Richard Burton's mentor) was the English
master and while she wasn't particularly aware of his influence at
the time, she would later admit to the impact he had on her development as a poet.[118] Her first poetry collection, *The Given Time*,
appeared in 1972. Her most recent, *Above the Forests*, was published
by Cinnamon Press in 2012.

A name conspicuously absent from the list is Sally's own and she
really should add it because after she moved from London to Port
Talbot in 1967 she had a significant impact on the Welsh writing
scene[119]. She was a founder member of the English Language
section of Yr Academi Gymreig/ The Welsh Academy in 1968 and
her first book of poems[120] was a Welsh Arts Council prize-winner in
1969. Since then she's published a shelf-full of her own writing –
poetry, history, criticism and children's literature – and promoted
dozens of other writers through her press, Alun Books[121], which she
set up in the 1970s with her late husband. She's also Chairman of
the Port Talbot Historical Society (founded in 1954) who meet at
the Carmel Chapel vestry, at Riverside Walk, on the first Wednesday
of the month between October and April. One of Sally's poems,
'Steel Town', was engraved into the underside of David Annand's[122]
sculpture, 'Order and Chaos', at the top of Station Road, opposite
the station.

This and two other sculptures were commissioned by Neath Port
Talbot Council in 2001 for a public art project funded by Arts
Lottery and European Community money. The bronze 'Mortal
Coil' by Sebastien Boyesen[123] is at the bottom end of Station Road,
beside Aberafan Bridge, while his relief sculpture spirals through
the pavement at the southern end of Bethany Square public car

park. Both bear poems by Port Talbot poets Haydn Harris and Eira Northcott.

Boyesen, born in Sussex in 1960, has lived and worked in Llangrannog, on the west coast of Wales, for over twenty years. He's responsible for dozens of powerful sculptures around Wales and England, sculptures that draw on a region's history and myths, the working lives of its people. 'Mortal Coil' has classical references: Da Vinci's 'Vitruvian Man' (the famous ink drawing of the ideal human proportions inscribed within a circle and square) and the Shakespearean phrase, "When we have shuffled off this mortal coil," from the 'To be, or not to be...' monologue in *Hamlet*. But Boyesen never forgets his contemporary audience: Port Talbot's steelmaking heritage was his primary inspiration, ordinary lives devoted to the industry as well as those lost to it. A Llangrannog farmer was the model for the central figure holding a ladle of molten metal; the coil that encircles him is literally the hot coil produced at the Port Talbot works and symbolic of the circle of life.

"Heat, havoc and humanity" is a phrase from Eira Northcott's poem in the car park sculpture, qualities that were present, but in an entirely different manner, in an event that unfolded in Station Road in 1958, the year I was born. There's no profound connection between my birth and an attempted bank robbery at the Midland Bank[124,] now HSBC, but I feel some kind of kinship because this was where I started work eighteen years later.

The man behind the attempted robbery, John Rivers, was never caught. The two brothers he recruited in Cardiff, Martin Thomas O'Brien and Dennis John O'Brien, weren't so fortunate. Or maybe they were. By the time the police burst into the shop opposite the bank, from where they'd tunnelled 35 feet under the road, shifting 10 tons of earth, between 3rd and 16th May, they were on the verge of breaking into the town's main sewer and very possibly could have drowned as well as providing the police with an infinite supply of 'shit' gags. They might never have been rumbled if they'd paid the rent on time: the landlord had called round on 13th and discovered the ground floor of the shop covered in earth and rubble and notified the police. When they did pop over to Bridgend a few days later to pay the outstanding £97 the police were watching them.

They were each given four years in prison, a sentence which recognised that the original idea, and its financing, had been conceived by the elusive Rivers who'd believed the steelworks payroll, which he estimated at £150,000, was held in the bank's vault over the weekends. Not that either brother was irreproachable; both had previous criminal convictions.

In 1978 the bank transferred me to their offshore corporation in Jersey and I had my leaving drinks at the Grand Hotel, opposite the station. Which bar? I can't remember now, but my memories of the Grand from that time play out under the orange glow of wall-lights, oak beams (who cared if they were fake), the rolling meniscus of a schooner of sweet sherry and the realisation that my prawn cocktail was served in the same kind of stainless steel dish as my scoop of vanilla ice-cream. But slip a main course of rump steak, gammon or plaice with chips and peas, between that starter and dessert and you were talking a good night out. Swap your ice-cream for a slice of Black Forest Gateau and finish off with an Irish coffee and you were living the dream. This was Berni Inn country, a chain of restaurants founded by Welsh Italian brothers, Frank and Aldo Berni, who took over the Grand in 1963. The Berni family came from Bardi, in Northern Italy, like so many South Wales Italian café owners[125] and who, from 1955 with the opening of their first UK restaurant, transformed the eating habits of millions. It's difficult to

explain the significance of a Berni Inn to anyone under the age of 40 but this was where my generation, and our parents', learned about eating out in an environment that felt risk-free, special, not too foreign and, above all, affordable.

The Grand was built between 1894 and 1904 on land owned by the Margam Estate, the site of the Tai storehouse and smithy[126]. Miss Emily Talbot's temperance sensibilities[127] are said to have dictated its Gothic design; a turret here, some castellation there, architecture to announce upmarket hotel rather than tavern or inn. It still does and since a makeover a couple of years ago the exterior has recaptured a sense of stateliness and allure.

I don't know what I was expecting from the interior but my first visit since those goodbye drinks in March 1978 made me feel as if I was trapped an Al Murray Pub Landlord sketch ("a pint of bitter for the gentleman and a white wine or fruit based drink for the lady") if the constant stream of glass-clutching women tripping back and forth from the bar were anything to go by. It was Saturday and bar duty had fallen to them due to the football on TV, the same match on four flat screen televisions that I had a quadrophonic appreciation of from just inside the front door. I'd arranged to meet an old school friend: both of us have since moved away from Port Talbot and The Grand seemed an obvious central choice. I was on the point of crossing the road and lying in the path of an oncoming Intercity 125 when he arrived.

A few months later one of my brother's bands, The Good Burghers,[128] had a gig there on a Sunday night, so I thought I'd go along with an open mind and give it another, football-less, chance. I lasted an hour for the music's sake but felt compelled to leave after a woman, defying science and gravity with the amount of alcohol she'd consumed and the platform shoes she was wearing, staggered across and grabbed the mic to sing along, and I use that term loosely, with the closing bars of Bill Withers' 'Ain't no sunshine when she's gone.' The lead vocalist had the look of a man whose whole life was devoid of light.

I've decided I'm not cut out for bars or clubs in Port Talbot, or even bars or clubs anywhere, but there are plenty of people, and let's be honest about this, decades younger than me, who will keep their spirit measures refilling, their tills pinging and their bouncers' muscles flexing. And refill and ping and flex they do in the Bacchanalian madness that can be Station Road on Friday and Saturday nights at B2M, Jimmy's and Eden. But despite feeling as if I've gained a few ounces of street-cred for working out that B2M stands for Back to Mine the truth is I've turned into my parents on the lookout for a nice country pub on those weekends in the 1960s. Dad would pop his head around the door of the bar and ask if there was a lounge or if it was alright to bring in the kids. Peace and quiet, an open fire, half a draught Guinness. Sometimes I even fancy a bottle of pop with a straw.

Notes

1. http://www.blancoshotel.co.uk
2. See South: Morfa Beach
3. After C.R.M. Talbot of Margam Park, a principal investor
4. Roberts Jones, *The History of Port Talbot*, p.77
5. Wales Online: http://tiny.cc/wv75qw
6. Wales Online: http://tiny.cc/zkf2lw
7. Wales Online: http://tiny.cc/cko2lw
8. Evans, Taibach, p.75
9. *Evening Post* 16.12.2011

10. http://www.thequinsrfc.com/history.htm on Harlequin Road

11. There's a chunk of stone, enclosed in an old wooden case, in Margam Abbey Parish Church inscribed with the words, 'This stone was found in Aberavon old castle which was taken by Meredydd in the year 1150 being 737 years old.'

12. See West: Vivian Park

13. A 1938 street map shows Pendarves Street but the years have eaten away at the e and made it an i.

14. Named for the landowner at the time, John David Rees.

15. http://home.maddogcasting.com/

16. Wales Online: http://tiny.cc/h5ollw

17. Ex-Carphone Warehouse manager, Paul Potts, has since released three platinum selling albums. He sold his two bedroom terraced house and bought and renovated the Art Deco villa, Sunray, between Port Talbot and Baglan. The house, built by the turf accountant Val D. Jones, is known locally as Mugs' Villa.

18. http://www.mtv.co.uk/shows/the-valleys

19. Port Talbot born James Hook, ex-Ospreys RFC player and Welsh International.

20. See West: Victoria Road

21. Jones, Port Talbot Gallery 3, pp. 33-41

22. Davies, Jenkins, Baines, Lynch, p. 943

23. Hospital Road, Sandfields Estate, closed in 2002.

24. Founded in 1906, the League, which took its title from a magazine of the same name, was responsible for the first Mr Universe competition in 1948 and was the forerunner of the National Amateur Body Builders' Association (NABBA) formed in 1950.

25. http://www.maxalding.co.uk/

26. Spong Jones, p.42

27. Voyle-Morgan, Brian, *Bryn and Tonic, The Life and Times of David Brynmor Thomas BEM*, Now Look Who's Talking Ltd, Cardiff 1996

28. Spong Jones p.135

29. *Ibid* p.136

30. *Ibid* pp.141-2

31. The nineteenth century Aberavon Borough Town Hall (demolished 1934) used to be at Green Park when it meant fields rather than the industrial park it became.

32. The oldest pub in Aberafan c.1850

33. BBC News South West Wales online: http://tiny.cc/emy2kw

34. Cadw record 22802.

35. Heilbronn, Germany, one of nine towns twinned with Neath Port Talbot

36. Includes St. Agnes, Forge Road, St. Paul's, Ysguthan Road and Holy Trinity, Sandfields Estate.

37. A stone vessel for washing the church service vessels, a reminder of the Roman Catholic traditions associated with the medieval church.

38. 1350: reputed headstone of Thomas, Rector of Avene who drew up the first Aberavon charter in Latin.

39. probably fourteenth century

40. www.parishofaberavon.org

41. *Ibid*

42. Roberts Jones, Sally, 'Richard Lewis and Dic Penderyn, The Man and the Martyr', *Transactions of PTHS* No 1 Vol III, p.6

43. Davies, Jenkins, Baines, Lynch, p.550

44. Roberts Jones, Sally, 'Richard Lewis and Dic Penderyn, The Man and the Martyr', *Transactions of PTHS* No 1 Vol III, p.14

45. *The Fire People*,

46. http://www.martynjoseph.net/

47. Welsh [better than] Brie from http://www.cawscenarth.co.uk/
48. www.bertevansartist.co.uk
49. *Evening Post* 9.4.2012: http://tiny.cc/p5o9jw
50. Application P/2009/1021: Report of the Head of Planning, Amendment Sheet: Planning & Development Control Committee Site Visit 10th February 2011
51. *Ibid*
52. There was no formal count of the vote only a record of majority approval.
53. NPT CBC Pre-deposit Local Development Plan (LDP) p.27- http://tiny.cc/j7i7kw
54. Application P/2009/1021 Ibid
55. *Evening Post*, 2.2.2011 – 'Concerns raised over toppling of historic building'.
56. Application P/2009/1021 Ibid
57. LDP p.24 - http://tiny.cc/j7i7kw
58. *Glasgow Herald*, 2.9.1980
59. *Port Talbot Guardian*, 4.9.1980
60. Dumbelton, p.33
61. 1911-1996. Headmaster, historian, author and artist who made an outstanding contribution to local history studies in and around Port Talbot. He was one of the founders of the Port Talbot Historical Society.
62. See West: Sandfields Estate
63. Roberts Jones, *History of Port Talbot*, p.36
64. See South: River Afan
65. Lewis, p.130
66. See North: M4
67. http://www.aberavonwizards.co.uk/
68. Parsons, In *War and Peace*, p.49
69. See West: Victoria Road
70. BBC *News South West Wales*: http://tiny.cc/yuwplw
71. http://www.npt-business.co.uk/PDF/Harbourside_property_brochure.pdf
72. http://www.twi.co.uk/
73. Used as the Magistrates Court since 1988, the building started life as the General Offices for the Port Talbot Steel Company c.1906. Cadw record 23152
74. Her Majesty's Court Services which became Her Majesty's Courts and Tribunal Services in April 2011
75. Wikipedia: http://tiny.cc/yrerlw
76. Cadw record 22136
77. Originally New Theatre opened in 1912. Hanson, *Profile* p.104
78. http://www.imdb.com/title/tt0028873/
79. Between World War I and World War II there were even more film venues, including Vint's Palace of Varieties and the Capitol in Aberafan and the Electric Cinema in Forge Road which all had live orchestras. Hanson, *Outline* pp. 77-84
80. Originally the Taibach Drill or Workmen's Hall and later The Picturedrome.
81. http://www.imdb.com/title/tt0031066/
82. http://www.imdb.com/title/tt0066011/
83. http://www.imdb.com/title/tt0068646/
84. See West: Aberafan Beach
85. Gloria Swanson, (1899-1983), Hollywood actress who engraved herself on filmgoers' memories as the fading silent movie star, Norma Desmond, in *Sunset Boulevard* (1950).
86. www.plazaporttalbot.co.uk
87. Sunset Boulevard: http://www.imdb.com/title/tt0043014/
88. Wales Online: http://tiny.cc/b9xylw
89. The Aberavon and Port Talbot District YMCA was founded in 1898 but changed its name

to Port Talbot YMCA at some point between that date and 1929.

90. *Evening Post* 6.12.2011

91. Wikipedia: http://tiny.cc/xd1ylw

92. http://www.imdb.com/title/tt0023582/fullcredits#cast

93. http://www.hollywoodsign.org/

94. You Tube: http://tiny.cc/sq4ylw

95. Hollywoodland (Images of America Series) Arcadia Publishing 2011, p.91

96. http://www.imdb.com/title/tt0057579/

97. http://www.youtube.com/watch?v=5RJOUrKXBZ8

98. Evans, Taibach p.39

99. Cadw record 23249

100. Cadw record 23251

101. Cadw record 23252

102. Cadw record 14174

103. 1821-1894, eldest son of JH Vivian and, after his father's death in 1855, director of the Hafod copper works at Swansea. It was under his influence that Swansea became the metallurgical centre of the world. His youngest brother, Arthur Pendarves Vivian, was co-director of the Vivians' copper mill at Taibach.

104. http://www.lamemobrasserie.co.uk/PortTalbot/index.html

105. Bon appetit in Turkish, courtesy of Mehmet at La Memo

106. http://giovannisporttalbot.com/

107. New coffee shop and bookshop, Book Bound, in Forge Road run by Coastal Project that supports people out of work through illness or disability. http://www.coastal project.co.uk/ Evening Post 9.2.2013

108. http://shah-restaurant.co.uk/

109. Hanson, *Profile*, p.79

110. Closed in the mid-1970s

111. Thanks to Lisa Thomas Jones and Andrew Tweed, Port Talbot Old and New Facebook Group, for the translation.

112. *Ibid*, p.89

113. This brief study, held in the Reference Section at Port Talbot Library, was expanded in her M.Phil. thesis, *The Literary Tradition of the Neath and Afan Valleys*, Swansea University and the National Library of Wales.

114. Welsh Biography Online: http://tiny.cc/kn77lw

115. http://en.wikipedia.org/wiki/David_Gwyn_Williams

116. *Cowslips and Chainies*, The Lilliput Press Ltd, Dublin, Ireland.

117. http://en.wikipedia.org/wiki/Ruth_Bidgood

118. Jarvis, p.3

119. Writers of Wales database: http://tiny.cc/i1a8lw

120. *Turning Away: Collected Poems 1952–1968*, Gomer Press 1969

121. www.alunbooks.co.uk

122. www.davidannand.com

123. www.boyesen.co.uk

124. Parsons, *In War and Peace*, 'The Robbery That Never Was', p.43-46

125. Hughes, *Lime, Lemon & Sarsaparilla, The Italian Community in South Wales 1881-1945*

126. Evans, *Taibach*, p.44

127. The stone built Eagle House on the other side of Oakwood Lane to The Grand used to be a hotel before the Grand took over its license. It subsequently became a Temperance Hotel.

128. https://www.facebook.com/GoodBurghers

NORTH

BAGLAN

The Treachery of Fields

That summer we turned eleven,
the shadow of school behind us,
we caught the bus to the last stop,
walked up through the new estate
past the unfinished houses to picnic
in a field at the top of the hill. We felt
the heat rise and stretch into the day.

Then the boys came crashing through
a low hedge and cornered us like dogs
chasing sheep. "Trespassers," they said,
herding us into the farmer's yard.
One boy laughed and wiped his mouth.
The farmer's hands buckled in his pockets.
"Shall I put them in with the bull then?"

The boys cheered and we cried until
he let us go, still crying as we ran,
our feet pummelling splintered shadows
on the lane, not daring to look back.

I didn't realise this was the place until I got out of the car and recognised the stone barn and the gate leading into a farmyard. I'm a little surprised at the clarity of the memory after forty-three years and I still don't understand why a grown man would choose to frighten three little girls like that.

This is Blaen Baglan farm[1] on the Bwlch Road just outside Baglan on the way to Cwmafan. The house is tucked behind the barns, out of sight from the road, but there's a public footpath through a latched metal gate that takes you right past it and up to the top of Mynydd Dinas. But you will stop here. You won't be able to help yourself.

There is beauty in certain types of brokenness. It's what Japanese poets call *wabi-sabi*: the kind of beauty that seems to be on the edge of defeat. Blaen Baglan has been on the edge of defeat for so long you feel like whispering, fearful that a raised voice might result in the whole structure – stone, slate and the remaining roof trusses –

collapsing into a pile of dust. If it wasn't Grade II listed it's likely that bulldozers would have achieved that long ago.

The earliest records I can find for the house date back to 1566 and despite a lot of architectural intervention over the centuries you can still make out the Tudor arched doorway and the blank stone frame above it that must have once held a coat of arms. There's a photo of the house from 1964 on the Royal Commission for Ancient and Historical Monuments of Wales's website[2] in which it looks quite robust. Even some 1997 shots, on the Welsh Ruins website[3], show the front of the house more or less intact. But the last sixteen years have beaten the stonework into submission and the front of the house is swamped by greenery.

I briefly entertain a renovation fantasy. I convince the owners to sell me the house and land. I bring the house back to its former glory so I can walk in and out of its stone doorway every day in awe of the panoramic views to the coast. I even buy a pet bull.

Baglan is purported to be named after St. Baglan, a sixth century wandering saint from Brittany[4] who, according to legend, was instructed by St. Illtyd to build his church where he found a tree "that bore three sorts of fruite". He wasn't convinced by the tree he first found with a litter of pigs, a hive of bees and a crow's nest and decided to build the church elsewhere. But when, each morning, he discovered his previous day's work had been destroyed, he decided on a more generous interpretation of 'fruite' and went back to the original site. What was probably no more than wattle and daub to begin with eventually became the stone built old St. Baglan, the ruins of which are at the back of St. Catharine's Church, on the corner of Church Road and St. Illtyd's Drive.

The houses I mention in the poem were the houses of Maes Ty Canol built in the mid-1960s, named after the demolished Ty Canol farm. My parents briefly contemplated giving up their council house on Sandfields Estate and becoming homeowners in Baglan, after their friends bought a house here, but in the end they decided that £2,750 was too much of a financial pressure for my dad's steel-worker wages. The new builds seemed awfully posh to me as a kid and the idea of owning a house must have contributed to that. But the location played a part too: the way the streets climbed the mountain, the trickle of steps down to each house was an exciting contrast to the featureless plain of Sandfields. And I still like the topography of Baglan, how the land rises up from the A48, and rolls around and rises again, leading you higher. It's no wonder that two grand country houses dominated the landscape here until the middle of the last century.

The public park, opposite the library, was the site of Baglan Hall built around 1600 to replace a late-medieval manor house, Plas Baglan, which would have stood to the east of the old church. In the fifteenth century Plas Baglan was the home of the Welsh Bard, Ieuan Gethin[5] and a centre of bardic activity for poets from all over Wales. His own poems are among the earliest surviving works of the Glamorgan Bards and include two moving elegies on the death of four of his children from the plague[6]. After being a private family home for over 300 years, Baglan Hall was bought by the Port Talbot Corporation in 1934 and met its doom in 1958, victim of a post-war cull that saw the destruction of so many country houses across the United Kingdom.

The only trace of the eighteenth century Baglan House is a section of wall in the corner of the garage compound at the top of Maple Avenue, at the Thorney Road end. Baglan House was built between 1760 and 1765 by the Rev. William Thomas (1734-1799), vicar of Aberafan and Baglan, although he spent more time at

Pembroke College, Oxford where he was a resident tutor and chums with the poet Thomas Gray, widely known for his 'Elegy Written in a Country Churchyard' published in 1751.

Gray's friend and fellow poet, William Mason[7], wrote his own country churchyard poem, in tribute to Gray[8], and there's been some argument as to which particular churchyard he waxes lyrical about. It seems that Mason stayed with both Rev. Thomas at Baglan House and with Lord Vernon in the neighbouring town of Briton Ferry. But Mason's poem specifically mentions the absence of any tower in the churchyard and as Briton Ferry's church tower had been erected long before Mason's time the tribute had to have been written in praise of the medieval St. Baglan. Or as historian, Les Evans put it: "the stark simplicity of the tiny church... would have made a greater impact upon his sensitive mind than its more pretentious neighbour at Briton Ferry"[9]. That's Baglan: 1, Briton Ferry: nil.

Baglan House was also snapped up by the Port Talbot Corporation in 1951 and demolished to make way for homes to meet the post-war housing shortage. Its original lodge house survives, at the top of Thorney Road, not a bad looking pad for the humble title of 'lodge'. To the left of its gates you'll see the entrance to Ladies Walk, named for the ladies of the Briton Ferry Estate, of which Baglan House was a part, who could trot through the woods between each other's houses, over the lower slopes of Mynydd y Gaer.

On Sundays they could have trotted downhill to St. Baglan, and later to the Victorian gothic monument that is St. Catharine's[10], built between 1875 and 1882 and designed by John Prichard, the leading church architect in nineteenth century South Wales. Local legend says that St. Catharine's benefactor, Griffith Llewellyn of Baglan Hall, insisted his church should take seven years to complete, inspired by the biblical legend of Solomon's Temple which also took seven years. This meant workers adhering rigidly to their allotted amount of work each day. It's also claimed that all the stone-dressing and preparatory carpentry work had to be done outside the boundary wall of the churchyard so the discordant sounds of hammers and axes would not be heard within the sanctuary of the new church (ditto Solomon[11]). I bet the builders loved him.

Add to that the church being named for his mother – which explains the variation on St. Catherine of Alexandria – and his likeness, as Patron, sculpted in stone on the frame of the main doorway, (on the opposite side of the Consecrator's, Bishop Ollivant of Llandaff), it wouldn't be unfair to surmise that humility wasn't one of Griffith Llewellyn's greatest attributes.

But I'm willing to overlook this peccadillo given the jewel his money and passion created. It's more mini-cathedral than parish church, but still, by virtue of its compactness, intimate and pretty. Dressed Bridgend and Forest of Dean stone in hues of green and red, pink alabaster from Penarth, Italian mosaic floors, Devonshire marble steps. There's even a stained glass window designed by Sir Edward Burne Jones in the Sanctuary at the front of the church and another by Burne Jones and William Morris in the south Transept. The choir stalls and pews are carved from Baglan oak; echoes of Solomon again and his cedars of Lebanon.

The Warden, John Victor, and Georgia Jones, the church organist, show me around one Saturday afternoon. Georgia is only the fourth organist the church has had since 1882, John has attended this church for almost seventy years and they both talk about it with genuine warmth. It is more than stone and glass for them, more than a receptacle of light and faith. It is home. And as all homes need a loyal pet, there's one here too: a little dozing hound carved from marble up on the right-hand wall towards the front of the

church. It's at odds with the angels and saints, the corbelled heads representing Life and Death. The sculptor's signature, perhaps?

A little bit of history from the Dark Ages interrupts the Victorian pomp in the vestry although you might miss it if you're pious as it's built into the wall at a height of about seven feet. I didn't. Somebody spotted the Brancu, or Brancuf stone[12], a ninth or tenth century gravestone carved with a Celtic cross, being used as a coping stone in the old churchyard wall around about 1850[13] and it was incorporated into the new church.

The new church made old St. Baglan[14] redundant. It aged gracefully and then disgracefully until a fire almost destroyed it in 1954. If I believed in burials and had to be forced into a box for eternity this is the corner I'd choose with the scent of sunlight on old stone, damp earth and shadows. Which brings us back to *wabi-sabi*.

A simple gravestone that dates from the 1880s, lying flat in the grass not far from the old church, is speckled with yellow lichen and splashed with sunlight on the day I visit. It bears the simple instruction: 'not to be opened'. Graves were, and sometimes still are, family affairs, but the family who had buried three children here by the beginning of the twentieth century chose never to disturb them.

The sprightly Baglan brook, or Pill (Anglo Saxon for 'creek') as it's referred to in the *Topographical Dictionary of Wales*[15], runs through a stone-walled channel past the churchyard, down to the A48 Baglan Road. It's been diverted underground at this point and emerges again, not far from Briton Ferry, where it runs towards the River Neath. But until the middle of the nineteenth century it was a waterway running parallel with the main road and big enough to carry barges of 20 or 30 tons, serving the industries along Swan Road. From east to west: Park Colliery, The Clay Mill Pottery and Limekiln, (which later became a brickworks), Swan Colliery, Torymynydd Colliery, Vernon Tinplate Works and Wern Pistyll Colliery. There's no trace of any of them at this level anymore, apart from the street names: Swan Road, Swan Walk, Swan Street and the dead-end Torymynydd. But if you peek over the garden wall of no. 6 Swan Road you'll glimpse a low brickwork arch: what remains of the pottery's kiln (*see p.66*).

What came first, Swan Road or Swan Colliery? Or maybe even the Swan Inn that once traded here in the middle of the eighteenth century? I'd like to think the swans themselves came first, centuries of them drifting along the brook. You can still see them sometimes on the Triangle Reservoir on the other side of the A48 and the M4.

The 'Res' lies between Baglan Bay Energy Park and the M4 but it's surprisingly peaceful, the traffic only a faint hum. At certain angles there's only water, trees and mountain in your point of view. If the swans aren't here you'll still find one on the sign at Baglan Railway Station on Seaway Parade, staring out over the dry rails and roads where water used to flow.

M4

I'm sure a lot of people heading west past Port Talbot on the M4 only know the town from that vantage point: a tangle of industry, rooftops and chimneys. This two-lane elevated section, before the motorway descends and runs past Baglan, then lifts again over the River Neath, glares with speed warnings of 50 mph. But keep below that and, on a sunny day, you can enjoy the gorse and sheep studded slopes of Mynydd Margam, before you pass the Dyffryn and Afan Valleys which frame the terminal moraine[16] of Mynydd Emroch. If it's raining, clouds blanket the mountains so thickly you won't be sure they're still there. At night the sparkle of lights from Tata Steel enchants you for miles, although don't believe the rumour that Port Talbot steelworks was the inspiration for Ridley Scott's *Bladerunner*. Scott came from the North East of England where industrial inspiration was equally rich[17].

The Port Talbot By-Pass, or the A48(M) as it was originally

called, (Junctions 39 to 41 of the M4), opened in 1966, the same year as the Severn Crossing. At 4.25 miles long and costing £5.06 million pounds[18], it was the first stretch of motorway to open in Wales, an accolade that might have been more celebrated if people hadn't been yanked kicking and screaming out of their houses to achieve the Welsh Office's goals.

Llewellyn Street, off Junction 41, at the back of the Aberafan Shopping Centre's multi-storey car-park hunkers below the gigantic viaducts that form the motorway's main thoroughfare and adjoining slip-roads. The single-sided street, from one end to the other, faces a thirty foot brick and concrete wall, a sub-station, or the concrete pillar equivalent of a magic-eye image. You know the kind of thing I mean? If you can relax your eyes enough another picture will miraculously appear, a picture that will make sense. The picture that should appear is Llewellyn Street's other half, its mirror-side of terraced homes that were demolished to make way for the new road. The street was known locally for its flourishing social life; people spoke of it as a community within a community. Old black and white photos show street party after street party. Their battle to protect that way of life was fought with passion and anger. And lost.

One of the principal scenes from Michael Sheen's *Passion* was played out here with the character of Alfie conjuring the past into the present with his litany of house numbers and names: "...the slow cricket game, a woman laying a table for dinner.., an old bloke reading his paper beside a fireplace, a kid building an Airfix plane on his bed."[19]

I understand the power of dramatic performance, the word on the page, and I don't expect to be similarly moved when I walk along Llewellyn Street, the thicket of concrete piles to my right leading to dead-ends and darkness. But I am. Perhaps the play and the words of Owen Sheers' novella have inscribed themselves onto my psyche more deeply than I realise. But it's more than that. Even 50 years after the houses were removed there's a sense of alienation and disconnection here. No-one's home is meant to exist like an island, hemmed in by a multi-storey car-park, a railway line and a motorway, grazed upon by the continual growl of overhead traffic.

Across from Llewellyn Street, on the other side of the motorway, up on Springfield Terrace, stitched along the side of Mynydd Dinas, there's a different view. Here the motorway traffic rolls past you at waist-level. On the other side of the road from the houses there are gateways puncturing an old stone wall at regular intervals, one or two blocked with ramshackle gates, others that invite you to tumble into bracken and bramble, or negotiate a few steep steps that end abruptly with a promise of broken bones. They look like the entrances to back gardens, or allotment gardens, before the town was sliced in two. And there was more loss to come.

The village of Groes, to the south-east of Margam, was built in the 1830s, designed by the architect Edward Haycock (1790-1870), supervisory architect under Thomas Hopper, (1776-1856) the head honcho for C.R.M. Talbot's gothic revival plans for his estate at Margam[20]. The problem of old Margam village standing rather too close to the ruins of his eleventh century abbey and his plans for improved fruit and vegetable gardens was easily resolved by uprooting the villagers *en masse* from their tenanted homes and demolishing most of the cottages. There's nothing like common people living outside your gates to put you off your pheasant shoot.

They were housed temporarily on another part of the Margam Estate, Cwrt Y Defaid[21], before being rehoused in the new Cotswold-like stone houses at Groes. They also got a school and a pretty roundish chapel. But at the beginning of the 1970s, residents at Groes found themselves in the way of someone else's grand plans: the completion of the new eastern section of the M4 to connect up with the Port Talbot By-Pass. To misquote Oscar Wilde's imperious Lady Bracknell, "To lose one village may be regarded as a misfortune; to lose both looks like carelessness."[22]

There was considerable local objection, as you'd expect, to the proposed demolition of the architectural gem of Groes. A village action committee was set up, chaired by Lord Heycock[23] and, at the Public Enquiry in 1972, Port Talbot Council's deputy engineer, M. Emyr Jones, suggested an alternative route for the motorway, to the south of the village, on the sea side of the A48, which only added an extra 51 metres to the motorway's overall length. The battle continued for another couple of years but in 1974 both the Inspector of the Public Inquiry and the Secretary of State for Wales, Conservative MP, Peter Thomas, chose to go ahead with the proposed route and consign Groes village to the pages of history books. The Beulah Welsh Calvinistic Methodist Round Chapel[24] was saved, dismantled and re-erected at the Tollgate Park in Margam in 1976.

Not everyone in the campaign gave up immediately. In 1975, one villager, Romeo Meli attracted the attention of the national news[25]: he was camping out on the grass verge in the middle of the A48 dual carriageway, not far from his Groes cottage. By then the other twenty-one families had already been rehoused and the village was

deserted; it was only a matter of time before Romeo's passion to protest, in the face of unbeatable odds, deserted him too.

If you want to see what remains of Groes village today you can read its faint name on the OS map, over a patch of green north-west of Margam Country Park. Although there is a little scrap of Groes installed in a cottage in rural Margam. Someone had the foresight to rescue a couple of stone windows from the debris of the old school before it was crushed to hard-core. I hesitate to reveal the location in case the occupants are hounded by Groes village pilgrims.

The missing link was also to be found at Port Talbot. Not the kind you can occasionally find stumbling out from J.D. Wetherspoons in the town centre on a Saturday night but the M4 kind: 6.5 miles of the A48 between Baglan's Sunnycroft roundabout, where the M4 ended, and its continuation on the other side of the Briton Ferry bridge. The difficulties of running a major motorway through this area of extensive industrial development – railways, soft peat, loose sand and flood-lands – had been discussed since the mid-1970s. They were finally resolved twenty years later when Alfred McAlpine and John Mowlem completed the job with 47,500m of concrete piles, 3,000m of temporary piles, 13,500 tonnes of steel reinforcement, 75,000 cubic metres of concrete and 350,000 tonnes of slag, most of which is underground and not even visible to the traffic.[26] This time round Port Talbot's residents managed to hang on to their homes.

CORLANNAU, BLACKWELLS AND PANTDU

It's less than two miles from Port Talbot town centre to the village of Cwmafan; a four minute drive north along the B4286 during which these three communities might not even register with you. Even on foot you'd be forgiven for overlooking them, so little of their existence remains.

The sign for Corlannau faces the road at the foot of a track that rises to a clutch of houses. Just before the sign, and again just after, there are breaks in the stone retaining wall. The first is more notice-able, a rusting wrought iron rail and block steps that blatantly invite

me somewhere. That somewhere is a bit of a fight through the gap in the wall at the top of the steps, pushing between brambles and tangled grass to trees and undergrowth on a lower slope of Mynydd Dinas. No tumbled down walls, no rubble, no trace of anything manmade. Perhaps I should be disappointed but the idea that there was something here once, and these steps are proof of that, is enough of a discovery.

> CORLANNAU. (Sheepfolds.) ...It is surrounded by rough wild mountain, but the spot itself, a small area of empty flat land, made it a convenient place to pen sheep... There are a few houses there now as well as a public house called the Mountaineer. Two small chapels[27] are also located there, one Baptist and the other Methodist.[28]

Graham Hughes[29], who translated the above text from Welsh, knew this place well. His father was born in Risca Row in Corlannau, in one of the four houses owned by his paternal grandfather, Richard Hughes. He remembers childhood visits to Corlannau to see his aunt Emma, a semi-professional contralto singer.

Old census returns list both Upper and Lower Corlannau and in a black and white photograph of Corlannau and Blackwells from the early 1900s I can make out a significant swell of homes with smoking chimneys. I convince myself of the outlines of the chapels and the pub too, enough to create a small village on the north bank of the River Afan, opposite where the footbridge and weir span the river today. Another photo, from 1918, shows the stack from the Myrtle Colliery that was also here, perched on the river's bank. If you cross the footbridge and head south along the river for a few hundred yards you'll come across a tumble of large stones and boulders breaking the water's flow. Nature doesn't produce stones with corners.

A little further north the sign to Blackwells is less obvious, tucked flat against the wall at the side of the road. Weather and time have rubbed away at the English name which has emerged victorious through the centuries over the original Welsh: Rhyd y Pwllau Duon, the Ford of the Dark Pools[30], named in an early sixteenth century sale of fisheries along this stretch of the Afan. Are Trinity Cottages, at the top of the steep drive, the result of a conversion of the second chapel in Graham Hughes's translation, above? Or were they built on or near the original site? There was no-one in to ask when I walked past last year, though the brick path to the front door of no.1 was treacherous with moss and rain, just like the path to salvation. Or is that damnation?

The appropriately dismal sign for Pantdu – black or dark hollow in English – is within the Cwmafan village boundary. A single street that curves off to the left and a house perched high at the end of a steep footpath hugging a cemetery wall. When the house was up for sale last year, the agent listed it as over 200 years old and still having the original footings of an old pub, the Tinmans Arms, in its front garden. You might think that a novelty to boast about until you learn that between 1840 and 1880 there were eight other pubs here in tiny Pantdu: Foresters Arms, George and Dragon, Greyhound Inn, Oddfellows' Arms, Prince of Wales, Union Tavern (known as the A.1), Welcome to Town and the Wellington Arms. And if none of those were serving the beer you liked you could trot back to Blackwells and try the Colliers' Arms or Alfred's Arms. And if you still weren't satisfied, or had been thrown out of any or all of the previous watering holes, you could wobble a few steps to Corlannau to the Forge and Hammer, the Mountaineer or Tumble Down Dick. At which point you most definitely would be.[31]

There are only a few houses remaining along the clipped back road that makes up Pantdu, where the steep sides of the Afan Valley start to give way to the valley floor, and it's difficult to imagine how significant rows of two and three storey houses ever fitted here. Particularly on the mountain side of the street, even allowing for some landslip over the decades since their demolition. A local story goes that a cow once fell down the mountain into one of the back gardens and the only way to get it out was to slaughter it.

Richard Derrick, Chairman of Cwmafan Residents Action Committee (CRAC[32]) remembers a couple of shops here at the time his aunt owned no.41 and tells me, with a wry smile, that he's a 'landowner' at Pantdu. The Council declared the terraced houses unfit in 1958 and agreed to demolish them on behalf of the owners for a fixed price. Richard still has the bill for £19 7s 0d which his aunt paid off in instalments of £2 with a final payment of £3 7s 0d wiping the slate clean in January 1964. He's not sure which patch of thistle and ivy bound ground is his although the ruins of one of the brick and stone arched cold rooms chiselled into the side of the mountain, by the people who once lived here, might offer a clue.

There was never a church or chapel attached to the cemetery. It was an overflow site for St Michael's Parish Church in Cwmafan; the graves mostly date from the late 1800s to the beginning of this century. I've wandered through a number of graveyards during my

research for this book and while at first I was seduced by ivy clambering over old headstones, the worn inscriptions pimpled with moss, I've recently felt less awe and more righteous anger. And that's principally down to the graves of children I keep coming across, from all centuries, their headstones carved with messages of faith: "God loved him best and took him home". No, I want to shout, if God loved him best he should have left him to enjoy life on earth. My brother and his wife lost their baby son a couple of years ago, days before he was due to be born. Words are sometimes all we have and we are both richer and poorer for them.

> For Florian
>
> We try to make sense of this –
> you were too tender for this world.
>
> We nurse the grief with words –
> you fell asleep in the safest of rooms.
>
> But nothing protects us against
> a death that comes too soon.
>
> You were loved, little one.
> So many of us would have given you
>
> the beats from our own hearts
> to watch you grow.

CWMAFAN

In 1971 I wanted to be a French translator but only for the thirty seconds it took me to say it while representing Sandfields Library in the final of the Inter-Library Quiz at the newly opened Cwmafan branch[33] on Depot Road. A chubby, bespectacled boy on the home team interpreted the question, "What do you want to be when you grow up?" in a totally different way. "A success in life," he replied and the audible approval rippled like a wave through the mainly adult audience. I immediately thought, That's not a proper job, but had a niggling feeling I'd missed some kind of opportunity. I was very literal at thirteen.

I still have a tendency to accept what people say at face value. Naïve, others might call it. So when, in the course of reading about Cwmafan at the same library, I came across a 1988 newspaper clipping that announced the unveiling of a plaque at a new housing development in Brynna Road for David John 'Afan' Thomas, the composer, I was looking forward to seeing:

> … a sort of 'Poets Corner', with two benches, a stone with a plaque inset and a landscaped area to provide an attractive seating area for the benefit of the new owners.[34]

I think I got over excited by 'Poets Corner', in spite of the missing apostrophe. The developer's aspirations for a seating area have disappeared but the stone is still there, at the edge of a wide grassy verge, close to where Afan's cottage once stood in Woodland Row. And a very nice stone it is too – still bearing the drill holes where the (presumably nicked) plaque once hung.

The D. Afan Thomas Memorial Award for Music was endowed in 1981 to perpetuate the memory of the violinist, organist and composer who was born here a hundred years earlier. In the Welsh music world he's probably best known for his choir and orchestra composition for Sir Henry Newbolt's poem, 'He fell among thieves', performed at the 1932 National Eisteddfod in Aberafan. He also founded the Afan Glee Society, one of the choirs that sang in *Blue Scar* (1949)[35], the British drama about a Welsh mining village in South Wales, directed by documentary filmmaker Jill Craigie. And then there's the Welsh lullaby, 'Suo Gân', memorably sung by the young Jim in J.G. Ballard's *Empire of the Sun*[36]. Afan wrote the piano accompaniment for the English and Welsh words by his close friend and biographer, Wil Ifan[37].

The first recipient of the award was, appropriately, from Port Talbot. Christopher Painter[38], who now lives in Barry, was commissioned to write 'Furnace of Colours' for the BBC National Orchestra of Wales in 2011. Last year, the award fell closer to home: twenty-two year old J.P. Williams who attended Cwmafan Junior School and graduated in 2012 with an honours degree from the Welsh College of Music and Drama in Cardiff.

Wil Ifan's idiosyncratic biography, *Afan, A Welsh Music Maker*, is written with unaffected admiration: a boy with a prodigious musical talent became a man whose passion and genius for composition earned him national recognition and acclaim. Though it seems he was appreciated most by the people he lived among: the miners and tinworkers, men and women, who flooded the streets of Cwmafan for his funeral procession from Woodland Row to Zion Chapel in May 1928. Zion was demolished in the 1970s but there's still a

stone plaque bearing its name in the retaining wall on a patch of waste ground on the left of the Cwmafan Road, B4286, as you approach the village proper. Thomas chose the name Afan, around 1899, to deliberately identify himself with the Afan Valley and the "rusty pebbled Afan River"[39] and I'm sure a local stonemason would willingly chip his name and dates into the stone at Brynna Road that is in danger of being forgotten.

I got lost trying to find Afan's stone. Dropping down over the Bwlch Road from Baglan I spent 15 minutes driving round the maze of streets that makes up Brynbryddan. It was like being trapped in an episode of *The Prisoner*, the graffitied, boarded up block of shops, that I passed for a third time, both numbingly hypnotic and threatening. It is an optimistic mind that hangs a 'shops and garages for lease' sign here. When a bus passed me, with Port Talbot in its front window, I did a swift U-ey and hung on to its tail but then, in no time at all, I was heading out of the village back towards town without ever having glimpsed its centre.

The truth is Cwmafan doesn't seem to have a centre, at least not in the sense of a lively hub of commercial activity and leisure. It has a few shops and three pubs (at the last count), a derelict club (auctioned in 2012 and converted into business premises) a community centre, a post office, a rugby club, the afore-mentioned library, the obligatory rash of chapels found in every self-respecting Welsh village and a church, but they're strung out south to north like a line of sparse bunting.

St. Michaels's and All Angels Church is a pretty church with a steeple and spire and a graveyard whispering the hymns of centuries. Its claim to fame is a pre-Reformation stone altar tomb with the inscription, 'Y Trymped Pan Kenir Y Meirw Y Gyfodir' – When the trumpet sounds the dead shall arise. It's the K in 'Kenir' that dates it prior to 1588 when the letter K disappeared from the Welsh language[40].

But Cwmafan hasn't always been so depleted. In his autobiography, *like it is*,[41] Chris Needs, the popular BBC Radio Wales presenter who was born and grew up in Cwmafan, remembers "a wonderful array of shops" in the late 1960s. Travel back another hundred years and Cwmafan was bristling with commerce and industry. Although another fifty years before that you'd have found yourself in a valley almost entirely given over to farming, echoes of which can be found in the suburbs and streets named after the many farms that used to be here: Brynbryddan, Pwll y Glaw, Dinas,

Cwm-Mawr, Tewgoed, Ynysafan, Ynysygwas.

While coal was being mined in the area from the middle of the eighteenth century it was at the beginning of the nineteenth that the topographical face of Cwmafan began to change through the ambition and vision of one man, Samuel Fothergill Lettsom, whose plans to build an ironworks led him to lease 1,000 acres of land here[42]. His story unfortunately dispels the belief held by local kids that a keystone built into the wall of Cwmafan School, bearing the initials SFL, stands for School for Lunatics. It actually came from the arch of Cwmafan's first blast furnace, built by Lettsom, which was all ready to start production in 1819. Before he achieved that goal he opened four coal levels and constructed one and a half miles of canal along the foot of Mynydd Foel[43] to Pontrhydyfen, to channel water down from the River Afan to power the furnace. After all that innovation and effort you'd imagine the road to being a successful industrialist was guaranteed but, allegedly, his wealthy father-in-law, Sir William Garrow, the Attorney General in 1813, wasn't responsive to his pleas for financial help and Lettsom was forced into liquidation. He then did what a lot of British people do when they're disappointed with this country. He went to France.

The happy chappies who took over Lettsom's leases, John Vigurs and Leonard Smith, powered ahead building tin mills, a chemical plant, a second blast furnace and a tramway for horse-drawn traffic down into Aberafan. It was Vigurs who set up the new copper works, designed by the Scottish engineer, William Brunton[44].

The Cwmavon Copper Works[45] was at the foot of Mynydd Foel though the only obvious trace of it in the village today is the name of the new Barratt Homes' estate in the south of the village: Copperminers. Other streets in the village remember the heavy industry of the past. Depot Road was the site of the Cwmavon Engineering Works (900 feet long and 45 feet wide)[46] known as 'The Depot' and said to have been the largest site of its kind in Wales in 1847.[47] Great Western Terrace and Rail Mill Lane mark the Great Western Works, a rail mill responsible for a 62 foot length of faultless steel rail exhibited at London's Great Exhibition of 1851 and another 83 foot length shown at the Paris International Exhibition in 1855.[48]

Changes in the iron and steel industry in the last half of the nineteenth century led to Cwmafan's decline. One by one the industries disappeared and the last remaining works, the Copper Miners Tinplate Works, ceased production in 1944.

The greenery around here today must be a dramatic contrast to the polluted slopes, tips, noise and smoke of last century. The population shot up from about 250 in 1800 to around 7,000 in the middle of the century though many of the rows of terraced houses, built to accommodate the influx of workers, were demolished in the 1960s, "a bid to renew the town and not allow it to fall into gradual decay".[49] The plan involved 1500 homes and was designated 'slum clearance' but local people didn't necessarily take the same view. The first stage of demolition went ahead, taking with it streets like Pelly and Gower named after the directors of local industries, but it was never fully completed.

I'm pleased that the houses around London Row survived the cull. Ebbw Vale Row, Jersey Row and Jersey Villas opposite The Afan Tavern[50], formerly The Jersey Arms[51] are unusual three storey terraces. The only other place I've noticed them is in Glyncorrwg, in the Afan Valley. Some of them have been rendered or coated with the ubiquitous pebble dash but others boast the original stone work. There were dozens of bog-standard two-up, two-down 'rows' built elsewhere in the village so what prompted the additional floor? The answer might be found in Ty'r Owen Row, opposite the Infants School, where there's another odd row, a central three storey house flanked by houses with only two. The middle house here was origi-nally provided for a Work's foreman: a higher level of employment

raised you, literally, above your neighbours.

Cwmafan library closes for lunch so taking the librarian's recommendation to try the Rolling Mill pub (another industrial echo) I park in Salem Road and walk across to the pretty hanging baskets but ominously unlit windows. So it's back down the road to Y Gegin Fach opposite the library, a burger/sandwich/hot potato van which suits me down to the ground given it's stopped raining and the benches back up in Salem Road will let me sit and gaze at the slopes of Mynydd Bychan while I munch.

I haven't lived in Wales since 1978 but my accent, as anyone who knows me will agree, has remained resolutely Welsh so I didn't anticipate a language problem in Cwmafan:

"C'n I help you?"

"Can I have a bacon, lettuce and tomato roll, please?"

"Sorry?" she said.

More slowly. "A bacon, lettuce and tomato roll."

"A bacon, lettuce and tomato roll?"

That's what I just said. "Yes."

"Sorry, we haven't got any lettuce."

'Okay, I'll have a bacon and mushroom roll.'

"A bacon and mushroom roll?"

"Yes."

At this point I really should have known better than to ask for anything else. "Could I have a sausage on the side?"

"Sorry?!" she said, accompanied by extreme Bette Davis eyebrows. So, can anyone tell me if 'a sausage on the side' is a metaphor in Cwmafan for something else entirely?

But we got there in the end. And very delicious it all was too.

I could have gone to Parc Siencyn Powell, opposite the rugby club on Depot Road, to eat my lunch (or dinner) but sad stories don't make for easy digestion. Until a few years ago it was called Parc-y-Llyn (Lake Park) even though said lake had been filled in with household rubbish decades ago. Before that local people called this sloping area above the school[52] the Wenglish Banc-y-Pond, named for a deep pond that used to be the header feed for the tin works. In January 1940 four little boys from the school, aged between six and eight, were skating on the frozen pond when the ice cracked. Jenkin Powell, an ex-collier and caretaker at the school, heard the shouts and dived in to save them but the mud, reeds and deep water prevented any rescue and led to his own death as well. A plaque was erected to the memory of the boys and Jenkin Powell in Cwmafan Infants' School but it was down to the efforts of local councillor David Williams that Parc-y-Llyn was renamed in 2009 for the quiet man who died a hero.[53]

The community centre opposite the park is home to the Cwmafan Communities First office. Led by Liz Randall. Communities First is the Welsh Assembly Government's flagship programme to empower local people in more disadvantaged communities to improve their living conditions and prospects.[54] It's one thing to write bureaucratic reports about 'community engagement and action for social injustice' and another to make a difference in people's lives without appearing condescending, didactic or overly worthy. But Liz and her team are doing something right because community spirit, effort and pride in Cwmafan are visible on the streets and from their activity on Facebook. Just in the course of one day I get CCF links to Mobile Skate Ramp Sessions, a water fitness class, a Summer Childcare programme, a Play Day for kids on Aberafan Beach and a call for any old denim clothes for another Summer project. Not all these events are organised by them but they're there in the background

offering advice and support, whooping with enthusiasm and spreading the news.

Liz Randall's work with the Cwmafan Residents Action Committee (CRAC) resulted in a walking group, with the gift of a name, Cwm Walking, who have organised local industrial heritage walks, nature and health walks, and even a Village Bat Walk to see bats feeding above the River Afan during the summer.

The transformation of two bus shelters on Depot Road began with a river and railway walk in October 2011 with artist and print-maker, Anne Gibbs[55]. She later worked with kids in Cwmafan Junior School and with the Cwmafan Youth Action Committee (CYAC) and the shelters include a piece of artwork from every child or young person involved with the project.

Groundwork, the environmental charity behind the bus shelter project[56], partnered with Neath Port Talbot Borough Council to install a way marker sculpture not far from the community centre.[57] It's sourced from local stone and cleverly incorporates historical and anecdotal aspects of the village. There's Stac y Foel[58] and old railway lines.[59] There's a carving of the night sky to represent the future musical and sporting stars of the village. And a little carving of Cwmafan's reputation as 'the land of the moving curtains'. You'll also see the initials PK there. They won't mean much to outsiders but everyone in the Port Talbot area knew, or knew of, Peter Knowles, or Mr Port Talbot as *Port Talbot Magnet* described him in their coverage of his funeral at St. Michael's church in October 2011.[60]

Peter Knowles was a press photographer for the *South Wales Evening Post, Western Mail, Neath and Port Talbot Guardian* and his own website, *Port Talbot News*. He'd held contracts with the Steelworks, BP Chemicals and had chronicled the construction of the M4 motorway. The list of his accomplishments as a voluntary worker is endless but more recently, as chair of CRAC, he was the driving force behind the creation of a traffic free walking and cycling route from Aberafan Beach to the Afan Valley as part of the national Sustrans Connect2 scheme.[61] His extraordinary vision, energy and humility have also been commemorated with a stone seat on the Cwmafan to Pontrhydyfen section of the walking and cycling route.

An earlier Cwmafan man with extraordinary energy was William Abraham[62], born in Copper Row in 1842. He was better known as Mabon[63], the eisteddfodic name he adopted as a singer and poet in the 1870s, and was a founding father of the trade union movement in Wales. He was also Labour MP for Rhondda West between 1918 and 1922, the year he died, but his entry in the Welsh Academy's *Encyclopaedia of Wales*[64] closes quirkily with, "His willingness to appear on tea advertisements made him a relatively wealthy man."

And the mention of groceries provides me with a neat segue into my Cwmafan man of the moment whose mother ran a grocery shop here – Siop Margaret Rose – while his father ran a fish and chip shop in Cattybrook Terrace where the Halima Tandoori Takeaway is today.

Chris is the popular and openly gay presenter of a night time show on BBC Radio Wales. My dad switches on six nights a week in the hope of 'a nice ballad from Boyo' whose playlist, all listeners' requests, can leap from Welsh hymns to Led Zeppelin, from Pavarotti to The Prodigy. And he's not alone.

The Chris Needs Friendly Garden Association Affiliated Limited (twice) has 50,000 members. Okay, the Friendly Garden Association might be imaginary in the physical sense but when I started teaching at the University of Kent, Canterbury, I spent a couple of semesters looking around the campus for The Centre for Modern Poetry. That was imaginary too. Conceptual, they called it.

Chris started working for the BBC in 1996 after winning the coveted Sony Award for Best Regional Presenter. He's also the recipient of a Lifetime Achievement Award from the Variety Club of Great Britain and was awarded an MBE in the Queen's honours list in 2005. But life hasn't always been so favourable.

Cwmafan in the 1950s and 1960s wasn't the most fertile of soil for a boy who preferred to spend an afternoon doing his mother's hair to throwing a rugby ball around and his autobiographies[65] rage against school bullying from other pupils and staff (what kind of teacher makes a kid write lines: "I am a nancy boy, I must change"?), his father's rejection of him and the repeated sexual abuse by a family friend he's always refused to identify. But in spite of the confessional material, and the shocking examples of the aggressive homophobic mail he occasionally receives, they're chirpy and entertaining books, evoking the familiar radio personality. I'd have loved to have been in the congregation at Bethania[66] that night in the 1970s when he played Tony Christie's 'Is This the Way to Amarillo?' on the chapel organ to accompany the deacons' collection.

Chris Needs in person is rather more complex. I call in to see him at the shop his mother used to run in Bethania Terrace, now called Siop Chris Needs and owned and run by Gabe, the love of his life and partner of twenty-two years, who serves me tea and custard creams.

"Gabe's a gentleman," Chris says. "I'm a complete git."

After talking to him for an hour and a half I don't believe he is. But he is angry, sad, thoughtful, rebellious, regretful and, above all, funny, with a range of camp put downs that would knock out a heckler as efficiently as a Taser-gun.

He's been living back in Cwmafan 'for Gabe', but he seems to collect homes like other people collect stamps. There's his mother's house in Cwmafan, a house in Porthcawl, two apartments in Cardiff Bay, a mobile home, a static caravan, and, until recently an apartment in Gibraltar which he's planning on replacing with a villa somewhere in Spain. Where is he happiest? Not in Wales where, he says, he's been attacked for being gay more often than anywhere else in the world. Someone spray-painted 'Queer' on the walls of his house in Porthcawl.

"I call myself queer now," he says. "And when I fill in a form that asks for marital status, I put 'poof'."

Talking of which, will he and Gabe ever get married? There's a pause then a cheeky, 'No comment,' before he tells me how an old family friend had responded with disgust when the same subject came up. "This was someone I'd known all my life. And she found me disgusting."

Experiences like that strengthen his resolve to move to Spain permanently although the weather is a big attraction as well. In one of his books he quips that he'd like his epitaph to read, 'Out of the rain at last'. I'm sure that his health worries play a part too.

Last year, after an extreme adverse reaction to medication, he was unable to eat and lost nearly six stone in a similar number of weeks. The media speculation about AIDS was boringly predictable but his listeners rallied into an airwaves equivalent of the Red Cross with one man sending him £40 pots of New Zealand honey every week to help heal the damage to his vocal chords. He still can't sing and he's looking at various treatments in the UK and, if they fail, consultations in the US. In the meantime his variety show projects are all cancelled and he had to find a lookalike for his theatre production, Encore! "People need some guts to play me," he told the *Evening Post*[67].

But I think that depends on which Chris they have to play. There's Chris Needs, 'Mr Brash, Mr Funny, Mr Caring', as he describes his radio show persona. Chris Needs the academic, M.A., D.Mus. Or Chris Needs the non-smoking, non-drinking showman whose professional life, perhaps like a lot of celebrity performers, spills into ordinary life. 'If someone tells you to bugger off, you think, What?! Why aren't you clapping?'

He doesn't believe in therapy, doesn't think it would help to ease any of the anger and hurt he carries around, including the raw grief at his mother's unexpected death a few years ago, at the age of 66, after which he developed diabetes. Perhaps he's right. But I'm more inclined to believe that what makes up Chris Needs, experiences that were good, sad and despicably ugly, are what makes him the person that appeals to his thousands of late night listeners. Take any of it away and you might lose the man who says, "As you drive into Pontrhydyfen there's a sign that reads, 'The birthplace of Richard Burton, Ivor Emmanuel and Rebecca Evans' When you drive into Cwmafan it says, 'Please Drive Slowly'."

"What are you going to write about me then?" he asks. "What a bloody fruitcake?"

No, I don't believe he's that either.

PONTRHYDYFEN

"It is spring, moonless night in the small town, starless and bible-black"[68]... You can listen to Richard Burton[69] reading the opening paragraphs of Dylan Thomas's *Under Milk Wood* on the Connect2[70] cycleway and footpath between Cwmafan and Pontrhydyfen. And sitting on a wooden bench in the cleft of the Afan Valley in the company of his rockily velvet voice is an experience worth pursuing alone. Well, you won't be entirely alone. Burton is standing next to comedian Rob Brydon[71] and former Head Ranger at Afan Forest Park, Dick Wagstaff, their three silhouettes cut from steel and fixed into a bed of stone. But they know better than to interrupt when you wind up the speaker at the side of the sculpture.

The bench is part of the Sustrans'[72] national Portrait Bench project, unique to each community who voted for the figures they'd like to see represented, and features on the Richard Burton Trail[73], as part of a network of trails originating in the Afan Forest Park. You can start from Cwmafan, outside the community centre, or a couple of miles up the B4286 at the Rhyslyn car park in Pontrhydyfen, the site of the former railway station that closed in 1964.

Everything that could have been written about Richard Burton[74], Pontrhydyfen's most famous son, probably already has been[75] but here are a few precise snippets about his early life which firmly establish him as a Port Talbot boy.

Richard Walter Jenkins was born at 2 Dan-y-Bont in Pontrhydyfen on 10th November 1925, the twelfth of thirteen children. In 1927, his mother died from septicaemia, six days after giving birth to her thirteenth child, and Richard was sent to live with his sister, Cecilia or 'Cis', and her husband, Elfed James, in Taibach. After attending school there he passed the scholarship for Port Talbot Secondary School in 1937 but left in April 1941 before obtaining his School Certificate to work at the men's outfitters department at the Taibach Co-op. It was one of his school teachers, Meredith Jones, who guided him back the following September allowing for a relationship to develop that would change the course of Richard Jenkins' life.

Between 1941 and 1943, his English teacher and commanding officer in the ATC, Philip Burton, nurtured and championed his talent, casting him in dramatic productions at school, the YMCA and the ATC. It was Burton who was probably responsible for the creation of that once heard, never forgotten voice by drilling him with parts of Shakespeare's *Henry V* in the mountains above Port Talbot. In March 1943 Richard moved into the same lodging house as Philip Burton in Connaught Street, Port Talbot. At the end of that year Burton became his legal guardian and Richard started to use the name that the world would know him by.

The Burton Birthplace Trail points out the house where he was born, Bethel Chapel[76] (which, strictly speaking, is in the adjoining community of Oakwood) where his memorial service was held in 1984, and leads you across the two magnificent bridges that dominate the village.[77]

The four bay Bont Fawr[78] (Big Bridge) aqueduct, 459 feet long and 75 feet high, was completed in 1827 by the Quaker ironmaster John Reynolds who was not to know that his considerable investment in water power, to drive the furnaces at his Oakwood ironworks, would soon be eclipsed by the coming of steam. The water course was filled in and a railway laid across it in 1841 but when the Oakwood ironworks was dismantled in 1874 the aqueduct's railway was abandoned. It was used as a minor road from 1903 and is now a public foot and cycle path.

The ten arch viaduct[79], the last railway bridge built in the Afan

Valley in 1898, is equally as imposing. Constructed from red bricks, rather than more expensive stone, it formed part of the Port Talbot Railway & Docks Company branch line to carry coal from the Ton Mawr collieries, via the Pelenna Valley, down to Port Talbot docks. The line closed in 1964.

If you walk down Aqueduct Terrace, from Bethel Chapel on the corner, towards the aqueduct, there's a view of the valley on the right that would make getting up each morning an act of pure joy. The names of the ten houses in this short terrace remind you of the one-time strength of the Welsh language in the valley. Bettws, the first stone plaque reads, Bryn Derw, Cartref, Bryn Cerdin, Arfryn, Pen Ton, Brynhir, Brynderwyn, Preswylfa and... Glenview House?? It's the last house before the aqueduct but why was it given an English name with the Scottish word for valley?

William Alun Jones who moved into Preswylfa eleven years ago, and is sitting in his front garden enjoying a cup of tea and the view, gives me some background information. His grandfather, also William Jones, bought the end house at the time of its construction in 1901. He was Welsh-speaking, but churchgoing not chapel, and the manager of the Oakwood colliery[80]. I wonder if he named his house in memory of Queen Victoria, who died in January 1901, whose passion for the Scottish Highlands was well documented during her reign. He wouldn't have been the only one: Glenviews, for houses, roads and hotels, proliferate across the English-speaking world. But nineteenth century commentators on Wales and the Welsh would have played a noxious part in the chipping away of any pride in Welsh culture too. The 1847 Royal Commission on Welsh Education is only one of many examples: "The Welsh language is a vast drawback to Wales and a manifold barrier to the moral progress and commercial prosperity of the people. It is not easy to over-estimate its evil effects."[81]

New lights were installed under the aqueduct in 2012 which has ratcheted up the drama of a night drive or saunter through Pontrhydyfen. Less obviously dramatic is the Kanji Wood across the road on the other side of the Rhyslyn car-park and picnic area. But before you reach it you'll have to swallow your disappointment when you discover that the stone sculpture in the car-park, carved with a steaming mug, is, frankly, lying. There is nowhere to get a cup of coffee around here.

The Kanji Wood, or the Japanese Garden, is part of the Afan Forest Park[82] and the result of a meeting in 1986 between the then Head Ranger, Dick Wagstaff, and Neath born writer, naturalist, environmentalist and martial artist, C.W. Nicol, a resident of Japan. It was after a visit to the Afan Forest Park in 1984, where Nicol witnessed the Forestry Commission's efforts to clean up and restore the industry scarred mountainsides of the Afan Valley, that he began to buy up neglected woodland, abandoned farmland and scrubby brush around his home in Kirohime, near Nagano, Japan with "the objective of restoring it to a diverse, healthy woodland that would be a haven for many species of creatures as well as a place for experiments in woodland management and education."[83]

In 2002 he handed over the 45 acre woodland to the Nagano Prefecture as The CW Nicol Afan Woodland Trust and it was twinned with the Afan Forest Park in two ceremonies, one in Japan and another in the Afan Forest Park the following year. If you browse through Nicol's columns in *The Japan Times Online*[84] you'll realise that Wales, and in particular the Afan Valley, are never far from his heart and mind.

The Afan Forest Park has been seriously affected by disease in recent years. *Phytophthora ramorum*, a fungus-like pathogen, was first discovered on the Japanese larch trees, deciduous conifers, in 2010 and the only way to eradicate it has been to fell vast swathes of plantations, a programme that was still continuing at the end of 2012. The larch trees in the Kanji Wood were felled in 2011, along with a number of other trees to allow for more light and to boost the

growth of those remaining. Once the felling programme is complete the Forestry Commission will design a redevelopment and replanting scheme for the whole park to improve and maintain it for the future.

Kanji is one of three styles of writing in Japan: Chinese characters or pictograms that were first introduced in the fifth century. The characters you see in the Kanji Wood represent Human, Life, and Forest, reminders of how crucial forest life is to the survival of the human race, and they've been made into sculptures, carved on their surfaces and also created in the landscape itself, by local and Japanese volunteers, through raised beds and picnic tables and benches.

There's also a haiku, a short form of Japanese poetry, by the Japanese haiku master, Issa, written in English, Welsh and Japanese on three rough slices of wood:

Flowing into/ my home village/ heaven's starry river
Afon serrenog y nef/ yn llifo i bentref/ fy maboed

The Kanji Wood was made up of around sixty different species, both conifer and broadleaf, so it hasn't fared as badly as other parts of the forest. The tree stumps cut to grass level and some clearings that feel unnaturally large do speak of absence but they also create tranquillity. And a few moments of stillness and contemplation in a simply decorated natural landscape is something we can all benefit from, even on a wet day.

> a raindrop
> balanced on a leaf of grass –
> someone is crying

> > all this green forgiving the rain

> after her death
> watching the rain
> meeting the river

As well as Bethel Chapel, Oakwood has St. John's Church on Oakwood Avenue, or rather it doesn't have St. John's Church because it's been converted into a private house. It's still so much like a church, down to the original boundary wall and gates, the owner must be used to people walking in for a look around. As I did. I later found out it was up for sale, at £325,000, but as the owner didn't volunteer this information I'm guessing I didn't tick the boxes for 'potential buyer'.

Jerusalem Chapel, on The Uplands, the opposite side of the aqueduct, boxed up its bibles and baptisms several years ago and, along with its previously converted Vestry and a deal clinching graveyard, was also up for sale in 2012 for £345,000. You'd be getting more for your money here than at St. John's (this is only an opinion – I'm not on commission) because the chapel has detailed planning consent for a ten bedroom guesthouse or bed and breakfast accommodation aimed at the rapidly growing tourist market for mountain biking in the Afan Valley which currently boasts 100km of trails.

The Glyncorrwg Mountain Bike Centre[85] is nationally known. There's accommodation for mountain bikers and a restaurant at the upmarket Afan Lodge[86] in Duffryn Rhondda. Cwmafan has the new Depot Road[87], a 1970s church conversion, and 'glamping' or glamorous camping in wooden pods at Tyle'r Fedwen farm[88]. And, by an odd quirk of fate, Gyfylchi Chapel above Pontrhydyfen, that

Jerusalem replaced, is the site of the Afan Valley Mountain Biking Centre and Bryn Bettws Lodge[89].

The moss-wrapped ruins of Gyfylchi sit on the Cistercian Way, an ancient long-distance path that linked the great abbeys of Wales and England: Margam and Tintern in South and East Wales. Take the B4287 out of Pontrhydyfen, turn right at Efail Fach, then right again at the Forestry Commission sign and up onto Mynydd Penrhys. The road's a bit rough and after you've listened to your teeth rattling in your head for half a mile you'll start to wonder if you've taken the wrong turn, but have faith.

Gyfylchi, which was re-built in 1776 on the site of an older chapel of ease, by William Davies (1729?-1787)[90] from Carmarthenshire, was an important centre of Calvinistic Methodism and, according to the information board, it inspired a special kind of devotion despite the considerable distances involved, by foot or horseback, for people to get here. A great deal of that, I'm sure, would have been down to William Davies and other travelling ministers preaching with evangelical chutzpah here. But perhaps its position on the Cistercian Way and on the boundaries of four old parishes played a part too. It even had a small extension built onto

one side: a small porch or ante-chapel where laymen, due to a short-age of ordained ministers, could preach to the congregation and not contaminate the main chapel. Industrialization and the shift from rural to town dwelling led to the building of Jerusalem Chapel in Pontrhydyfen in 1826 and Gyfylchi was abandoned.

There's another attraction worth checking out while you're here: the cheese and onion toasties in the Bryn Bettws Cafeteria. This was one of the best toasted sandwiches I've ever had: the cheese like melting fondue, the onions cooked through but retaining their bite. But the best thing about it was the outside of the bread: it had been lightly buttered beforehand so it had a sweet, toasted flavour reminiscent of those stove-top single toastie makers from the 1960s. It takes a special kind of devotion to make toasties that good.

BRYN

A couple of years ago my nephew, Gareth, married Jemma, a girl from Bryn[91], north east of Port Talbot. During his wedding speech he thanked everyone for coming.

"Lynne, who's flown in from the south of France," he said. "And some of Jemma's family who've come all the way from Nantyffyllon."

The best gags contain an element of truth and Nantyffyllon, as you've likely guessed, is a brisk jog from Bryn through the hills into foreign territory: the Borough of Bridgend. There's a further grain of truth in that people from small, enclosed communities, separated in some way from the wider world, cherish their difference, a difference that gives them a specific identity.

Eben Jones's book on Bryn is subtitled, 'The Village in the Hills' and that's pretty spot on. Hills are what surround you on the drive here, branching off the Cwmafan road, the A4107, and picking up the B4282. At one point, as the road rises and falls between the clefts, I begin to doubt I'll find any trace of civilisation, as the map promises, although the occasional car that attaches itself to my rear bumper before pulling out and roaring past suggests differently. I feel like a virtuous tourist when I pass the village's electronic speed sign and the warning light that had flashed the car in front goes out.

At an historical exhibition[92] in Bryn Community Centre a number of people come up to me.

"Are you from Bryn?" they ask expectantly.

"No, I'm from Sandfields," I say, "I was born and grew up there." And then, "but my parents are from Llanelli." I sound as if I'm apologising for having a personal history only dating back to the 1950s when the estate was built. Perhaps that's one of the reasons why the exhibition is so well researched and so well attended: the memories that hold people together here are closely woven, there's a shared history, going back centuries, that wraps them like a blanket. But there's no need for anyone else to feel left out: the pride the villagers have in their heritage means they're delighted to share their stories. The historical exhibition starts at 6.30 but I arrive a couple of hours early to see if I can find one of Cadw's less well-known listed monuments in the Port Talbot area: kiln block at former Bryn Brickworks[93].

The directions are rather vague: "Approximately 1.7km SE of Bryn village in a field on N side of the former Port Talbot Railway". And while the grid references seemed useful when I was looking at Google Earth they make no sense to me at all at ground level. I don't recommend the confused route I took via the public footpath just before the Maesteg boundary sign, across the golf course, over or under, depending on your height and gender, a barbed wire stock fence, and down into the valley over a tract of reed studded land where I fell in a bog. Instead, start from the path behind the Royal Oak Hotel in the village.

The Bryn Brickworks was operational from the end of the nineteenth century to the 1920s and the kilns are the only trace that remains. They're rare examples in South Wales of intermittent kilns associated with small nineteenth century brickworks, i.e. they were left to cool after firing rather than having their heat maintained.

The 'former Port Talbot Railway', mentioned in Cadw's record, opened in 1898 mainly for the needs of colliery owners, in this and two other valleys, who wanted their coal delivered to the docks at Port Talbot. And it was the Port Talbot Railway & Docks Company, formed in 1894, that built the railway and a tunnel for it to run through the mountainside. It started at Port Talbot's Central Station, behind Plaza cinema, and ran up the Dyffryn Valley towards Bryn and then on to Maesteg via the Cwmcerwin tunnel[94], over 1,000 yards in length. You can still see the tunnel's entrance, bricked up in 1989, a little further east of the kilns.

I'm intrigued why the brickworks had such a short life and it's guesswork that brings me to the conclusion it might have been instrumental in producing bricks to construct the tunnel and was subsequently of less use.

Developing an interest in bricks has come as a surprise, but here I am digging one up from the soft ground to try and find the name BRYN pressed into it. They're as much to do with our industrial past, and our living history too, as coal, iron and steel, and I'm not the only brick enthusiast around. There's a wall of them at the South Wales Miners' Museum in the Afan Forest Park Visitor's Centre on the A4107 north of Port Talbot. And the National Waterfront Museum in Swansea has a display of bricks manufactured in South Wales next to their brick press, and more in their stores.[95] Bryn is a little known brickworks; I might be adding to their history records.

Why the clay preparation and drying sheds, as well as the round chimney stacks once linked to the kilns, were destroyed and the kilns left standing is another mystery. But the kilns' brick domed ceilings are a work of engineering beauty and worth a visit: they could be little more than rubble within another decade if nothing is done to preserve them. They're virtually the only evidence of how a farming community was radically transformed by the expansion of heavy industry in the nineteenth and twentieth centuries and then re-transformed after its decline in the 1960s.

The gorse pocked hillsides and forestry commission land surrounding Bryn could be how the landscape looked in the early 1800s with a sprinkling of tenanted farms[96]. Coal was mined in this area as early as 1249 by the monks of Margam Abbey while they lived and worked at the abbey grange of Penhydd.[97] But the harsh industrial landscape of pithead, coal shutes and slag-heap arrived centuries later with the peak of coal production taking place between 1851 and 1871, due to the demands of the copper industry. There were four operating mines here at one time but the Bryn Navigation Mine[98] was sunk in the late 1890s and worked until 1963[99].

A miner from Bryn, forty-three year old Bryn Tudor from 1 Coronation Street, was a recruitment poster boy for Ernest Bevin's wartime scheme to keep Britain's mines supplied with essential labour. At the beginning of World War II the Government had underestimated the value of experienced coalminers and proceeded to conscript over 36,000 of them into the armed forces. A subsequent plea for enough volunteers to work in the mines failed and by 1943, with continuing hostilities preventing imports, there was a desperate need for coal at home and for the wartime effort.

From 1943 one in ten physically fit conscripts was allocated to

work in Britain's mines; 48,000 of them over a period of five years. The Bevin Boys[100], as they came to be known, came from all professions, did the hard, dirty work of miners, and were often unfairly treated and criticised as draft-dodgers, victims of bigoted attitudes towards conscientious objectors, a small number of whom were also sent to work in the mines. Families in Welsh towns and villages also resented their presence when their own fathers and sons were fighting and dying in Europe. When the programme came to an end in 1948, the Bevin Boys were expected to return to their old lives with no acknowledgement of their war contribution and no right to their previous jobs, as was the case with armed forces personnel.

It might have been a case of too little, too late but amends were eventually made in 2007, under Tony Blair's government, to award a Veteran's Badge to the thousands of conscripts who worked down the mines during World War II.

Bryn's most famous and possibly most respected miner was Billy Beynon[101], 5' 2" local hero as fit and fertile as a ferret, who became British and Empire Bantamweight champion when he beat Digger Stanley at the National Sporting Club in London on 2 June, 1913. His win over Stanley was the pinnacle of his career but he carried on boxing until 1928.

Beynon was born on 8 April, 1890 in the Goytre area of Port Talbot. He took up boxing as a teenager to supplement his collier's wages and used to train by running between his Port Talbot home and the colliery, and on the hills around Bryn, before and after putting in a full shift. He also found the energy to father somewhere between eleven and fifteen children: accounts vary on the exact number.

On 20 July, 1932, while Beynon was working on the coal-face at Bryn with his fourteen year-old son, the noise of an imminent roof collapse prompted him to push his son to safety while he took the full weight of the fall.

His popularity was evident at his funeral, attended by several thousand mourners, including the Canadian boxer Del Fontaine and Jack Peterson, the first Welshman to win the British Heavyweight Championship[102]. His youngest son, eleven week old Ivor, was christened over his dad's coffin on the same day. A couple of years later, in May 1934, 5,000 people turned up in his honour when a marble memorial was unveiled in Goytre cemetery[103] by the Chief Constable of Glamorgan.[104] His gravestone is framed by a pair of boxing gloves.

Graham Rowland and other members of Bryn Residents Action
Group[105] are working to officially change the name of one hill,
alongside Drysiog farm, to Billy Beynon's Hill. In the meantime,
running up hills is still very much a part of the village with the
annual Bwystfil y Bryn – Beast of Bryn – Alpine Trail Running
Races[106]. The runs are not for the faint-hearted, not even the half-
size run of 6.8 miles. If you're planning to take on the full 15 miles
then make sure you've eaten your three Shredded Wheat. Even the
organisers don't underestimate the challenge: 'backbreaking' they
say. There's also a 2km fun-run. I can't say if the switch from
Imperial measurement to Metric is a subtle comment on what Bryn
runners think of the capabilities of their European counterparts.

The Bwystfil is named for the sightings of several big cats
reported in the hills around Bryn over the years. The people I talk
to at the historical exhibition seem pretty sincere about the sightings
– no Hound of the Baskerville theatrics attached – but I don't meet
anyone who's actually seen one. However, there is a nasty claw-
mark at the entrance to the Bryn to Goytre and Port Talbot Cycle
Path, just at the back of the Royal Oak Hotel, built in 1898, that
follows the route of the old railway.[107] You have been warned.

notes

1. Cadw record 14147
2. http://www.coflein.gov.uk/en/site/18038/images/BLAEN+BAGLAN/
3. http://www.welshruins.co.uk/photo2076465.html
4. Evans, *Baglan*, pp.19-20
5. Welsh Biography Online: http://tiny.cc/kv33qw
6. Evans, *Baglan*, pp.29-30
7. Drabble, p.628.
8. Ibid, pp.412-413.
9. Evans, *Baglan*, pp.129-131
10. Cadw record 14171
11. King James Bible, I Kings 6.7
12. An early historian, J.O. Westwood, in *Lapidarium Walliae: The Early Inscribed and Sculptured Stones of Wales*, The Cambrian Archaeological Association, 1876-1879, is convinced by the letter 'f'. A. Leslie Evans (*The Story of Baglan*) states that the 'f' is a weathered, early Christian Chi-rho symbol which invokes the crucifixion. (http://en.wikipedia.org /wiki/Chi_Rho).
13. Royal Commission on Ancient and Historical Monuments in Wales (1976) *An Inventory of the Ancient Monuments in Glamorgan Volume 1: Pre-Norman. Part II: The Early Christian Period.* Cardiff: HMSO
14. There is another St. Baglan in the village. The National School (1873), on Old Baglan Road, educated the munchkins of the parish until 1951 when a new Primary School opened on Elmwood Road. The school was dedicated as a church of ease to St. Catharine's in 1959.
15. Lewis, Samuel, *A Topographical Dictionary of Wales*, 1849: http://www.genuki.org.uk/ big/wal/GLA/Baglan/Lewis1833.html
16. End moraines, or terminal moraines, are ridges of unconsolidated debris deposited at the snout or end of the glacier. Wikipedia: http://tiny.cc/r6g3kw
17. "I see things in a certain way. It probably goes back to industrial England, and, a lot of people would say, that's why you get Blade Runner. There were steelworks adjacent to West Hartlepool, so every day I'd be going through them, and thinking they're kind of magnificent, beautiful, winter or summer, and the darker and more ominous it got, the more interesting it got". From 'Director Maximus', interview with Monahan, Mark, *The Telegraph*, 20.9.03: http://tiny.cc/dug3kw
18. The Chartered Institution of Highways and Transportation: http://www.ciht.org.uk/
19. Sheers, p.66
20. See East: Margam Park
21. Ruins opposite the junction of the A48 with the B4283 to North Cornelly.
22. The original quote reads, 'To lose one parent, Mr Worthing, may be regarded as a misfortune; to lose both looks like carelessness'. From, *The Importance of Being Earnest, A Trivial Comedy for Serious People* by Oscar Wilde.
23. Llewellyn Heycock, Baron Heycock CBE (1905-1990), born in Margam, was a respected and powerful voice in South Wales politics. He was made a life peer in 1967. Wikipedia: http://tiny.cc/lah3kw
24. Cadw record 14172. The Round Chapel, built in 1838, was actually octagonal.
25. *Daily Mirror*, 14.4.1975
26. Chartered Institute of Highways and Transportation: http://tiny.cc/ich3kw
27. One of these identified as Soar Calvanistic Methodist Chapel, Corlannau, built 1849: http://www.genuki.org.uk/big/wal/GLA/Aberavon/Chapels.html
28. Fychan, p.24
29. Graham Hughes was born in Port Talbot in 1929. He attended the old secondary school

in Talcennau Road, read English and Law at Cambridge and moved to the USA in 1956 where he became a Professor of Law at New York University. He perfected his Welsh while in the States and also translated, *Dechreuad a Chynnydd Gweithiau Cwmafan* by John Rowlands, a winning entry in the Ivorites Eisteddfod held in Aberafan in 1853.

30. Lewis, Ivor, *The Afan Fisheries*, Afan Valley Angling Club 1999. 'The pools themselves are no longer visible but lay beneath the artificial bed which was created when Corlannau weir was erected.' p.15
31. Roberts Jones, *Welcome to Town*
32. http://www.cracwales.org.uk/about%20crac.html
33. Opened 28.9.1971
34. *Port Talbot Guardian*, 5.11.1988
35. http://en.wikipedia.org/wiki/Blue_Scar
36. http://www.imdb.com/title/tt0092965/
37. Welsh Biography Online: http://tiny.cc/kua4qw
38. www.christopherpainter.co.uk
39. Ifan, p.34
40. www.parishofcwmafan.com
41. Y Lolfa 2007 www.ylolfa.com
42. Eaton DT, 'Cwmavon and some Early Notabilities', *Transactions of the Port Talbot Historical Society*, No.2, Vol 1 (1965)
43. The second highest peak in the Afan Valley
44. http://en.wikipedia.org/wiki/William_Brunton
45. Went into production in May 1838, Eaton, Ibid
46. Rees, W&C, p.43
47. Lewis, Samuel, A Topographical Dictionary of Wales, 1849, pp. 273-276, www.british-history.ac.uk
48. Rees, W&C, p.43
49. *Western Mail*, 6.2.1965
50. http://www.afantavern.co.uk/
51. The Earls of Jersey were successive significant landowners in the area. Lettsom would have leased his 1000 acres from the sixth Earl (1808-1859). http://en.wikipedia.org/wiki/Earl_of_Jersey.
52. The school fronts Ty'r Owen Row but stretches back towards the park. It was built in 1910 after the Education Act of 1902 abolished local school boards.
53. http://www.walesonline.co.uk/news/south-wales-news/port-talbot/2009/03/05/village-s-memorial-to-true-hero-jenkin-powell-91466-23053513/
54. http://wales.gov.uk/topics/housingandcommunity/regeneration/communitiesfirst/?lang=en
55. http://www.annegibbs.co.uk
56. Funded through the Rural Development Plan for Wale, and with the support of Baytrans, the Swansea Bay Sustainable Transport and Tourism Partnership: http://www.baytrans.org.uk
57. Funded by the Welsh Assembly Government through the European Regional Development Fund and Western Valleys Regeneration Area scheme. CCF 'Putting Your Community First' Issue 34, Summer 2012
58. A 13 metre brick chimney built on the top of Mynydd Foel as an outlet for fumes from the copper works and demolished in 1940.
59. The Rhondda and Swansea Bay Railway and the Port Talbot Railway, later Great Western Railway, ran through Cwmafan on top of a network of rails serving the industries there. See an old freight weighing mechanism outside the community centre.
60. http://www.lnpt.org/2011/10/19/hundreds-bid-farewell-to-mr-port-talbot/
61. http://www.sustrans.org.uk/

62. For a full account of his life see, Jones, *Port Talbot Gallery 3*, pp.161-175
63. Heol Mabon is named after him.
64. Davies, Jenkins, Baines, Lynch eds., University of Wales Press, Cardiff 2008, p.11
65. Needs Chris, *like it is* and *And there's more*, Y Lolfa 2007 and 2009. *Highs and Lows*, a third volume, is due in 2013.
66. Bethania Independent Chapel, Salem Road, built 1850, rebuilt or enlarged 1858
67. Evening Post, 10.8.2012
68. Thomas, Dylan, *Under Milkwood, A Play for Voices*, JM Dent & Sons, London 1954, p.1
69. Official website: http://www.richardburton.com/
70. http://www.sustrans.org.uk/what-we-do/connect2
71. Rob Brydon was born and grew up in Baglan.
72. A UK charity enabling people to travel more often by foot, cycle or public transport. http://www.sustrans.org.uk
73. http://www.afanforestpark.co.uk/default.aspx?page=7390
74. www.richardburton.com
75. Also see East: Taibach
76. Cadw record 23021
77. 'Pont' is bridge in Welsh and village's name is likely to be a compression of 'Pont ar Rhyd Afan', the bridge at the Afan ford. Evans, Daniel, *Place Names of the Afan Valley*.
78. Cadw record 23022
79. Cadw record 23024
80. Oakwood Mines, Pontrhydyfen. 1918 workforce: 308 underground, 57 surface. Mgr: W. Jones. Closed 1927. www.welshcoalmines.co.uk
81. Wikipedia: http://tiny.cc/04a2jw
82. http://www.afanforestpark.co.uk/
83. http://www.japantimes.co.jp/text/fe20030807cw.html
84. *Japan Times Online*, Old Nic's Notebook Index: http://tiny.cc/04a2jw
85. http://glyncorrwgpondsvisitorcentre.co.uk/mountain-biking/
86. http://www.mountain-bike-accommodation.com/index.html
87. http://www.depotrd.co.uk/
88. Tyle'r Fedwen Farm, Cwmafan, Port Talbot, SA12 9YA http://www.thisissouthwales.co.uk/Carry-glamping-new-farm-pod/story-17245276-detail/story.html
89. http://www.brynbettws.com/
90. http://wbo.llgc.org.uk/en/s-DAVI-WIL-1729.html
91. The village's full name is Bryntroedygam, the hill of the twisted or crooked foot. The OS Explorer Map 165 shows an outline of a hill above the village that, with a little imagination, looks a bit like a club foot.
92. Organised by the Bryn Residents Action Group: http://www.bryn-porttalbot.btck.co.uk/
93. Cadw record 22167
94. Its red bricked archway bears the letters PTR and 1897.
95. From the collection of Lawrence Skuse www.pemmorfa.com/bricks: South Wales Argus, 24.11.2009.
96. Part of the Margam Estate, owned by the Talbot family.
97. Evans, *Margam Abbey*, pp.40/41
98. The Bryn Navigation Mine slag-heap was referred to locally as 'Amy', after Amy Johnson, the first woman aviator to fly solo from England to Australia, because it appears that locals thought the coal drams (wagons or tubs) looked as if they were about to take off as they travelled up it.
99. *Evening Post* 6.12.2012: The site of the former colliery declared as a local nature reserve because of its biodiversity and community interest.
100. http://www.museumwales.ac.uk/en/rhagor/article/2041/

101. Jones, *Port Talbot Gallery 2*, pp.1-18

102. Hanson, *Profile*, p.57

103. See East: Goytre

104. *Daily Mirror*, 21.5.1934.

105. http://www.bryn-porttalbot.btck.co.uk/

106. http://www.bwystfilybryn.btck.co.uk/

107. Bryn railway station was at the back of the Royal Oak. The passenger service only lasted thrity years and was closed after the construction of the main road from Port Talbot to Bryn and Maesteg.

WEST

BAGLAN BAY

'Wasteland turned into a Wonderland'[1] was the announcement at the official opening of the BP Petrochemical works at Baglan Bay in 1963. Wonderland was an accurate description for the completed site at night: the plant lights, visible from miles around, glittered like an industrial Las Vegas. And wonderland it would have been too for the boost to the South Wales economy and the creation of jobs. By 1968 it was one of the largest petrochemical sites in Europe covering 500 acres and at its peak, in 1974, employing 2,500 people.

The accuracy of 'wasteland' depends on your point of view: a small bay[2] at the mouth of the River Neath[3] backed by saltmarsh, sand dunes and moorland, framed on one side by Sandfields housing estate and separated from the village of Baglan on another by the Swansea to London railway and the A48 main trunk road. The land had always been undeveloped. The 9th Glamorgan Rifles, a volunteer artillery unit, used it in the mid-nineteenth century as a range and battery point in expectation of a French invasion that never arrived. It was used again as a rifle and practice range during World War I and by the Home Guards during World War II.[4] Older people remember the moors as an open, natural habitat for wildlife, punctured with streams and pools.

There were inevitable problems associated with manufacturing huge quantities of hazardous chemicals on the doorstep of densely populated residential areas during BP's peak years in the 1960s and 1970s: pollution and noxious fumes, washing turning black or even disintegrating on the garden line were some of the complaints from the neighbouring communities.

I attended Sandfields Comprehensive School between 1969 and 1976, a cough and a choke away from BP, and I remember the warning sirens to stay inside until an all-clear. I also remember a monstrous open-mouthed effluent pipe that used to cut through the sand dunes from the works onto the high tide line of the beach in the 1960s. I checked with a few other people to make sure it wasn't a figment of my childhood imagination.

Market changes in the industry brought a partial site closure in the mid-1990s but the final shout came in 2004. We're back to wasteland now, but in a more accurate sense: a scraped and scarred plain where the plant has been demolished, dug up and carted away. A few small brick compounds and electricity substations are scattered across it and, on the horizon, towards the River Nedd, there's the high-tech sheds of General Electric's gas turbine power plant built in 2003. Post-apocalyptic desolation is the impression I get when the rep for St. Modwen[5] drives me around the perimeter in 2012.

You wouldn't think there's anything here worth nicking but the hunks of reinforced concrete from the demolition work, dumped in front of some of the vulnerable wire panels along the old BP boundary fence, help to keep out the idiots who believe there is. What does remain, mostly hidden underground, is potentially lethal: high voltage cables. Not all of them are live but you can bet that some troglodyte will accidentally find one and the grunts for compensation will be loud.

St. Modwen acquired the 1,000 acre site in 2009 and they're overseeing the redevelopment plans and continuing with land remediation work voluntarily advanced by BP. Some areas, like the site of the old Styrene plant, are heavily contaminated, down to 3 metres in depth, and it could take another five years before the work is complete.

I was surprised there's no legal stipulation to clean the land but the standard of remediation work depends on its eventual use. What's required for housing or schools would far exceed the acceptable level for industry. Up until now development has been limited to industry: the most recent announcement was for a £15 million solar energy farm with 25,000 photovoltaic panels generating enough electricity for 1,500 homes[6]. But plans for a new £40 million super-school on the site have also been spoken about.[7] If, post 2016, Port Talbot's schoolchildren grow extra toes or start glowing in the dark we'll have a pretty good measure of what the acceptable levels are. Just kidding. Really.

The natural landscape annihilated in the 1960s is making small encroachments. South-east of the General Electric power station, and nudging right up to the southern end of a plot intended for the construction of a second, larger gas turbine power station, there's a seven hectare Lapwing site, the largest remaining Lapwing population in the borough.

Lapwings became a fully protected species after changes to farming destroyed their natural nesting grounds. They're now highly dependent on brownfield sites, like Baglan Bay, where scrub and ground vegetation supply the varied habitat they need. It's not easy being a lapwing egg: you're laid in a scrape of ground at risk from predators. Being a chick doesn't get much better: your parents lead you to and from feeding sites for about 5 to 6 weeks until you can fly.

There is good news for the Lapwings: gas turbine power plants are cleaner and less harmful to wildlife than the petrochemical industry. And Neath Port Talbot Council's bio-diversity programme is committed to protecting the birds and perhaps even expanding the breeding ground. But the reality of multi-million pound developments, the money they are capable of generating, means that directions and policies can change. But for now I'm going to think positively and take some advice from Winnie the Pooh who unexpectedly turned up in a water pipe on my site tour.

"Tigger is all right really," said Piglet lazily.
"Of course he is," said Christopher Robin.
"Everybody is really," said Pooh. "That's what I think."[8]

The whole site is owned jointly by BP, the Welsh Development Agency and Neath Port Talbot County Borough Council. The northern end has been developed into the two phase Baglan Energy Park, home to a diverse collection of companies from the ethical beauty-product business, Montagne Jeunesse, to Wales' first

Hydrogen Research and Demonstration Centre, exploring the use of hydrogen as a fuel of the future. General Electric's power station supplies electricity at a discounted rate to the tenants on Phase 1 with the rest being fed into the National Grid.

It's surprisingly straightforward getting into the power station. I phone up and ask if I can have a tour and it's arranged within a few days. There's a security barrier where I have to page reception before it lifts but there's no handbag search, although, come to think of it, I left my handbag in the car. I wanted to do my best for womankind in an environment that feels particularly intimidating. I was rubbish at science in school. And when Kelvin Hood, Operations Manager, tells me I have to get my PPE, I have a rush of exam panic. But PPE is Personal Protective Equipment: hard hat, high-vis jacket, and earplugs that are satisfyingly colour-coordinated with the yellow jacket.

When it opened in 2003 the GE plant was equipped with the most advanced combined steam and gas turbines in the world, at 500 MW (megawatts), powerful enough to supply electricity to 500,000 homes. Technology has continued its relentless advance and their soon to be new neighbour, Abernedd Power Ltd, will almost double that production with 875 MW. But the high-tech aspects of this facility are still impressive.

Now that it's fully operational, the whole plant can be run from the control room by three technicians. A room next door, packed out with hundreds of metal lockers, is the electronic heart, each door protecting the millions of cables that are its veins and arteries. If you remember that as late as 1995 an IBM mainframe could take up a whole room that will give you some perspective.

A new gas pipe had to be laid on to supply the needs of the plant, a whole 11.5km of it, from the Transco feeder main in the north. If you look up at Mynydd y Gaer from the A48, where Baglan meets Briton Ferry, you'll see the swathe of land that was cleared to lay it down to the bay. The old lower pressure one running across the River Neath and through the site, that used to supply BP, now delivers gas to the houses on Sandfields Estate.

Modernisation extends to the external construction too. Those old hyperboloid cooling towers that used to dominate industrial landscapes are becoming a thing of the past. Although still called by the same name they now tend to be long sheds, reminiscent of big out of town DIY stores. The science we take for granted in cooling systems, this one as well as those in our restaurants, hotels and cars, is the same science, if not properly monitored, that can kill us with Legionnaire's Disease. And this monster-sized 10 cell water cooling tower has the capability to do exactly that in significant numbers. It won't, of course, by the simple addition of chlorine that inhibits the growth of the bacteria responsible. Sometimes the simple things are as astonishing as the futuristic.

A relatively simple thing is happening in the southern corner of Baglan Bay, on the edge of Aberafan Beach, where a local company run a ragworm farm for bait and dried fish food. The security at the ragworm farm is in stark contrast with my visit to GE: I can't get past the office. The worm business is, I am told, highly competitive and they are anxious not to reveal any of their secrets by letting me walk around the raised troughs where the worms are fed and fattened. Given I have no idea what a ragworm even looks like I doubt I'm a good candidate for worm espionage.

But I am allowed a peek in a shed where a man wearing thick gloves (these babies bite) is scooping a mound of wriggling flesh onto a large wooden paddle. Between ragworm, lugworm and mudworm, the ragworm wins the prize for good looks with its frilly body fringe but none of them pick up points on body odour. The air is sodden with damp worm-flesh, a smell I remember from my childhood when my dad came back from digging for lugworm on the beach at low-tide.

As I leave the shed I notice one on the wet, concrete floor and I think about picking it up to add to my growing Port Talbot souvenir collection. I'm sure it'll air-dry quite nicely. But the proprietors' concerns about malicious competitors and rumour-mongering seem quite genuine, and they're nice people too, and I don't want to do anything that might come across as suspicious. Or just plain weird, I think in retrospect.

ABERAFAN BEACH

It was mecca for day-trippers from the valleys during the summers of the 1960s, those days of innocence when a warm bottle of pop and sunburn were the quintessential components of a good day out. When using sun-screen meant sitting in the shade of a canvas windbreak, a beach accessory that, according to American Bill Bryson, you have to be British to understand. "Why, pray, are you there if you need a windbreak?"[9]

I was born and grew up a street away from the beach, could roll up a towel and be running across the sand within two minutes, a fact I was eternally grateful for when it came to calls of nature. There were no toilets at the western end of the beach so anything more than a pee created a pressing problem. If the quality of the water was anything to go by then a few people overcame their inhibitions though it was more likely that the occasional fragment of floating faecal matter was the result of careless sewerage disposal in the bay. Add to that the little oil slicks and glittering drifts of coal dust we jumped over to get to the scum-frothed waves and we couldn't have had more fun. But we did. We didn't know any better than a beach framed by a petrochemical works and a steelworks, and the country as a whole was yet to be seduced by the sun and ulcer-inducing wine of cheap Spanish holidays.

In 2013 the beach couldn't be further from its contaminated past: a stretch of gleaming, soft sand that's tractored clean every day. Its Blue Flag status was renewed every year from 2008 but it narrowly missed out on the award in 2012: tests for water quality in the bay only achieved 15 out of 20 'excellent' readings rather than the required 16. (I blame the water washing over from Swansea.) And it remains a popular beach with surfers[10] with areas at the eastern end reserved for boards and for water craft.

THE PROM

We didn't have a toilet at the western end but we did have one of the original beach shops, double-sided seating pavilions with a shop at either end, topped with flat overhanging roofs where you could buy your sweets and ice-cream, your bucket and spade, and be sheltered from the sun. Or the rain.

The beach-shop is long gone, abandoned, vandalised and demolished by the 1980s (along with the original prom attractions: funfair, seaside pavilion, tea-gardens, toilet blocks, the putting green, paddling and boating pools, trampolines and a roller skate rink) after the last proprietor, Mrs Johns, a short, plump woman with hair the colour of Brillo, relinquished the lucrative business of counting four-a-penny Black Jacks and Fruit Salads, White Mice, Flying Saucers and Rainbow Drops into white paper packets for the kids from the western end of Sandfields Estate.

> crowded promenade
> a little boy jumps
> the long shadows

Work on the first stretch of promenade began in 1901 at the eastern end of the beach where the Jersey Beach Hotel used to stand, now the site of the Jersey Quay residential development. It had been the spot favoured by day-trippers since the middle of the nineteenth century[11] because of its proximity to the town and railway station though facilities for visitors were limited to bathing machines, some official, and unofficial, refreshment stalls and sheds, and a bandstand that popped up in 1891. The new promenade project was funded by the proprietors of the hotel, Lord Jersey[12], and the Aberavon Corporation and opened in the spring of 1902 along with the renovated wooden pier, the old north breakwater. Built on a concrete sea wall, it stretched for 640 feet with the kind of trimmings every self-respecting Victorian prom deserved – tubular railings, cast iron lamps, seating, and steps to the beach – but, unfortunately, no bandstand. That was sold by the Corporation for the princely sum of £5, to make way for the new prom, and never replaced.

But the major building works that gave us our modern day prom began in the 1950s when the sand dunes running along the shore,

the Aberavon Burrows, were levelled to make way for the building of Sandfields Estate which would house the massive influx of workers at the new steelworks. Building houses on sand, over 3000 of them by 1956, meant that some kind of sea defence wall was essential and when it was completed in the late 1950s the prom extended for 1¼ miles.

The 'prom' is what all the locals call it, never the promenade. And despite a shift away from tourism at the western end, where a significant development of independent care homes has sprung up, and the loss of the attractions that gave it a traditional 'tiddly om pom pom', some of the council's recent projects, around the theme of Art & Energy, have definitely reinvigorated the seafront.

The old rough concrete arches and rusty two bar tubular railings, that were meant to protect you from the eight foot drop over the seawall onto unyielding stone, but were actually kindergarten-easy to climb, have been replaced with white curved posts and a triple rail. Their modern design is intended to be anti-climb but they could equally be curving inland from the force of the westerly winds that push in from the bay. They're made from white ferrocast polyurethane because of its resistance to rust and corrosion, and while the name on the page is hollow with an absence of poetry, their sleek lines and Persil-brightness sing against the skyline as refreshingly as Port Talbot's adopted tenor, Paul Potts.

These, along with the new benches, the resurfacing with pedestrian and bike lanes and the white lampposts with their happy blue caps make the prom a delight to walk, jog or cycle along. And, unfortunately, to hop, skip and jump along if the piles of dog excrement are anything to go by on the morning I head east.

There's a skate-board park, a toddlers play park, and a new adventure playground that shouts with lots of bright plastic. It was built in 2012 as a replacement for a wooden version that had greyed and weathered beautifully in the salt air. It seemed pretty sturdy but I imagine that splinters are high on the list of Public Enemies as far as Health & Safety are concerned. Far more satisfying is Franco's, the prom's renowned fish and chip shop. Raymond 'Franco' DiFrancesco started frying in a blue shed in 1970, not far from the current purpose-built brick building, and the place is still going strong. Fish and chips and longevity: that's art and energy enough for me.

It's outside Franco's that you find the first of two steel sculptures by Carmarthenshire based artist, Andrew Rowe[13]. 'Taper' is a column of steel weighing 4 tonnes that rises 13 metres into the sky, kinked like a ripple of cloth at its peak. 'Kite Tail', a few hundred

yards further along, is the largest single piece of artwork to be installed in Wales at 14 metres high, 17 tonnes in weight and made from one continuous band of steel looping through itself that seems to defy gravity. It's an extraordinary feat of engineering and a dramatic symbol of the industry the town is famous for, and of the more contemporary allure of this stretch of coastline for wind and kite surfers and stunt kite flyers.

A twenty-first century paddling pool, the Aquasplash, has replaced the 1950s boating and paddling pools and at the midpoint of the prom the Coastguard[14], Aberavon Surf Life Saving Club[15] and RNLI[16] buildings cluster around the slipway off the roundabout.

Until 2012, when a futuristic steel and glass booth appeared at the western end of the prom[17], you had to make it past this midpoint to find a cup of coffee: Café Remo's was opened by the DiFrancesco family in 2005 and tends to be packed to the scuppers day and night.

You'd also have to make it here to find a toilet. The Piazza and Toilets, better known locally as Telly Tubbies Hill due to the raised grass mound the toilets shelter beneath and its crown of futuristic railings, was a long awaited replacement for three 1950s toilet blocks dotted along the prom.

I find it a bit too military bunkerish for the seaside, although the choice of steel cladding is undoubtedly linked to anti-vandalism objectives. But the £945,000 the council spent on them does seem a bit steep for a few flushing toilets built into a bank of earth even if there is plenty of room in the Piazza out front to form an orderly queue.

The only original feature remaining from the glory days of the 1960s are The Sunken Gardens, beyond the 'Kite Tail', which after metaphorically living up to their name for decades had a twenty-first century makeover last year with geometric granite paths and wooden benches thanks to a European grant of £135,000.

The upkeep of the oddly popular Blue Whale is less of a drain on public funds: a lump of painted concrete from the 1980s submerged in the grass next to the Jersey Quay. A few years ago the council put forward a proposal to create a car-park on the site but following a flurry of local protests the planners appear to have backed down. It's a popular hang-out for teenagers who usually sit on it with their backs to the sea, preferring, with true adolescent indifference, the view of the waste ground on the other side of the main road.

The whale brings us back to the prom's beginnings. The Jersey Quay townhouses and apartments are on the site of the old Jersey Beach Hotel, built in 1900 for a syndicate of local business men. Its imposing three storeys of red brick met the needs of wealthier beach visitors for several years before it was reduced to a shell by a fire in 1908. It was rebuilt the following year, with a roller skating rink appearing on its flat roof in the 1920s, and it remained as a hotel, bar and wedding venue until its closure in 1999. When the Welsh Development Agency bought it a year later there was hope that this iconic Port Talbot building would be preserved but in 2001 history repeated itself and the hotel was destroyed by fire with the blaze visible as far away as Devon, across the Bristol Channel[19].

THE PIER

The concrete breakwater, that splits Aberafan Beach into its large and small sides, runs along the same line as the old wooden pier that opened to the public in 1902. It used to mark the entrance to the docks and was the site of several shipwrecks[20].

The *SS Ethelwalda* floundered in a violent gale here while trying to enter the docks in October 1911. The crew was rescued but the cargo of pit props was tossed into the sea and the ship itself stuck fast in the sand despite attempts to free it. In 1913 the Blue Star Liner *S.S. Brodland*, taking Welsh coal from Port Talbot to Puntas Arenas in Chile, was parted from its tug in a fierce gale and driven ashore more or less in the same spot. Once again there was no loss of life but the ship suffered the same fate.

The seductive wrecks were the scene of several tragic accidents in the following decades[21] and it wasn't until the early 1960s that the remains of both ships were finally blasted out of the sand. The *Brodland*'s anchor is displayed outside the Coastguard station on the prom.

The wooden pier, pummelled by storms and high winds, was patched up every decade between the 1920s and the 1950s until the only thing left to do was to encase it in concrete. The problem of additional protection against the strength of the sea was solved with 'tetrapods'. Not alien life forms but concrete, four legged jackstones, 2,147 of them, that sea water could flow around and over rather than crashing directly into the breakwater wall.

While the tetrapods protected the arm of the pier, problems from sand erosion and ground movement over the following decades threatened the 1950s sea wall supporting the prom. In 2009 major coastal protection works laid nearly 4,000 tons of stone at both the western and eastern ends of the beach, tumbles of giant rocks that have a likeable Flintstone charm to them.

I'm quite fond of the tetrapods that still nudge the concrete pier. They might have been placed there as coastal defence but as kids they were our climbing frames, and in teenage years, an outcrop to look particularly moody on as you stared out to sea. Although you were advised only to strike that pose at low tide. And I hadn't realised how many still survived until a particularly low tide early in 2013 exposed them at the end of the pier in their beached mountainous glory.

The pier, in its more watery state, hosts the annual round-the-pier swim organised by Aberavon Green Stars RFC[22] who celebrated their 125th anniversary in 2012. The club badge is a shield bearing a shamrock, an Irish harp, the Welsh red dragon and the Prince of Wales' feathers: a symbol of the club's origins in the town's Irish community.

The Great Irish Famine[23] of 1845-1852 saw a significant increase in emigration to Liverpool and Glasgow and the port towns of industrial South Wales. The first Catholic church in Port Talbot was established in 1851 at Capel Moriah, Clifton Terrace, Aberafan, built by the Baptists in 1822 but used by a bundle of different faiths through two centuries before it was demolished to make way for the M4 motorway in the 1960s[24]. The first purpose built church, St. Joseph's in Aberafan, was consecrated in 1860 and rebuilt in 1931, developments which reflected the growth of the town's Catholic population from 200 in 1850 to 3,300 by 1925.

The Green Stars opened their clubhouse on the Little Warren Playing Fields, at the back of the small side of the beach, in 1962 and properly earned their nickname of 'The Fighting Irish' in the following three years when they created a record in world rugby by being the first team to achieve one hundred consecutive games without defeat.

All of which you can ponder while you watch a flock of men clad in speedos hurtling towards the pier every August because the swim begins and ends with a sprint from and to the club. Okay, there aren't only men, and not all of them are wearing speedos, but they're the ones who tend, for some reason, to catch my eye.

The Green Stars came up with the idea of a race around the pier, originally called the Prince of Wales Investiture Cup Annual Land and Sea Race[25], in response to Port Talbot Borough Council's request for clubs to organise a special event for the Investiture year in 1969.[26] It proved so popular they kept it going and it's currently supported by the local authority and Tata Steel.

In 1969 5,000 people watched 22 entrants take part. Robert Phillips was declared the winner with a time of 18 minutes and 11 seconds. Bernard Donovan, who has organised the event from the outset, tells me that a lot of rugby players made up the original entrants but fitness levels and times have improved since more triathletes and lifeguards have taken part. Marc Jenkins, the Olympic triathlete from Bridgend, won the event in 2004 and 2006. In 2012 there were 65 entrants and local lifeguard, Garod Thomas, was first back at the club, completing a 2 x 700 metre run and the 800 metre swim in 15 minutes 49 seconds. Bernard, who was born in 1934, took part in the race every year between 1969 and 2010 which makes him the longest serving entrant, a record that'll take some beating.

Another piece of history attached, literally, to the pier is a rusting spear that pushes up at an angle from the concrete floor and leans towards the prom, what remains of the rail sidings laid to transport sand and cement for early pier repairs.

There's no logical reason why I'm so fond of it but it feels like a symbol of the town I was born into – the sea, the iron industry – and a metaphor for strength and survival. Of course, there's also the irony of a rail designed for forward movement being permanently immobilised in a bed of concrete. Sometimes I think too much.

> sun along the shore
> even the grey cockleshells
> surprise me

PRINCESS MARGARET WAY

The road that runs parallel to the prom, dividing it from the houses of Sandfields Estate, was granted its royal title in 1959, three years after Princess Margaret, on a visit to the Steel Company of Wales, unveiled a commemorative tablet in a section of the new sea defence wall.

The first pub to open along the new road, at the midpoint round-about, was the Marine Hotel in 1960 although the name was changed almost immediately to the Four Winds. The hardy bloke showing his belly on its roof in all seasons today is called Windy Man who has his own Facebook page[27]. His uncomfortable looking

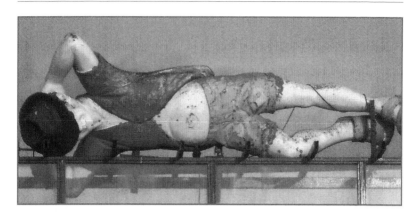

position is due to the fact that he started life on his back as part of a Foster's Lager promotion in London's Leicester Square. The Bay View Social Club was the next to open, a little further east, in 1962 and both premises were welcome oases for thirsty fathers and uncles in the booming summer months of that decade while the women struck up camp on the beach and kept an eye on the kids. The Bay View closed in the 1990s, was demolished after a fire and houses and a car park were built around the site.

The present Best Western Aberavon Beach Hotel opened as The Hotel Executive with a million pound bang in 1973[28]. I had to wait a couple more years, until the summer of 1975 when I was 17, before my parents allowed me to go to the Sunday night discos in the grandly named Snowdon Banqueting Suite (now The Ballroom). This was Port Talbot's very own Sunday night fever two years before the hysteria of the official Saturday Night version. The Stylistics, Van McCoy and the Hustle, George Macrae, KC and the Sunshine Band, Barry White (the first time round). And, just before 11pm and lights up, 10cc and all that slow soul-wrenching faux-denial of being in love. We were young hearts running free. The real thing.

Talking of which, it was around that time that Richard Burton and Elizabeth Taylor stayed at the hotel, in that brief wedge of rekindled happiness between their second marriage in October 1975 and second divorce in July 1976.

But the venue that dominated Princess Margaret Way was the Afan Lido. You probably wouldn't expect to find chlorine foot baths, Pink Floyd and the National Union of Mineworkers under one roof but the Lido was home to them all during its lifetime.

Plans for a championship swimming pool, cafeteria and roller skating rink were approved by the Borough Council in 1959 though it was 1963 before the first foundation stone was laid for the newly named Afan Lido. By the time the Queen and Prince Philip arrived for the official opening on 25 June, 1965 the complex housed a 50 metre pool and diving boards, a restaurant, cafeteria and ballroom. Its first manager was Graham Jenkins, brother of Richard Walter Jenkins, better known as Richard Burton.

It rained that day, torrentially, as anyone who lined the route from the railway station, or stood outside the Lido, or along the streets of Sandfields Estate for the send-off journey, will remember. And it didn't stop me from waiting at Western Avenue roundabout for nearly an hour to catch a glimpse of the Queen in her shiny black car and wave my little Union Jack at her.

The Afan Lido was a landmark building in Wales, a symbol of the prosperity in the town, and the following year a Sports Hall was added, a venue big enough to host large scale concerts and sporting events. Pink Floyd played there in December 1969 at the Afan Festival of Progressive Music[29]. Over a period of forty years it welcomed performers and bands as diverse as Vera Lynn, Spencer Davis, Tom Jones, UB40, Coldplay, Catatonia and McFly.

In November 1984 the atmosphere in the hall was considerably less celebratory when TUC leader Norman Willis addressed a mass rally of the National Union of Mineworkers[30]. In September the TUC had passed a resolution supporting the now historical miners' strike of 1984-85 but had offered nothing in the way of solidarity action. The NUM's funds were to be sequestrated, a legal move designed to crush the miners, and the TUC had one last opportunity to show their active support with a one day general strike to rattle the bones of the courts, the National Coal Board and the Conservative government. But in front of an audience of thousands, with thousands more lining the streets outside, all Willis could do was condemn the violence by the pickets. The mood was hostile but not without humour on the part of the working class men who felt abandoned by their leaders. During Willis' speech a noose was lowered in front of him carrying a placard that read, 'Where is Ramsay McKinnock?', an ironic grafting of Neil Kinnock, the then leader of the Labour Party, and Ramsay MacDonald, MP for Aberavon in 1922 and the first ever Labour Prime Minister, who had refused to support the General Strike of 1926.

My dislike of the swimming pool – cold changing rooms, gritty foot baths and swimming instructors with long poles – was in stark contrast to my enjoyment of the Sports Hall where I played badminton during my last couple of years at school under the guidance of a coach called Terry. A mate of Terry's used to run karate classes at the same time, a small, red haired man whose fierce demeanour made me shiver. But away from the dojo, when the pair of them partnered a couple of us girls for mixed doubles, he was the ultimate clown, racing to reach impossible shots, making us all belly-laugh.

Although I knew him as Ritchie, it was years before I discovered this was Ritchie Noblett, one of the founding fathers of karate in Wales. Irish born Ritchie came to Port Talbot in 1970 and opened the first karate club in the area in the Walnut Tree Hotel in the centre of town. When the hotel was demolished he moved his club to the Afan Lido and began to dominate the Welsh karate scene. In 1980 he founded the Welsh Bushi-Kai Karate Association[31] that continues to teach traditional Wado Ryu Karate. After retiring from the tournament circuit Ritchie coached the Welsh National Squad for fifteen years and was honoured by the Sports Council of Wales as Local and National Sports Coach of the Year in 1997 and 1998. The charismatic Shihan Ritchie Noblett eighth Dan died in Port Talbot in 2009, after losing his battle with cancer. In 2010 he was inducted into the Welsh Karate Governing Body Hall of Fame.

The Lido survived fire damage in 1978 then, in the 1990s, wrapped itself in plastic slides and called itself the Aquadome. The Sports Hall continued doing what it said on the box. At the end of 2009 another fire[32] ripped through the pool area and the demolition of the whole complex began in October 2011.

In December 2010 Neath Port Talbot Council had unveiled proposals for a £13.6 million replacement leisure and community centre: pool, sports hall, dance studio, a twenty-first century glass atrium, (there's always a glass atrium), library, IT room, crèche. Nearly 3,000 people took part in the public consultation. The word was it could be open by 2013. "The Council has given full consideration to a number of sites within the Sandfields/Aberavon Area, and has concluded that the site of the existing Afan Lido provides the best location for the rebuilt facility",[33] the consultation brochure announced. So it came as a surprise when an article appeared in the local paper at the end of 2011[34] in which the council's Chief Executive, Steve Phillips, proposed to house the replacement (and

smaller) pool in a redundant, developer owned, bowling alley on the ill-fated Hollywood Park site next door.

Hollywood Park, at the beginning of 2013, was a far cry from the plans announced seven years earlier for a "20-lane tenpin bowling alley complex with brasseries and restaurants aimed at families"[35] to sit alongside the multiplex cinema that opened there in 1999. But the bleak industrial looking unit that should have been the bowling alley never opened. A drive-thru burger bar, that made headlines in 2007 when it went through three operators in less than two months, shut down in 2009. It was no real surprise when the Water Margin[36], a popular Chinese restaurant, situated between the burger bar and the fire ravaged Afan Lido closed at the beginning of 2011. Abandoned was the word that came to mind when you stood and looked at the empty car park, the boarded up premises and broken glass, and the lonely cinema sign.

The abrupt change of direction might have been better received by the electorate if officers and the councillors involved had explained their reasons for back-tracking on previous assurances. What was perceived as arrogance and a lack of insight into an appropriate 'fit for purpose' facility for the town led to public protest meetings and the presentation of a 10,000+ strong petition[37] that effectively helped block approval of the new plan in July 2012.

A cross political party Task & Finish Group subsequently set up spent six months and more than twenty meetings wading through the bureaucratic swamp of insurance pay-outs, funding proposals, procurement processes, existing leases to developers on the Hollywood Park site, one of which had plummeted from £15,625 to £1 per annum in 2009[38], as well as analysing which choice and mix of facilities would best serve the borough.

Rumours that the old Afan Lido site had already been sold for housing were refuted by the group's chairperson, Cllr. A.J. Taylor, in February 2013 when the group's recommendations were formally announced and endorsed. But the economic legacy of Hollywood Park, the futility of building a spanking new facility next to a lot of dereliction and neglect, and the continuing programme for the seafront's regeneration, means that Afan Lido: The Sequel will necessarily be rebuilt there. The old site will be sold, for mixed use (housing, retail, leisure and hotel amenities) the report said. But no social housing. Campaigners could celebrate other successes though: an 8 lane pool instead of the original 6, adequate spectator facilities, a contingency plan for a 6 court sports hall instead of 4, and they get to keep a library on Sandfields Estate that the previous proposal would have closed. Work was scheduled to start in 2013 with a workable 18 month timetable and quarterly progress reports back to the group.

I don't have to say, 'watch this space'. The affirmative action of 10,000 people means that everyone involved with this project, at every level, will have their eyes and ears wide open, their antennae twitching.

For sixty years the beach has been determined to reclaim the land Princess Margaret Way was built upon. After storms and high winds, the council still have to close the western section of road to clear the carpet of sand that's treacherous for drivers.

"What happens to it all?" I asked one of the guys working there.

"After it's been cleared of contaminants," he said (for contaminants read 'dog poop'), "it's put back on the beach at the tide break." And then, "If you mess with nature…"

He meant the complete removal of the natural defence of the dunes[39] (some as high as 50 feet) in the 1950s that would have held back the blown sand. Now, no sooner has one lot of sand been

cleared then another storm wallops around Swansea Bay and the whole process starts again.

Sand isn't the only danger present at this end of the road: a long straight run followed by a sweeping curve inland used to surprise motorists and bikers and speed ramps have been installed all along the seafront. It's still known locally as Jeff's Bend, even though the identifying graffiti was removed several years ago, named, as far as I can find out, after an overly-indulged local lad who smashed up a couple of Escort Turbos here not long after taking his driving test. But in 1980 this stretch of road changed the life of a Port Talbot girl beyond all recognition.

Melanie Davies was fifteen when she was thrown from her boyfriend's motorbike, her spine shattered by the fall and the bike slamming into her while she lay on the road. After two months in bed and five months of rehabilitation at Rookwood, a spinal injuries centre on the outskirts of Cardiff, she was confined to a wheelchair, paralysed from the chest down. Her book, *Never Say Die*[40], is an inspiring read, a catalogue of trials, indignities, challenges and life threatening illnesses that she struggled with and conquered. In 2000 she set up the charity, TREAT (Treatment, Rehabilitation, Exercise and Therapy)[41], to raise money for a centre, providing sports facilities and therapies for people disabled through illness or injury, on land next to Morriston Hospital in Swansea. She was nominated for the Evening Post Pride Awards in January 2013.

Melanie has said that her life would not have been half as rich without the accident. One of those riches is undoubtedly her husband, Mike Davies, the surgeon she married in 2004, twenty-four years after he operated on the fifteen-year-old girl with the broken back.

SANDFIELDS ESTATE

It's a snare of contradictions. A burst punching bag spilling its black entrails hangs outside one house; new Georgian replacement windows decorate another. One driveway boasts cracked concrete and tufts of grass; further along there's a shiny black 4x4. There are an increasing number of disabled ramps and railings; in Mozart Drive there's an award winning stage school[42] whose kids have appeared on Sky 1's *Got to Dance* and in *Britain's Got Talent*. I watch a couple of yobs give the finger to an old man shouting at them on Southdown View while at the end of the same road three lads on bikes stop and chat to me when I ask them what R35P3C7 means on the wall of one of the Afan Way underpasses. "Respect?" they intonate, as if I must be a bit thick. And they have a point as 'RESPECT' is painted in full at the other end of the wall.

"You have to write it like that when you get detention in the Comp," one of them says. The answers to my inevitable next questions are, "Yes" And, "About 400 times."

The mural[43] was designed in 2011 by pupils of Sandfields Comprehensive School, which opened in 1958 as the first purpose

built school to provide comprehensive education in Wales, and the painting was carried out by young offenders. The project's aim was to help young people develop a sense of pride in their community and two years later the mural is still graffiti free so the philosophy seems to be working. There are more underpasses in the same area and it would be great to see similar projects decorating their bare walls.

But initiatives like this take money and the local authority wards of Sandfields West and East, along with Aberafan, are identified as among the most deprived in the Port Talbot area, according to WIMD statistics (Welsh Index of Multiple Deprivation[44]), with parts of the wards in the top 10% of the most deprived wards in Wales.

It's a depressing judgement but, of course, not everyone living in a deprived area is deprived, and it's not an area itself that's deprived, it's an average of the circumstances and lifestyle of people living there that affects the ranking. In other words statistics can create inaccurate general impressions.

But I'm used to wrong impressions of Sandfields, and of people, like me, who were born and grew up here. As recently as 2011, when I was MCing the Swansea launch of *another country, haiku poetry from Wales* (Gomer 2011), a woman stuttered, "Oh, you've done well for yourself!" when I told her where I was from.

Sandfields because that's how it began: over 600 acres of sand dunes and sparse grass, known as the Aberafan Burrows, between the sea in the south and the old Rhondda & Swansea Bay Railway line in the north, the route of the present Afan Way.

Housing was a problem that had to be tackled swiftly in the post-war era. A few streets had already sprung up in the south east of this area by the late 1930s but nowhere near enough to meet the 1946 council house waiting list of 3,200[45]. And then the newly formed Steel Company of Wales (1947) put in a request for 2,000 more to meet the housing demands of men and their families who were flooding in to work at the plant from Wales and beyond.

Aberafan Burrows was actually the second choice site for a new satellite town, the first choice being a lower land value 500 acre site between Margam Castle and Pen-y-Bryn to the east of Port Talbot. But that site was opposed by the Ministry of Agriculture & Fisheries and the Ministry of Fuel & Power because of the seams of coal there[46]. So despite the higher cost of site preparation the council re-focused their attention and set about shifting millions of

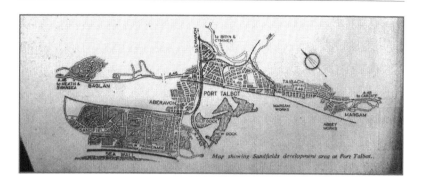

Map showing Sandfields development area at Port Talbot.

tons of sand and draining and stabilising the area ready for building.

By 1951 a thousand houses had been built on the 'Sandfields
Neighbourhood Unit', over 3,500 by 1957, both the popular, at the
time, Cornish houses[47] and the new Wimpey 'no-fines' houses. The
latter speeded up construction time enormously through on-site
assembly, pouring a mixture of chippings (rather than a 'fine' sand
aggregate) and cement into specially made moulds. 'Durability' was
the architectural description for the hardness of these walls. My
Llanelli-born parents took possession of their 'no-fines' Wimpey
house in Chrome Avenue in the summer of 1957, at a weekly rent
of £1 17s 3d, and my dad soon discovered how hard they were
when he tried to put up curtain rails and shelving. Drill bits
bounced off them like ping-pong balls.

Today there are nearly 6,000 homes here though many of the
original council houses transferred into private ownership in the
1980s as a result of Margaret Thatcher's 'right to buy' social
housing policy. My parents bought theirs in 1986 for £6,405
which, given the intervening three decades, wasn't that distant from
the 'Sandfields Site Cost per House' reported in the *Municipal
Journal*, December 1957 of £1,497.

The estate now sprawls across 800 acres. And, to me, it still feels
more like a collection of villages rather than a single community, a
legacy perhaps of the original building project that crept west in
stages, adding an extra bus terminus, a shopping centre (what we
call a row of shops these days), a primary school as it grew. In the
late 1960s our 'shops' were in Fairway, even though we were
equidistant from the 'shops' in Parry Road, a few streets further
west. And we had a Co-op, pronounced, of course, Cwop.

The same with the compounds where our dads built their garages: un-made up tracts of land they leased from the council, often tucked at the back of a close. And with the children's play areas, or 'parks' as we called them. The Steamroller Park, behind the roundabout where Golden Avenue meets Western Avenue and long since demolished and built upon, was our park, named for the full-scale iron steamroller fused onto the tarmac along with a see-saw, swings and roundabout.

VIVIAN PARK

The only park on the estate, in the traditional sense of the word – one with grass, flowerbeds and railings – was Vivian Park which opened in 1931. It's a notable quadrangle of green on the street atlas in Sandfields East and is named for Sir Arthur Pendarves Vivian (1834-1926), Liberal MP for West Cornwall and local landowner, who came to Port Talbot in 1855 to manage the family's copper works at Taibach. In the second half of the nineteenth century he bought a sizeable amount of land in this area and the park was built upon a parcel he donated to the town.

Park House, a rather prestigious detached building for a park-keeper's cottage, still stands inside the park's boundary at the Moorland Road entrance, though the house is now privately owned. Between 1943 and 1951 it was occupied by Mr. Flur Carey[48] and his family. He'd been appointed foreman gardener at a weekly wage of £2.11.5d and his war-time responsibilities included growing substantial crops of tomatoes, cucumbers and lettuce in the park's greenhouses.

Where the greenhouses used to be there's a wild garden, a corner rescued from the old-fashioned manicured approach to the rest of the park, intended to encourage... well, wildness. I started to wonder about the degree of wildness when the gates to this section were padlocked on the three occasions I tried to get in. On the fourth I went over the top and hoped for the best, in both risking my middle-aged bones and any possible danger lurking inside the steel fence. I needn't have worried about the latter. For wildness read biodiversity, the encouragement of butterflies, birds and insects in a naturally evolving environment.

There's an information board and a couple of rough timber benches: the kind of place you could easily overlook but come and

have a sit down here and contemplate the little things you can do in your garden to help nature along. The nice lady at the Parks Department has since assured me the gates will be open between 8 and 4. I'd prefer to see the whole park given over to this approach: I'm paralysed with boredom just watching the current gardener hoeing between primroses and daffodils in the geometric beds. Some rough sandy tussocks, some nettles and undergrowth, a few paths through indigenous trees and bushes: the kind of landscape that pre-dated the estate. What would be wrong with that?

During the summer holidays in the 1960s I used to hang around the park with my sister while my mother played tennis on the hard courts at the back of the bowls pavilion. We'd wander to and from the children's playground, circle the old bandstand, or walk the paths and glare at the Keep Off The Grass signs. Or we weighed up the risks of using the public toilets equipped, in those days, with wooden toilet seats and the hallowed graffiti: 'It's no good not sitting on the seats, the crabs in here can jump three feet'. I had no idea what crabs were but I knew they'd pinch.

The bandstand was demolished in the late 1960s and in its place there's a war memorial. The stone cenotaph, carved by local stone-masons Roderick & Son, was originally erected in the Mansel Tin Works, later the Byass Works, in Aberafan to commemorate 29 employees who lost their lives in the 1914-18 war. The names of the Port Talbot men who died during World War II were added before the works closed sometime later. Thanks to a group of ex-Mansel and Byass men, re-employed at the steelworks, the cenotaph was moved here from the derelict site and rededicated in November 1969[49].

War never closes though. It continues to haunt families and communities, as the more recent names of local boys killed in the Falklands and Afghanistan remind us.

> roadside bomb
> another soldier
> comes home

Sir Arthur also donated land, in the years leading up to the First World War, for the building of the Port Talbot and District General Hospital which opened in 1916 and emptied its last bed-pan in 2002. Hospital Road runs east from Victoria Park Drive but all that remains of the hospital[50] is the anachronistic street sign and some sections of the hospital's boundary walls that hem in a 'mews' development of houses.

There's an element of irony attached to Sir Arthur's gifts of land as records indicate that a lot of the property he bought, at considerably less than its true value, actually belonged to the people of Aberafan. It appears that the local burgesses responsible for the sales, who have been described as uneducated men, partial to their beer[51], were no match for Sir Arthur's business acumen.

THE PORT TALBOT GOLF CLUB

The origins of the plain, double fronted, white bungalow on the corner of Hospital Road are completely hidden. There are no signs, no clues on the outside of the building, except maybe for a couple of wooden picnic tables in the car-park out front that might vaguely suggest, in the more investigative mind, a private club. And that's exactly what it is: The Port Talbot Golf Club, infamous for its complete lack of golfing facilities. It must be the only club in Wales, if not in the entire United Kingdom, that never plays on a home green. But it wasn't always so.

The benevolent Sir Arthur opened the club in 1911 and the links were laid out across the sandy landscape by J.G. Hutcheson of Porthcawl. According to 1923 records, a local solicitor, E.T. Tennant was the secretary, there were 150 members, male visitors could enjoy a day of play for 2/6, with ladies bringing up the rear at 1/6. No play allowed on Sundays, of course. The first tee was at the end of Vivian Park and the front nine ran parallel with the beach; the back nine came back along the Rhondda & Swansea Bay Railway where the old Aberavon Seaside Station was handily located.

The club played its last tournament in 1947 and soon after the bulldozers began their preparatory work. Golf Road, Fairway, St. Asaph's Drive, even Sandy Ridge perhaps, are echoes of its existence. But the little bungalow still continues as a 19th hole though I am yet to find it open. But when I do I hope women are allowed because I have my 7½p ready.

PUBS, CLUBS AND THE GLORY OF THE LORD

The first pub to open on the estate was The Red Dragon on Moorland Road in June 1955. It was designed by a local man, Tom Gibbs, and the deputy mayor at the time, Alderman G. Griffiths, congratulated the owners, Ansells Brewery Co, for providing, "an important amenity to satisfy the needs of the seven to eight thousand population of the estate".[52] Fortunately, to avoid a particularly long wait at the bar, four more venues opened in the following decade: The Dunes in Wyvern Avenue, The Amazon (named after the ship wrecked on Morfa Beach in 1908[53]) in Parry Road, The Royal Naval Club in Purcell Avenue, and The Seaside Social & Labour Club in Dalton Road.

At the last count they were all still pulling pints though they have an air of tiredness about them, these double and triple bar, dance floor/function room, thousands of square footage pubs and clubs whose faithful flocked in from the estate and local industries and happily drank, smoked, danced and bingoed through their way through the decades. But demographics have changed and the smoking ban undoubtedly took its effect too: I'm a non-smoker but can understand the intimate relationship between a pint and a fag. It's going to take more than a lick of paint and chicken and chips in the basket to secure their future.

The five pubs were thoughtfully balanced with five churches. They're all still open for the business of the Lord too. Sandfields Methodist, Holy Trinity, St. Therese's, Elim Pentecostal and my own childhood haunt that took longer to say than any venue, religious or otherwise, reasonably should: Fitzclarence Forward Movement Presbyterian Church.

I wasn't a particularly rebellious child but Sunday School brought out the worse, or the best, in me. If my older sister wasn't around, I encouraged my next door neighbour, Anne, to practice our swearing on the way home. "Bugger bloody bugger. Bloody buggering buggers." There was only so much variety we could conjure with the two swear words we knew. We started our incantation at the boundary wall of the church in Western Avenue, across Briar Road and down Marine Drive, stopping at the bend in our street in case our mothers could read our lips from 500 yards away.

The big event at Fitzclarence was the Whitsun March followed by the Whitsun Tea. Garibaldi biscuits were a main feature, hardly

an inspiration for participating but we did, in our Courtelle suits
and Mary Poppins shoes and straw bonnets.

Whitsun Walk

We gathered on the grass outside at two,
pools of children pressed into Sunday clothes
and rallied into lines to march for Jesus.

At half past we set off on a temporary
swell of feeling, fired by banners,
the smiling white teeth of Reverend Steed.

In the better streets people waved, smiled –
Western Avenue, around the roundabout,
up Fairway. It was past the Co-op

where our troubles began, the rough kids
mocking us from the kerb – Jesus wants me
for a bum-beam – and waggling their rear-ends.

The Reverend and the faithful sang on,
unperturbed, while I stuck the hymn-sheet
up against my face and followed the heels

of the person in front, blind to the glory
of the coming of the Lord. In Southdown Road
we picked up speed: not even a miracle

could have slowed us down, a river
of hot children in uncomfortable clothes.
We were back at the church at five past three,

queued up for our free tea. A thin minister,
his face full of shadows, stood at the only door
and stamped our hands in indelible ink.

BOOM, BUST, BEYOND

The 1960s were the boom years followed by recurring recessions in the 70s, 80s and 90s. The estate showed the strain. 'Hotbed of Crime', 'Wave of Vandalism', 'Skid Row' were some of the newspaper headlines feeding outside negative opinions and demoralising the residents who did have pride in themselves and their homes. But there's been a turnaround in the last twenty years, even more so in the last decade. Not that the estate is without its problems but a programme of renovation and regeneration has made a significant difference.

New Sandfields Aberavon (NSA), based at Tŷ Arian in Silver Avenue, is a regeneration organisation that has the word 'community' stamped through it like 'Aberafan' through a stick of pink rock. You can't turn on the estate without reading the name somewhere and the energy it's created is a tribute to Chief Executive, Ian Isaac.

Between 1974 and 1991 Ian worked as a miner and pro-active leader in the NUM[54], pretty far removed from his subsequent role as Wales Development Manager within the National Schizophrenia Fellowship[55]. When he asked his new employer why he'd been given the job he was told, "Because you looked like someone who could pick up a rugby ball, run through the long grass and score a try at the other end." He's been with NSA for over ten years and the tries keep coming: IT projects, a beach festival, employment training, a community café, free solar panel installation, workshops in hair and beauty, construction and business admin, and a carpentry project, Unit 19, that recently went independent.

He sees no benefit in just chucking money at people. He believes a community needs to participate in its own regeneration so all of NSA's projects are focused on working with people, in partnership with other organisations, helping them take control of, and responsibility for, their own lives.

The description of the BASE project (at Bevin Avenue) in the 2010/11 Annual Report is wrapped in the language of bureaucracy – "a programme of soft entry points for individuals who are furthest away from the labour market and who have developed barriers to engaging in basic community activities" – but in real language this project began, in 2000, with 50 of the most disengaged kids in the area with a history of car theft and anti-social behaviour, kids that have continued learning, or gone onto employment, or have started work as volunteers. NSA also bought the building, an old West Glamorgan Community Centre from the early 1960s, as part of their asset building programme, and it now houses a Cyber Café as well as an ICT training suite.

I was lucky. I had a solid family background. I got my first job in the 1970s when the economy was breathing. In an ideal world all kids would have that advantage and opportunity. There's no such thing as an ideal world but Sandfields has NSA to help improve it.

It also has Captain Beany, an orange, caped super-hero from Planet Beanus who currently lives in a council flat off Moorland Road and runs The Baked Bean Museum of Excellence. The day I visit the museum Captain Beany is in civvies, which is rather less distracting than sitting opposite a man wearing orange tights, because, as you've probably guessed, he's not really from Planet Beanus.

Everyone in Port Talbot knows Captain Beany who was born Barry Kirk in 1954 but changed his name by deed-poll in 1991. It all started five years before that when he came up with the idea to lie in a bath of cold baked beans for 100 hours in the foyer of the Aberavon Hotel to raise money for The Gateway Club for handi-capped kids. The inspiration for the stunt came from the album

cover of *The Who Sell Out* featuring Roger Daltry in a bath of beans; Barry emerged from his bath, four days later, a distinctive shade of yellow (not orange, as you'd expect) but with £1,500 for the minibus appeal.

Since then, as Captain Beany, he's run over 20 international marathons, has been filmed by crews from as far away as Korea, stood for The New Millennium Bean Party in local elections, won first prize in the Eccentric Club's Greatest British Eccentric in 2009, and was interviewed by Hunter Davies for his book about whacky museums, *Behind the Scenes at the Museum of Baked Beans*[56].

The museum, which was officially opened by TV presenter Danny Wallace in 2009, is in his spare bedroom. It's compact, as you'd expect, but extremely professional: there are baked bean brands from the UK and the USA and a whole bunch of bean related memorabilia. Did you know that Biba made baked beans back in those days?

Not that many people visit: the odd hen party, someone who's stumbled across an entry on a 'Welsh attraction' website. But the local council have been happy enough, so far, for Barry to advertise his 'hobby'.

It does all feel a bit weird, other-worldly you could say. Here's a man who paints his face orange and talks about farting. But if the puns ('artefarts', 'full-blown', 'half-baked') start to grate think about the £100,000+ Captain Beany has raised for local and national charities and he shows no sign of flagging. Also, for an alien, he makes a damn good cup of tea.

READING THE SIGNS

You don't hear a lot of Welsh spoken around the estate though you see it more these days. As part of their regeneration work the local authority have re-greened corners of streets and roundabouts and replaced the English only street signs with bilingual ones. Heol and Rhodfa sit below Street and Avenue. Some of the translations produce an ironic smile: Rhodfa Arian, in Sandfields West, is both Silver Avenue and Money Avenue in English.

My parents come from Welsh-speaking families so the language has always been a part of my life. But the outdated belief that kids learning two languages would be slower combined with the only Welsh language school in the 1960s being miles away at

Pontrhydyfen persuaded them to bring up their three children to speak English. I regret not being fluent in Welsh, not because I think I would feel more attached to my country, but because all the research shows that having more than one language from a young age builds confidence, provides a more expansive world view, and triggers patterns in the brain that facilitate learning.

There was a smattering of Welsh at Tir Morfa Infants School on Marine Drive. 'Ble mae Tedi? Dyma Tedi! Ble mae Doli? Dyma Doli!' were the components of my first Welsh lesson in the temporary classrooms, or the Terrapins as we unquestioningly called them. They were nothing to do with soft little turtles but the trade name of a modular building manufacturer, years before the appearance of Portakabin.

Tir Morfa was one of five primary schools built on the estate, a sign of the baby-boom of the fifties, with the Infants and Juniors connected by a shared dining hall. The two halves still share it but since 1987 the Infants is now Rhosafan, the only Welsh medium school in Port Talbot for three to eleven year olds. It comes as a bit of a surprise when the head, Julia Griffiths, tells me that apart from a handful of children the rest come from English speaking families. And almost a third of those are 'walkers' from the surrounding estate.

The school is popular, so popular it is bursting at the seams, every available space used for teaching, and a second mobile classroom for the playground was ordered for September 2012. Are Port Talbot parents enthusiastically supporting the Welsh Government's vision of creating a bilingual Wales? Or is it more to do with the standards the school achieves? In 2011 a delegation of European educators visited the school, impressed by the standards of excellence there.

One of my reasons for visiting was to reacquaint myself with the huge mural in the assembly hall, four panels each measuring about 12 feet by 12 feet, by Port Talbot born artist, Andrew Vicari. Vicari, whose parents moved to South Wales from Italy in the 1930s, was born in 1938 in Water Street, Aberafan, in a flat above a shop that sold, of all things, paint. The family moved to Neath shortly afterwards, he attended Neath Grammar School for boys and the Swansea School of Art. At the Slade, in London, he was mentored by Francis Bacon and brushed canvases with other luminary artists of the era, including Lucien Freud and Craigie Aitchison.

He moved to Monaco in 1975 following his appointment, a year

earlier, as official artist to the Saudi Arabian King and Government; an event that propelled him to international acclaim and astonishing wealth. In 2010 the *Sunday Times* calculated his wealth at £85 million. There are three museums dedicated to his work in the Middle East, hundreds of his paintings are displayed in other museums and public buildings around the world. More recently in Wales he created a seven foot mural, 'The Millennium Stadium Vigonade' (2002), was the official artist at the Ryder Cup at the Celtic Manor Resort in Newport (2007) and, in 2008, completed a triptych drawing of rugby legend, Shane Williams. In January 2013 he was in London preparing for a portrait of the Mayor of London, Boris Johnson[57].

I don't expect him to get in touch with me personally when I contact him via his website, but he does, and he happens to be in London, so why don't I come up to his club for tea?

His club is the East India Club in St. James's Square, behind Piccadilly. The address I have is no. 16 but neither its name nor its number are of much use as the building is magnificently anonymous, half of which I feel while I wait for him in the teak-panelled, chandeliered reception. So I'm very pleased when he appears and he's as far from intimidating as imaginable: not very tall, a little rotund and quietly spoken but still with a trace of his welsh accent that gets stronger the longer we talk. When I show him a photocopy of one of the Tir Morfa School panels he seems genuinely moved at seeing his work from over 50 years ago. "Oh, look at them," he says, "These make me feel I must be a good painter."

The Tir Morfa murals were commissioned in the late 1950s by Llewellyn Heycock, Chairman of the Glamorgan Education Committee, later Baron Heycock of Taibach, who paid for the materials out of his own pocket.

Vicari worked *in situ*, in oils over gesso-ed wooden panels, and directly from the faces of teachers and children who posed for him, standing on a plank as each panel grew in size and neared completion. He didn't earn a penny from it. You might expect that's no longer the case but Vicari has been described as having a 'Robin Hood' attitude to art commissions and he confirms it's true. "Expensive commissions enable me to do paintings for free for friends and people I want to work with," he says. And that goes for his home town as well. Over the years he has given free master-classes to students at Neath Port Talbot College and to sixth formers at a three day event in Margam Abbey.

I don't really want our interview to end, and it's not just down to the second glass of champagne he insists we have, or because he tells me I look like Ruth Hussey, "a beautiful actress from the 1940s," he says. It's because he's a man full of stories to fill a book or two, a project that's in the pipeline, and animated by life and art.

"Why don't you come back to Wales and live?" I ask him.

"I'd feel too comfortable," he says, "too much at home. There'd be no tension to paint."

The mural is a product of its era – stylised lips and eyes, strong outlines – and perhaps more of a social statement and a nostalgia trip for me than a landmark of art history. It takes me back to a time of home knitted jumpers, when the toys children carried didn't require a power source. The children feel unfamiliar to me but the faces of the women are the remembered mothers of my childhood: Mammy, Aunty Ruth, Aunty Phil, Aunty Beryl. They were the soapsuds and steam of a Monday's laundry, the warnings of being in trouble when our fathers got home, letting us stay up late on Fridays for *Bonanza*. Women their daughters took for granted until they feared they might lose them.

welcome hug
each time I come home
my mother is smaller

I leave the school feeling physically warmed by the welcome, the journey back into my past, but also excited by the idea that this icon of Welsh education is happening here, in 'deprived' Sandfields West: welsh culture, history, language, tradition, pride, enthusiasm and confidence are thriving. And it starts even before Nursery with free Language & Play and Number & Play sessions for mothers and toddlers.

And there's another satisfying link too. Llewellyn Heycock was a passionate supporter of bilingual education in primary and secondary education. He believed that the crux of the Welsh culture was the Welsh language. And over half a century later the paintings he commissioned from a promising young artist are mounted amongst the living representation of that belief.

The future should look bright but there is uncertainty in the air. The English side of Tir Morfa Primary School is scheduled to close in 2013 and merge with Glan y Mor in a new combined school in Sandfields East. It would be wonderful if the crowded Rhosafan could overflow into the vacated section and continue to expand and excel in a way the community obviously supports and benefits from. According to Richard Gordon, Programme Manager for SSIP (Strategic School Improvement Programme), that might be a possibility.[58] I hope so.

VICTORIA ROAD

Victoria Road is an architectural map from the late nineteenth century to the beginning of the twenty-first. Dressed stone, red brick, render, decorative gables, mock Tudor fronts, round and squared bay windows, art deco curves, post war concrete, late twentieth century ugliness, the town planners' recent builds: they're all here in the terraces, the semis, the detached houses, the villas, the blocks of flats and the shop buildings.

The road itself, the main thoroughfare out of town towards the beach, and the easterly boundary of Sandfields Estate, was given its first makeover in 1887. Thirty years earlier the *Cambrian*'s Aberavon correspondent, after championing the facilities for holidaymakers at the beach, bemoaned the challenge of getting there: "The only drawback to us placing Aberavon as A1 is the want of a good sound road." He then took a harder line: "...Our Corporation must shake off its character for torpidity and stupidness to expect this much to be done[59]."

Shaking off the torpidity, and maybe the stupidness, took some time but they were eventually galvanised into action by Queen Victoria's Jubilee and spent £900 on a new road surface of quarry work ballast and tinwork ashes. The 'New Road to the Sea Beach', or Jubilee Road as it was first called, officially opened in June 1887 with appropriate razzmatazz: a procession, a bonfire and fireworks, and free oranges and buns for the kids[60]. The name was changed in 1901 after the death of the Queen. There wasn't a great deal to see along the road at the time of the official opening and it's difficult now to imagine walking south with only sand-dunes for company. The opening ceremony took place on a field owned by our friendly neighbourhood industrialist, Sir Arthur Pendarves Vivian, land he'd bought from the Aberavon Corporation with the proviso that a right of way to the beach be kept open. In 1883 there'd been a kerfuffle when he erected a couple of locked gates and placed them under private police guard, effectively blocking anyone's access to the beach. An incensed group, including the Mayor, some burly councillors and a crowd of local people, marched to the gates and forced them open. Sir Arthur, perhaps wisely, did not argue.

In 1905 the Vivian Hotel, later called the Vivian Park Hotel, was built on that field by Morgan Cox & Son for the brewery Truman, Hanbury & Co but a few years ago it was demolished and replaced with the contemporary Jubilee House. While it's not too bad as modern builds go – some variety in the roof line, corner balconies, render in white and café crème – it's not what most people were expecting to see.

In 2006 the council approved plans for the construction of flats and commercial premises that retained the facade of the original building. The plans show the inclusion of the original features, the arched brick windows, the parapet above the second storey as well as the dormers projecting from the roof. But then a second application was submitted and approved in early 2009 to pull the whole structure down.

The Viv, as everyone called it, its bars, function and hotel rooms, had been a part of Port Talbot life for a century. Admittedly, it wasn't listed by Cadw but it was one of the few remaining monuments to Port Talbot's industrial past and a symbol of the network of the railways[61] that led to the growth of tourism and culture in a rapidly expanding town.

There was a fire at The Viv too. I've added an endnote[62] so you don't think I'm making up these fire stories. It broke out in July 2009, a few months after the second planning permission was granted. I don't know whether it made the demolition easier or trickier, but it definitely sealed The Viv's fate.

But Victoria Road still retains some of the lovely late Victorian and early twentieth century red brickwork, which makes me think of aspidistras and corsets, in the terraced houses that run south along both sides. No. 3, on the corner of Addison Road, stands proud from the row, its elevation higher than the rest. It's currently a hairdresser's salon but it was Antolin's for seventy years.

Dolores[63] and Angel Antolin came to Britain from Spain for their honeymoon in 1910 and never left. They moved from Newcastle to South Wales in search of work and settled in Port Talbot in 1919. A year later, with three children, they rented 3 Victoria Road and opened the shop that would become a Port Talbot landmark.

In 1932, when he was only forty years old, Angel Antolin contracted TB and died, leaving his widow with eight children to support. But the indomitable Dolores continued to run her shop, offering credit to customers suffering in the economic crisis of the decade, and, because of her limited knowledge of written English, identifying each account, so the local story goes, with ingenious little sketches of a large nose here, or a shock of curly hair there.

By the outbreak of World War II the shop had progressed from an immigrant's struggling concern to a reputable Port Talbot business, complimented by shops run by other members of the family, and at different times, in Corporation Road, Station Road, Cwmafan Road and Newbridge Road.

In 1963, the family opened the Ros-a-Mar Function Suite above the Victoria Road shop. Dolores's grandson, Gary Antolin, who was a year above me at Sandfields Comprehensive and who has worked at the steelworks since 1973, remembers his grandmother making her celebrated ice-cream in the restaurant's kitchen. And the exquisite taste of it. His own parents, Nin and Betty Antolin, were the first caterers at the Afan Lido, running the restaurant, cafeteria and Sportsman's Bar for over ten years as well as operating a Meals-on-Wheels service. He is constantly reminded by people who know his family, or recognise his surname, of the Antolin legacy, of the ice-cream, the birthday and engagement parties, of wedding receptions, memories and events that shaped people's lives.

Dolores Antolin never went back to Spain. She passed away in 1966 in the town that had shaped her life, the town she called home.

My sister had her wedding reception at the Ros-a-Mar in September 1975. The event is memorable for two additional reasons: the schooners of Harvey's Bristol Cream I was allowed to drink and the journey in my dad's Austin 1100 taking the happy couple to Port Talbot station for the London train. When my mother had encouraged me, 'Go with them and wave goodbye,' I hadn't anticipated the embarrassment of driving across town with a clatter of cans bringing up the rear and people squealing and waving from the pavements. At seventeen, there is only one state you want to exist in. The state of cool.

sisters

38 years ago I cried when my sister got married and left home. For fifteen years she slept on the other side of the room from me. We hit each other with clothes hangers and hairbrushes. I hid behind the bedroom door to jump out and frighten her when she wandered back from the bathroom at night. She called me 'child' just to annoy me. And now she was leaving and becoming a wife. In wedding

speeches fathers of the bride and groom talk about
gaining a son, a daughter. But all I knew was that I was
losing my sister.

mobile blackspot
I sing happy birthday
to my sister to myself

There's another elevated roofline next door to Victoria House, no. 49, which stares directly down Newbridge Road towards the docks. The ground floor was a hairdressing salon at the last check but it started out as a boarding house for sea captains before it became The Rhondda Restaurant, named for the proprietors from Porth, Rhondda, in the first decade of the twentieth century. It still continued to attract the attention of sailors staggering up from the docks, the unwanted kind that meant boarding up the windows in late afternoon.

There's the suggestion of aspiration in its architecture: the decorative gable and inset of fancy brickwork set it slightly apart from the previous builds. And some of the villas further down the road mark the growth of the middle-class and their desire for houses of distinction. After all, this was the 'west-end' of the town, a new suburbia, a place where the residents could be relatively free of the smoke and smells of industry delivered by the prevailing westerly winds, as was the case in many areas of the British Isles, to those less fortunate in the east.

When Melville Thomas, a shoe-shop owner known locally as 'Thomas the Boot', had the art-deco 'Briar Meades' built for him in 1937, he would have been the talk of the town. At that time the nearest house on the town side was 200 yards away and the 1950s social housing that would soon crowd around him wasn't even a faint cry. It's a different story now with every available space built upon, right down to the Prom, with only a whisper of air between some houses. 'Briar Meades' attracted a few showy neighbours before the Jac Codi Baws[64] started their sand clearance: some buxom bow-fronted bay windows here, an overhanging gable and a sprinkling of Arts and Crafts timbering there. Stand in front of one of the palm tree planted gardens on the western side of the road and you'd be forgiven for thinking 'Torquay'.

The Grove Park club and function room at the beach end was built as a private house in the 1920s and extended in the following decade to become the Beach Restaurant. In 1952 the RAFA bought it as a clubhouse, painted a large RAF roundel on the beachside wall, and named it Gremlin House, for reasons that are lost in the mists of time. Phil James MBE, the club's Chairman, who flew with 192 Squadron and still lives on Sandfields Estate, organised the sale of the building in 1990 when the cost of maintaining and running the club became too big a financial burden. The whole £106,000 from the sale was handed over to RAF charitable associations. It was renamed Grove Park, in memory of its RAFA years, when it became a private club in 1991. RAFA headquarters are in Grove Park, London.

The Bar Gallois, opposite, was also built in the first decade of the twentieth century. It opened as the Alexandra Café and Hotel, shrunk to The Alex Grill, changed identity entirely in the 1980s as The High Tide before becoming 'Welsh' in French. We celebrated my parents' silver wedding anniversary there in December 1977 when it was still a sophisticated late supper club with live jazz at the weekend.

1977. I was sizzling with first love, dating Stephen Collins, son of the Aberavon winger and Welsh rugby international, John Collins. John's test debut for Wales was in 1958 at Cardiff against Australia where he scored their only try and took them to victory. Everyone knows John in Port Talbot. His portrait is among Port Talbot's famous faces on a mural in Blanco's Hotel and Restaurant, near the town centre, where he has free coffee every weekday at 12.30. When I bump into him there the first thing he apologises for is a cut and swollen lip. "I scored a try in the gutter last week," he tells me. Then he says, "You're still pretty", as funny and charming as I remember. He's in his 80s now and still plays piano at Bar Gallois where he gets a free pint on Sundays. Hanging around with John is getting higher on my list of things to do when I'm in town.

The beach end of Victoria Road was definitely the party end in the 1970s: the RAFA, the Alex, the Jersey Beach Hotel, the Sandman nightclub, the Bierkeller at the fair, and, at a 500 yard trot, the Sportsman Bar at the Afan Lido. I met Stephen at the Sandman in 1976, three years before its owner, George Deakin, made the national headlines for being arrested and charged in connection with the Jeremy Thorpe scandal[65] for conspiracy to commit murder. Although all four defendants, including Thorpe, were eventually released without charge the case had all the elements of both film noire and British farce: a top politician, a male

model, a carpet salesman, a nightclub owner, a hitman, a Great Dane called Rinka, the moors, blackmail and class warfare. It's a book in itself. And it is[66].

The town end of the road was the working end. 1 and 2 Victoria Road, or Gasworks House, were originally built, as you'd guess, for the manager of the turn of the century gasworks. A second, 'modern' gasworks, including the huge cylindrical gasometer that dominated the landscape here for so many years, was dismantled in the 1970s. For a while there was a scattering of light industrial units here; currently it's rubbled grassland awaiting redevelopment.

The gasworks site is one of a number of plots around Port Talbot that Paul Farley and Michael Symmons Roberts would call 'edgelands' in their book of the same name[67]. Edgelands are the places you glimpse from a car or a train window, neither townscape nor rural landscape, though nature is often doing its best to reclaim them. Places at the edge of other developments that you pass and dismiss, abandoned places, old industrial sites waiting, without holding their breath, for change.

The old flat-roofed Gas Showroom is still standing by the gates, but gas cookers, 'joking'[68] fires and boilers have been replaced by pet and garden products. It's a Sunday and the gates alongside Beachways Pet Food & Garden Centre are padlocked so I head down an alley at the back of Victoria Road and clamber up a low wall and through the broken fence. In the middle of the site there's a set of low stone steps leading nowhere but I still climb them. Perhaps the extra height will provide some clarity as to why this site has remained derelict for so long when there's been new development on the other side of Victoria Road and to the south at Harvey's Crescent. Given its previous use perhaps land contamination is an issue although in 2011 it was included in the council's plans for development with residential and light industrial use[69].

But this area already has its 'derelict land to leisure venture' story, one that Harvey's Crescent and the nearby Lake Road are named for. Frederick Harvey was a Cardiff man who either bought or leased an area of marshy ground with a pool next to the old gasworks with the idea of creating a similar venture to Cardiff's Roath Park boating lake[70]. Earlier references to the pool, called both The Sinking Pool and Victoria Lake, can be found in old Aberavon Town Council records between 1903 and 1905 but around 1908 Frederick Harvey and his son, George, who came home from sea to join him at Port Talbot, opened a boating lake to the public. They even constructed their own boats in a little boathouse on the edge of the lake and the business went well until the depression of the 1920s.

George Harvey stayed on in Port Talbot as a marine store dealer at the docks and would have seen his father's lake filled in during the post-war period with sand taken from the bottom end of Victoria Road as the construction of the Little Warren housing estate began.

The Little Warren Beach or the Small Side. The name changes amongst local people but it's the old harbour beach between the

concrete pier, the old north breakwater, and the River Afan: a quiet corner of captured water and a few sand dunes. In 1999 the private townhouses, detached houses and apartments of Mariner's Point and Mariner's Quay began to fill the area between the coast and the older Little Warren housing estate, where Port Talbot Town Football Club[71] has its grounds. This is 'new' Port Talbot: nothing like the town I grew up in. And I struggle with the conflict of wanting to live in one of the twenty-first century beachfront properties with a breath-taking view of the bay and the giant cranes in the deep harbour and the feeling that I don't belong here. Perhaps it's about the preservation of memory: my childhood framed by physical and emotional boundaries I am trying to keep intact. This was where the Miami Beach Amusement Park opened in 1963[72]: candyfloss and diesel fumes, the ghost train and bumper cars, the smell of warm bronze pennies in your hand, plastic ducks and goldfish. And boys in leather jackets who spun the Waltzer even faster when you screamed.

ebb-tide not knowing where home is

notes

1. Strawbridge & Thomas, p.23
2. Within Swansea Bay which stretches from Mumbles Head in the west to Port Talbot deep harbour in the east.
3. *Real Port Talbot* covers an area between the River Nedd in the west and the River Kenfig in the east. The River Afan runs through the middle.
4. Strawbridge & Thomas, p.5
5. UK's leading regeneration specialist
6. *Evening Post* 23.1.2013
7. Strategic Schools Improvement Programme, NPTCBC, Cabinet Report 25.6.12
8. Milne AA, *The House at Pooh Corner*, Methuen & Co, 1941 edition, p.107
9. Bryson, Bill, *Notes from a Small Island*, Harper Perennial 2001, p.130
10. http://www.surfschoolwales.co.uk
11. *The Cambrian* newspaper of 27.6.1856 reported a crowd of 1200-1500 people. Hughes, JV, 'Aberavon Beach: Aspects of its History', Port Talbot Historian 2005, p.81
12. The Earls of Jersey were significant landowners in South Wales.
13. http://www.dar-design.com/
14. http://www.coastguard.ukf.net/
15. http://aberavonslsc.co.uk/
16. http://rnli.org/findmynearest/beach/Pages/Aberavon-beach.aspx
17. Public toilets and a kiosk that's home to Gelato Gatti: takeaway coffee and home-made Italian gelato.

18. Hughes, John V, 'Aberavon Beach: Aspects of its History', *Port Talbot Historian* 2005, p.88
19. Ibid, p.103
20. http://www.swanseadocks.co.uk/Port%20Talbot%20Wrecks%20&%20Groundings.htm
21. Perry, Walter, *Shifting Sands Vol II – Turning Tide*, privately published, p.20
22. http://www.aberavongreenstarsrfc.co.uk/
23. an Gorta Mór in the Irish language, the Great Hunger
24. *Port Talbot Guardian* 27th January, 1961: Notice given of the removal from Moriah Chapel's attached graveyard of the remains of 28 named persons owing to the M4 construction. The remains were reburied at Goytre Cemetery.
25. Aberavon Green Stars Fixture Card 1969.
26. Prince Charles was created Prince of Wales by Letters Patent in 1958 but was not invested until July 1969 at Caernarfon Castle, North Wales.
27. https://www.facebook.com/windy.man.5?fref=ts
28. Hughes, John V, 'Aberavon Beach: Aspects of its History', Ibid, p.102
29. http://www.ukrockfestivals.com/pinkfloyd12-6-69.html
30. http://www.marxist.com/Europe-old/miners_twenty_years_on_part2.html
31. http://www.welshbushi-kai.org.uk
32. You would be forgiven for imagining more than a whiff of smoke in the vicinity. The Jersey Beach Hotel, the Bay View, the Afan Lido. Port Talbot has had more than its fair share of bad luck when it comes to old buildings bursting into flame.
33. Afan Lido Consultation brochure 2010
34. *South Wales Evening Post*, 15.12. 2011
35. Turner, Robin, *Western Mail*, January 2006
36. Renovated for potential re-opening at the beginning of 2013. Evening Post 15.1.2013
37. *Evening Post* 18.7.2012: http://tiny.cc/3ty3qw
38. Report of the Cross Political Party Task & Finish Group, Cabinet Scrutiny Committee 20th February 2013.
39. A natural dune range still stretches from beyond the western end of the prom, along the old BP/Baglan Bay site to the River Nedd.
40. Davies, Melanie & Barrett-Lee, Lynne, *Never Say Die*, Harper True 2009
41. http://www.treattrust.org.uk/
42. TDM Stage School http://www.tdmstageschool.co.uk/
43. *Evening Post* 2.4.2011
44. Calculated on income, employment, health, education, housing and geographical access to services.
45. *The Municipal Journal*, 13.12.1957
46. Plans for a new Margam mine stretched across the decades of the last half of the twentieth century. In 1985 West Glamorgan County Council supported a new £850,000 road improvement scheme for the planned £78 million drift mine which never materialised. BBC online: http://tiny.cc/e08zqw See South: Steelworks for Tata Steel's plans for a new drift mine under Mynydd Margam.
47. A successful design for the Central Cornwall Concrete & Artificial Stone Co but the roof and wall insulation contained asbestos and over time concrete decay around the timber trusses led to an alarming level of horizontal and vertical cracking.
48. Jones, *Port Talbot Gallery 2*, pp.77-88.
49. Hanson, *Outline* pp. 165/6
50. A fire also broke out at the hospital but after planning permission had been granted to demolish it and build houses on the site.
51. Hughes, John V, 'Aberavon Beach: Aspects of its History', Ibid, p.83
52. *Port Talbot Guardian*, 3.6.1955
53. See South: Morfa Beach

54. Isaac, Ian, *When We Were Miners*, Ken Smith Press 2010
55. Rebranded as Rethink.
56. Virgin Books 2010
57. *Evening Post* 19.1.2013
58. Email correspondence 4.12.2012
59. Hughes, John V, 'Aberavon Beach: Aspects of its History', Ibid, p.81
60. Ibid p.84
61. The Rhondda & Swansea Bay Railway ran through the Aberafan Seaside Station at the back of The Viv.
62. http://www.thisissouthwales.co.uk/ravages-Port-Talbot-hotel/story-12434045detail/story.html
63. Jones, *Port Talbot Gallery Vol 1*, 'Dolores Antolin' pp.79-96
64. JCB: codi = to lift, baw = earth (Welsh) - Jack who lifts earth.
65. http://www.express.co.uk/posts/view/99798/The-downfall-of-Jeremy-Thorpe
66. Freeman, Simon with Penrose, Barry, *Rinkagate: The Rise and Fall of Jeremy Thorpe*, Bloomsbury 1997
67. *Edgelands, Journeys into England's True Wildernesses*, Vintage Books 2012
68. A 'joking' fire as opposed to a 'real' fire. I'm not sure how far that expression travelled outside of Port Talbot but I'm talking about gas fires with artificial coals licked by a blue gas flame.
69. NPTCBC: Port Talbot Harbourside & Town Centre Development Framework SPG, April 2011
70. Jones, *Port Talbot Gallery 3*, p.35
71. http://www.porttalbottown.co.uk Formed initially in 1901 and playing as Port Talbot Athletic the team changed their name to mark their centenary season.
72. The amusement park continued to operate until the 1980s. The site was cleared in 1988.

SOUTH

RIVER AFAN

Allen Blethyn is a local and family history researcher and a descendant of the Roderick family, Port Talbot stonemasons founded around 1827 who still have a yard near Tan y Groes Street. If you have a local history question that needs answering Allen is the one to ask and he's been my companion and guide on countless expeditions since I started writing *Real Port Talbot*, pointing me towards the little known, the overgrown and the forgotten.

If I had to guess how many bridges cross the River Afan from Aberafan to Pontrhydyfen I'd say about a dozen. When I check the A-Z and OS Explorer map I'm surprised to count twenty-one. Allen reckons there are twenty-four. Guess who was right? But on top of that twenty-four his painstaking research has located another seven long-demolished crossings connected with the coal, tin and iron industries, traces of which can sometimes still be found pressed against the riverbank or hidden beneath a new span of iron or steel.

Newbridge[1] is the most southerly existing bridge, a plate-girder bridge[2] engineered by one of Allen's ancestors, J. Roderick Esq., and opened in 1903 between lower Aberafan and the docks. If you look up-river at low tide you should see the wooden stumps of a rail bridge that preceded it.

The 'new bridge' still sports the bases of its original gas lampposts and is a link in NPTCBC's riverside foot and cycle path network. I remember when it was open to traffic, driving across in the 1960s next to my dad on the front bench seat of his red and cream Hilman Minx. It was a common, if unofficial, short cut through the docks and the steelworks to the eastern end of town. Some of the river bridges, like this one, are protected by Cadw. Others, like the arms of the Afan Way roundabout and the town centre flyovers, are anonymous roads in a kind of nowhere land, everyone who uses them on their way to somewhere else, oblivious to the river flowing below. There's only one rail bridge left: the main GWR line from London to Swansea through the centre of town.

One of the oldest footbridges is the Halfpenny Bridge, west of the Aberafan shopping centre, which pre-dates the opening of the new docks in 1837. It's been rebuilt at least three times, swept away by floods: the latest reconstruction took place in 1988 as part of major flood alleviation works. I'd love to confirm that at some time in its history you had to pay a halfpenny to cross it, but I can't. Although there used to be a passenger ferry in the docks from the Rio Tinto Wharf to Llewellyn's Quay that would have set you back a penny, so a halfpenny for hoofing it across the river sounds reasonable.

ABERAFAN BRIDGE

The triple arch stone bridge[3], a walkway into the Aberafan Shopping Centre, used to be the main A48 thoroughfare for road traffic, joining Station Road on the south bank of the Afan with High Street on the north, before the planners' blitz in the early 1970s. The modern canopy might protect shoppers from rain, and even be a shining example of contemporary engineering, but when I'm under its low shadowy span I feel like Chicken-Licken[4].

The bridge's keystone is marked with two dates: 1842, the date it was built to the design of William Kirkhouse, engineer of the Tennant Canal, and 1893, the date it was widened, in time for the new century's evolution of horse-drawn into horse-power. The 1842 bridge replaced one built by William Edwards (1719-1789) from Groeswen, Caerphilly[5] whose early bridge-building efforts were seriously thwarted. In 1746 he built a three arch bridge across the River Taff that he promised to keep in good repair for seven

years. It was destroyed by a flood two years later. He started on a replacement single arch bridge but the centring was washed away by another flood. He rebuilt it but it only stood for a short time before that collapsed too. Fourth time lucky, as no-one says, but his next bridge, with a 140 foot span, remained stable. Knowing that Edwards' father died in 1726 while trying to ford the River Taff adds a certain amount of poignancy to his son's determination.

In July 1768 when Aberafan's old bridge was swept away by a flood that rose to five feet, destroyed crops and homes and left the area covered in mud and slime, Edwards built a 70 foot single span stone bridge in its place. It survived, thanks to all the practice he'd had, until Kirkhouse's replacement in 1842.

Most of the current footbridges crossing the Afan are relics of the industrial past. The pedestrian four arch stone bridge at Velindre, shared between river and road, was originally a rail bridge. Cadw list it[6] as an early nineteenth century horse-drawn railway bridge but Allen believes the horse-drawn rail must have run along the Cwmafan Road, on the north bank, and straight down to the Aberafan wharfs because there wasn't any need to cross the river before the opening of Port Talbot docks in 1837. But rails were laid here with the coming of steam and, according to old maps, engines were running down the valley and across this bridge with their cargoes of coal in 1839.

The remaining river bridges from here to Pontrhydyfen, apart from one road-bridge at the foot of Ynysygwas Hill in Cwmafan, are foot and cycle bridges, replacing the rail bridges that carried trams, engines and wagons from the collieries towards the coast. Some have been spruced up in recent years and painted NPTCBC blue – a strange colour choice[7] for a local authority in a firm socialist grip – and they're worth searching out for the views up and down river, at varying heights from the rush and roll of water below.

There are three footbridges heading north from Cwmafan: Ynys Afan, Ynys Dafydd and Maes y Bettws, the names of three farms at these sites. 'Ynys' can mean both island and plot but historians reckon there was once an island at Ynys Afan where the river divided to create a fertile tract of land in its centre. The modern bridge at Ynys Afan[8] sits on top of an early nineteenth century stone viaduct that carried the horse-drawn Bryn railroad across the river.

Ynys Dafydd, or Dafydd's plot, seems to have been named for Dafydd Davis, a wool carder and maker of carding frames, who lived at his farm on the south side of the river in Margam parish[9]. The entrance to the bridge is off Afan Terrace in Pwll y Glaw, down a narrow path between the houses and guarded by a sunburst of wrought iron work that surely must have been manufactured in Cwmafan's rail mill.

Maes y Bettws footbridge, between Pwll y Glaw and Pontrhydyfen, is my favourite for the rush of water over the weir, the view of the mountains above the south bank and the remains of an old stone structure that's history in the raw – unnamed, un-tidied and patched up – and just asking to be climbed.

All three farms were swallowed up in the nineteenth century by the advance of industry and two collieries were sunk here, named for the Ynys farms. An accident at the Ynys Dafydd mine in 1856 resulted in the loss of thirteen lives.[10]

The word bridge is common currency in our language: we talk about building as well as burning bridges. Literally and metaphorically they represent cooperation and communication, surmounting an obstacle, the meeting of two sides. Industry once stitched the two sides of the Afan Valley together. It's good to see the bridges still doing their work, if for a different reason.

Bridges
For Allen Blethyn

All day we crossed them, arches of stone, spans of steel
and concrete, looking down at the rush of weirs, tracking
bends in the river from the sea towards the head of the
valley, in the company of swans, a cormorant, a rippling
curve of ducks, once a wagtail dipping on a hunk of
granite, the flash of a goldfinch. The sun shone, clouds
burst, at times our maps betrayed us, but the bridges,
when we found them, told us their stories: floods, a
halfpenny, lost islands. And above the sound of the river,
when we stopped and listened, other footsteps, the faint
rumble of drams and engines, voices we felt sure we
recognised, the past meeting us there, suspended between
two banks, mountains ahead, the sea behind us, hills rising
on each side. Shadows and sunlight.

THE RIVER

The River Afan has its source in the mountains near Cymmer –
formed out of three main tributaries, the Corrwg, the Gwynfi and
the Pelenna – and drops around 1,600 feet on its thirteen mile
journey to Aberafan, literally, 'the mouth of the Afan'. The
eighteenth century historian, Edward Williams, better known as Iolo
Morgannwg, suggested that its name derived from *a* (from, in
Welsh) and *ban* or *fan* (height) so Afon Afan would be the River
from the Heights[11]. That's a term you could probably apply to
hundreds of rivers in Wales and Iolo Morgannwg's scholarly reputation is a little smeared even if his passion for all things Welsh was
undeniable[12]. Glan Williams, one of the founders and former chairman of the Afan Valley Angling Club[13], had the idea it evolved from
the Welsh word for beaver, 'afanc', animals that were native to Wales
until Medieval times, and that the name lost its true meaning and
closing c as Afon Afanc was passed down through generations[14].

Rights to Afan fisheries were granted as far back as the twelfth
century and the history of disputes over those rights illustrates how
lucrative they were. The first Afan fishing lease was issued by Abbot
David of Margam Abbey in 1509, covering a section of the river
from above Pontrhydyfen down to Blackwells, outside Cwmafan,
with payment being "4 gillings, 40 sewin and 17 salmon.[15] After the
dissolution of the abbeys, subsequent landowners continued to
issue leases but the nineteenth century industrial development of
the Afan Valley – weirs built to harness water power and the
dumping of industrial waste and small coal – dramatically reduced
the stocks of migratory fish.

In *The Afan Fisheries*, Ivor Lewis tells the story of how, in 1950,
two ex-servicemen and keen fishermen, Viv Evans and Glan
Williams, met on the bank of the river at Reginald Street in
Velindre, a meeting which resulted in the launch of the Afan Valley
Angling Club at The Jersey Arms in Cwmafan in 1951. Two of the
club's principal aims were to acquire fishing rights and improve and
maintain the purity of the water but they could not have known the
scale of the battles ahead.

In August 1952 a creosote spill from Nantewlaeth coal washery
on the River Corrwg wiped out the Afan's fish stock. After a great
deal of pressure the National Coal Board accepted responsibility
and the club's actions, and the publicity surrounding the spill,

brought them national recognition. But even after a programme of fish restocking, and introducing plant life, snails and shrimp in the late 1950s, the river continued to be polluted with bad coal water, toxic chemical waste and leaks from the main trunk sewer. The height of the weir at Green Park, the point where the river was cut and diverted in the first half of the nineteenth century to create the Port Talbot docks, presented an additional problem. Fish that did enter the river, and managed to survive were often trapped here during ebb tides.

The club developed a militant reputation but given the size and strength of their adversaries – principally the NCB and Glamorgan River Board – I doubt they had any other option but to be stridently vocal and pro-active. By the late 1960s iron water from pit closures further up the valley had so badly polluted the river the club were again fighting to protect fish and aquatic life. But by the end of that decade, with the last of the pit closures and the pending closure of Port Talbot docks following the opening of the tidal harbour, the future was looking more optimistic.

Weir repair and replacement in the 1970s and 1980s, the laying of thousands of tons of limestone blocks in the river to protect the main sewer, and, over the years, the dedication of club members to fishery management – the acquisition and protection of fishing rights, restocking, bank clearance and snag removal – have undoubtedly made the river what it is today. They were true eco-warriors[16] before the term was invented.

The most recent intervention in the Afan was in 2012: a £200,000 fish pass[17] at the Green Park weir which had been a major obstacle in the river's recovery for a long time, something which Glan Williams, affectionately known as Glan of Afan, would have been delighted with. His passion for the river and his contribution to the club was commemorated in 1989 with the unveiling of a stone bench on the banks of the Afan near the Afan Argoed Visitors' Centre[18].

If you follow the river east from its mouth the path takes you past a number of iron and wood sculptures, studded with tokens of seascape life designed by local schoolchildren. I like their un-sculptured roughness, an echo of the cargoes of iron, tin and wood that once docked here blending with the natural world. And they mark the continuing passage of time too with their reaction to the salty air. Yes, you can still lean over one of the Afan's bridges and see a supermarket trolley crocked at the bank, or a crush of soggy litter,

but swans, ducks, geese and cormorants are commonplace along this stretch of the river now. Further east, sewin jump the weir on an incoming tide. Seals occasionally come in to feed.

On the flood prevention walls near the Civic Centre in town someone painted, 'CLEANED RIVER OUT 13.7.93'. Well done, mate. Where the river bumps around Velindre there are two handprints on the road side of the riverbank wall, a large one in red, a smaller in white. The kind of graffiti that whispers, Our river.

> day moon
> the river and I
> don't say a word

THE DOCKS

There's a great view from the Docks Café, towards the end of North Bank Road, but not of the docks or the open sea. With your back to the caf and a cup of steaming tea in your hand you can enjoy a panoramic view of all three of Port Talbot's mountains:

Dinas, Emroch and Margam. And as your tea's too hot to drink you might as well pull up a chair because the mountains are worth more than a glance.

I always thought Mynydd Dinas meant City Mountain but Madog Fychan[19], in his prize winning essay at the Cwmafan Eisteddfod in 1889, suggests its true name is Mynydd y Danas, Deer Mountain, for the deer herds that once roamed there. There are two ancient fortifications on Dinas and a Bronze Age round barrow[20] so it does make sense that the name derives from human settlements. But Madog argues that deer names (including hydd and carw, both meaning stag) are a popular choice for places in Wales. And Deer Mountain is prettier too.

These days the deer are on Mynydd Margam[21] and Margam is thought to be a corruption of Morgan. When the Cistercian abbey was established in 1147 it was known as the Abbey of Morgan and the name persisted until the mid-sixteenth century[22].

Emroch is more of a mystery: there are no Welsh words that are recognisably similar. Thomas Gray, in his early twentieth century study of the granges attached to Margam Abbey, converts Mynydd Embroch, as he calls it, to: "Hen-brembch… the old steep mountain; from hen, old; bre, synonymous with bryn in the twelth century, hill or mountain, moch, steep, shortened into easier Embroch."[23]

Sold. On the grounds I could not be more inventive.

This view might not be around for too much longer. The mostly disused docklands are part of Neath Port Talbot County Borough

Council's regeneration plans which, as at July 2012, included sports venues, a college, residential, retail and leisure development, offices and light industry, and a bulky goods retail park[24]. Some of the land is contaminated brownfield so there's some work to be done before the transformation can begin so this might be an appropriate time to put in a request. Can we keep the Docks Café, please? Starbucks and Costa Coffee don't do egg and chips.

The first steps to improve road access for the redevelopment, and supposedly relieve traffic on the M4, were taken in 2010: the new Peripheral Distributor Road (PDR), or Harbour Way. It'll run for 4.8km from Junction 38 of the M4 at Margam, across Tata Steel land, through the docklands and join up with the Afan Way south of the town centre. Waste material from the steelworks – 400,000 tonnes of slag and 35,000 tonnes of crushed concrete by the time of the road's completion in Autumn 2013 – has been used as fill material and the overall cost of the project is £107 million. However, before construction could begin, 1,800 *Anguis fragilis*, or slow-worms[25], had to be moved from the steelworks' site and relocated. That's a lot of snake or, to be accurate, legless lizard: slow worms have eyelids. I hope they kept them closed during the move.

And there's likely to be a lot more protected species – birdlife, plants, animals and reptiles – to look out for on the docklands site where nature has been quietly reclaiming the vacant lots. In 2009 Sand Martins that were nesting in a sand and gravel extraction quarry at the docks were relocated to a custom built nesting bank, with a feeding pond below, as part of the mitigation strategy[26] for a controversial, and, as at the beginning of 2013, yet to be built £400 million wood-chip biomass plant[27].

The parcel of docklands that's still (unofficially) accessible is relatively peaceful. Most of the people crossing the gorse scrambled landscape, to the left of Riverside Road as you come out of town, are there walking their dogs. But the number of wharfs and landing stages still marked on the map, the four distinct basins and the old entrance to the Graving or dry dock, tells you this wasn't always the case.

The Port Talbot Docks were built between 1836 and 1841 by diverting the course of the River Afan at Green Park. Prior to this small vessels had berthed at wharves on the Aberafan side of the river and at the Old Bar in Taibach but rapid expansion of the iron and copper industries required improved shipping facilities. The new floating docks were named for C.R.M. Talbot of Margam Park, one of the principal investors and a keen yachtsman. When the Suez Canal opened in 1869 Talbot's *Lynx*[28] was the first private yacht to steam through it.[29]

By the end of the nineteenth century the docks were again inadequate – big ships were being unloaded at Swansea and their ore brought in by smaller vessels – so in 1894 the Port Talbot Railway and Docks Company obtained parliamentary approval to extend them. Their completion in 1898 made Port Talbot the natural outlet for coalfields in South Wales.

The docks hit a slump in the depression of the 1930s but geared up again with the outbreak of World War II. Between 1943 and 1944, under a cloak of secrecy, American ships arrived and unloaded their cargo of tanks and military vehicles which were loaded again onto railway wagons and shunted off to South East England. American troops billeted around the town staged mock landings on Morfa Beach, south of the docks, in preparation for the D-Day invasion. Denys Parsons, author of *The Dock Street Story*, recounts how every child in the street learned to say, 'Got any gum, chum?' and how "the older boys walked about like the American Gangster actor, George Raft, with Chesterfield cigarettes hanging out of the side of their mouths."[30] History books tend to credit Cardiff and Swansea for their D-Day support but Port Talbot Docks, the railwaymen and the dry dockers, made a significant contribution too.

Docks that could handle ships carrying 10,000 tons of iron ore in the first half of the twentieth century were becoming dinosaurs with the development of the new bulk carrying vessels. In May 1970 Queen Elizabeth II officially opened a £20 million tidal harbour to the south east of the docks: the first dry-bulk cargo terminal in the UK capable of accepting ships in excess of 100,000 DWT[31]. Further dredging in 1996 deepened the harbour to 16.5 metres allowing ships up to 170,000 DWT to berth and unload. These were the biggest capesize vessels in the world, i.e. ships too big for the Panama and Suez Canals that had to sail via the Cape of Good Hope or Cape Horn. Standard capesize ships are still around 175,000 DWT but bigger ones have and are being built.

The tidal harbour is currently used exclusively by Tata Steel, who manage their own discharge operations with the three huge cranes that are an iconic part of Port Talbot's landscape, but Ralph Windeatt, Commercial Manager for Associated British Ports in South Wales, says a feasibility study is being undertaken to see how much deeper the harbour can be dredged. Which would increase

the draught, which would mean bigger ships, which would mean more opportunities for ABP.

What surprises me, when we stop at the south breakwater, is how close the *Cardinal Victory* from Panama, in the final stages of unloading at the jetty, is to the shoreline – a fringe of white sand that rises to an expanse of dune grass and wild flowers. I know sea distances can be deceiving but the sea bed must drop away from the shore at an alarming angle. Not the place for a paddle in what you'd imagine to be the shallows.

At the opening of the tidal harbour, the Queen also unveiled, "a remarkable inscribed sun-dial... The large gnomon of Welsh stainless steel, standing in the centre of a circular stone and slate structure, indicates the time in Port Talbot and six of the world's major ports."[32]

In the background of a black and white photograph of the sundial, which looks remarkably like a deep barbecue pit filled with stones stirred with a steel rod, I can see the top of a castellated tower. And the reason why I'm jogging towards it today in the blustering wind and thrashing rain to take a photograph is because it's one of only two buildings left that commemorate the history of the old docks.

The Grade II listed octagonal Harbour Watchtower[33] was built around the middle of nineteenth century, outlasting the sundial whose presence as "a permanent memorial to Her Majesty's visit"[34]

wasn't so permanent. It's either been removed, filled in or disguised. The lookout tower is on the south side of the mouth of the River Afan but unless you have a pass to get through docks security you'll have to be content with viewing it from the north bank.

In the 1920s HM Coastguard moved here and used it as their official lookout until 1974 when they moved to the prom at Aberafan Beach. With those sturdy walls of rubble and dressed stone and a kettle simmering on a Valor paraffin stove it must have been quite cosy. Until you had to step outside into the wind-wrapped and gull-shrieked dark for a pee. Or when you peered out through the door during your watch and a bomb dropped on a sandbank opposite and blew you across the room.

This is one of the wartime stories that Bill Matthews tells me. Bill was born in Dry Dock Cottages – phone number Port Talbot 8 – in 1930. His father, W.H. Matthews, was watchman at the dry dock, in charge of the Coastguards and awarded the B.E.M.[35] for his services during the war. But there was one duty he and his colleagues were never called on to perform: to blow the dry dock, the lock gates and the cranes on the wharf in the event of a German invasion, the dynamite for which was stored in a large padlocked box in the cottage's garden.

Bill worked as a shipwright at the docks between 1946 and 1970 when, after the opening of the tidal harbour, the old docks became redundant and closed in December 1971. When Civil & Marine started processing slag[36] from the steelworks' blast furnaces the docks re-opened, in the mid-1990s, for exports from the Rio Tinto[37] Wharf. These exports, and imports for Dyfed Steels at Talbot Wharf and for Talbot Block, a builders' merchant next to The Docks Café, hardly amount to the same bustling existence – a couple of ships through the lock gates a week is the norm. But the completion of Harbour Way, allowing HGVs to travel between these acres of development land and the M4, without rumbling through the town, could change all that.

Turn left off Riverside Road and follow the road to the edge of the quay and you'll come to the Grade II listed Harbour House[38], built in 1838 for the harbour master at the site of the original lock gates. Harbour operations are now controlled from the modern Puckley House, on the southern side of the docks, and Harbour House, along with the red corrugated shed opposite, is used by Port Talbot Sea Cadets. The roof of the shed announces its former identity: the Missions to Seamen[39]. When the docks were in their heyday sailors could have chosen between Christian literature and pastoral care here or the (allegedly) best pint of Trumans in town at The Dock Hotel[40] a few hornpipe steps away. For a shed it's had a variety filled life: before it arrived here it was part of the cottage hospital at Broom Hill above Taibach, built in 1893 by Emily Talbot.

Along with Dry Dock Cottages, on this triangular spit of land between the docks and the River Afan, there was also Wharf Row facing north towards the town with the Dock Police Station right in the middle and a dance hall in front of it, built by the people who lived there. (Bill Matthews tells me that The Wharf Row Social Club had a championship table tennis team and some stylish sequence dancers.) And I've already mentioned Dock Street on the other side of the lock gates: a row of 25 houses sandwiched between a railway embankment and Morfa Beach, demolished in 1955. At one time Dock Street had its own football team, the Dock Stars formed in 1905[41], and their own ground. One of the Dock Stars' most famous players was Port Talbot-born Tommy Bamford who played for Manchester United between 1934 and 1938 and was capped for Wales[42].

A working docks, housing, a football ground, a hotel and dance

hall, an active sports and social club. In twenty-first century speak that would be: a mixed and thriving community built around commerce and industry, residential and leisure development and sporting venues. History could be repeating itself in NPTCBC's regeneration plans.

There's already been an independent strike for leisure at Llewellyn's Quay, opposite the slag processing plant. I only found the jet-ski club by accident on a sunny spring Sunday when I wandered through an open chain-link gate. I wasn't expecting a dozen men in tight black neoprene but some days work out better than others. The South Wales Jetski Club[43] has been going for 15 years. They're a non-profit making group whose members pay £250 p.a. to ski this 20 acre freshwater lake.

Jet ski-ing isn't a cheap sport during any economic climate (a new ski will set you back around £9,000, a second-hand one about £2,000) but the recession has bitten away at club membership in recent years, from around 70 six years ago down to 30 in 2012. Paul Taylor, one of the founders, told me they used to lease the lake from Associated British Ports for £4,500 p.a. but when ABP sold the land to a property company the rent almost doubled overnight.

The club is hanging in there and the regeneration plans are one good reason to do just that. Another is the uniqueness of the lake. The water that Tata Steel use in their energy plant is recycled in this lake which means the temperature stays around 10 to 14 degrees. When lakes around the country are sealed with ice during the winter this one stays open.

The club has open days, master-classes and fund-raising events and on a day like today, the sun glittering off the water and a canopy of blue overhead, the industrial background is dramatic. I'd like the club to do well: their passion and initiative pre-empted any action by the local authority to exploit the docks' potential.

If jet-skiing holds no interest for you I'd still recommend a trip here because Bro's Café[44] is just around the corner and if you're not frightened by the F-word (not that one) then prepare yourself for the simple deliciousness that is Mark Mizen's tray-baked faggots. The neighbouring town of Neath likes to think of itself as the faggots and peas capital of Wales[45] but the gauntlet is down, my little Neathlings.

MORFA BEACH

Until Michael Sheen's *The Passion*, and Dave McKean's subsequent film version, *The Gospel of Us*[46], unzipped Port Talbot like a corset and everything fell out for the world to see, I doubt the town would have sprung into people's minds as a film location choice. But Port Talbot has featured in more movies than you might know, one of the most recent being *Hunky Dory* (2011)[47] starring Minnie Driver. It was fictionally set in Swansea but I bet I wasn't the only Port Talboter to squeal when the scenes at Port Talbot docks and Newbridge appeared on screen.

Morfa Beach has been the specific location for a handful of films. It is also one of the town's best kept-secrets: even I wasn't fully aware of it and I lived in Port Talbot for the first nineteen years of my life. Of course, I wasn't short on sand and sea, living only a street away from Aberafan Beach, but it just didn't occur to me that this unspoilt stretch of coastline, popular with surfers, anglers, horse-riders and walkers, existed on the other side of the docks. To say unspoilt you have to stand with your back to the land and look out to sea. If you look inland it's less picturesque, but still dramatic, looking across the peat beds at low tide to the steelworks whose land

and plant run the length of the beach from the tidal harbour in the north, almost to the River Cynffig in the south.

But to get back to the movies. The desert scenes from *The Man from Morocco* (1945)[48] were shot at Morfa Beach so there was a lot of interest when the film was eventually shown at Plaza cinema. And more than a few laughs "when a familiar local locomotive steamed on to the scene, its G.W.R. sign concealed by one on which was printed 'Etat', and its driver made up as an Arab".[49]

According to information gleaned from IMDb's website, Anthony Brockway's *Babylon Wales* blog[50] and local memories, the beach and other parts of Port Talbot appeared in the following diverse collection. *Nine Men* (1943)[51], starring Gordon Jackson; *The Bed Sitting Room* (1969)[52], a slapstick, post-nuclear black comedy with Peter Cook, Dudley Moore, Spike Milligan and a host of usual suspects; the apocalyptic *Hardware* (1990)[53] starring Iggy Pop; *A Kiss Before Dying* (1991)[54], a remake of the Robert Wagner and Joanne Woodward 1956 film of the same title; the disturbingly enjoyable *Twin Town,* (1997)[55], number 4 in Love Film's list of the Top 10 Sweariest Films[56]; and *I Know You Know* (2008)[57] starring Robert Carlyle. In 2012, Lindisfarne Films shot scenes for *The*

Darkest Day, their Viking invasion epic, in the mountains and along the storm battered shore.[58]

A film that wasn't shot here, but whose director was inspired by the landscape, was *Brazil* (1985)[59]. Terry Gilliam discovered Morfa Beach while on location for his solo directorial debut in *Jabberwocky* (1977)[60]:

> Port Talbot is a steel town, where everything is covered with a grey iron ore dust. Even the beach is completely littered with dust, it's just black. The sun was setting, and it was really quite beautiful. The contrast was extraordinary. I had this image of a guy sitting there on this dingy beach with a portable radio, tuning in to these strange Latin escapist songs like Brazil. The music transported him somehow and made his world less grey.[61]

So, if you're a producer or director who gets your kicks from military conflict, dystopias, the apocalypse, bumping off your nearest and fucking dearest, espionage and heathens, Port Talbot's your ticket.

One event that began here in the 1960s had all the ingredients of a movie: a message in a bottle that led to a friendship lasting 40 years and still going strong. In July 1968 8-year-old Sandra Morris, from Pennsylvania USA, slipped a piece of paper into a Mateus Rosé bottle and threw it over the side of a cruise ship into the Atlantic Ocean. Three months later 8-year-old Rosalind Hearse (now Causey) was walking along Morfa Beach with her father when she spotted it, pulled out the cork and found the message inside. The two have been in touch ever since.

Local and national newspapers[62] reported the celebration of their fortieth anniversary in 2008 with photos of them supposedly sitting on Morfa Beach, although they were actually taken at Rest Bay, Porthcawl because of the difficulty of accessing Morfa Beach, a private beach owned by the steelworks, operated by Tata Steel.

The issue of privacy aside, Morfa's not the most straightforward of places to get to. If you'd asked me for directions a year ago I'd have instantly told you to turn up Longlands Lane, off the A48 at Margam, past the Crematorium, around Hank's Bend leading into Heol Caer Bont, over the railway crossing (pay attention and don't dawdle), carry straight on and over the works' Haul Road (look right, look left, look right again) then down the slipway onto the beach. But that route, mapped as Footpath 92, is at risk and Tata insist the footpath never extended onto the beach. The Save Morfa Beach (Friends of Morfa) Facebook Group[63] disagree.

The creation of the 870 mile All Wales Coast Path[64], from Chester in the north to Chepstow in the south east, highlighted the obstacle of heavy industry along the Port Talbot coastline: the steelworks, the tidal harbour and the docks. I really don't know if Health & Safety concerns could have been surmounted and a safe route created for the public from Kenfig in the south, along Morfa Beach and through these sites to Newbridge over the River Afan, but the whole issue is immaterial now. This section of the AWCP has been diverted away from the coast, over land owned by Tata Steel, following an agreement between them and Neath Port Talbot Council[65].

While the Welsh Government states that the creation of the AWCP is entirely independent of any issues concerning existing footpaths it is difficult to divorce it from Tata's almost simultaneous request to extinguish Footpath 92 which also runs across their land. Closing it will remove access to Morfa Beach at this point.

Tata's argument revolves around securing their COMAH[66] designated site, which Footpath 92 crosses, to prevent unlawful entry to operational areas and to eliminate the danger of people crossing the Haul Road (there are monster trucks operating there). They also say that while the company has previously allowed access, through tacit consent, this does not mean a right of way has been established to the beach which is also their private land.

Members of Save Morfa Beach are adamant about the right of way: they have evidence of continued usage over a period in excess of 20 years, and evidence of public access predating the building of the steelworks in 1947. Health and safety issues can be met, they say, by appropriate fencing. They are also investigating how the beach ended up under steelworks' ownership. The land originally belonged to the Talbots and the Margam Estate, was requisitioned during World War II then derequisitioned, and they can't find any records, as yet, about transfer of ownership. And the group have attracted a lot of support, through its Facebook members, an online petition, local councillors and director, Terry Gilliam: "Morfa Beach inspired a beginning. Let it inspire a happy ending. This is no dead parrot, squawk loudly and long and you will win in the end."[67]

The group are anxious not to present themselves as anti-Tata: the lawful protection of Footpath 92 and access to the beach remain the focus of their battle. And Tata management have reiterated their commitment to work with and listen to the local community too.

Tata have also stated that they have no plans for expanding their operations in this area but public knowledge of a potential on-site deep drift mine and the phased sand extraction for the progressive site restoration of the Morfa Landfills have fuelled rumours about their application to close the path and prohibit beach access.

The deadlock should be broken by a Public Inquiry sometime in the autumn of 2013. In the meantime, the group keeps walking Footpath 92.

Paths

We are diverse,
concrete, paved brick,
or a stretch
of beaten earth,
sometimes straight
like the way
to an open hearth
or with a twist
or two, the horizon
obscured. Even lost
for years we wait,
unperturbed,
for you to glimpse
more light
than growth
through a hedge,
the knock
of firm ground
hidden by grass.
We serve you
through and beyond
our making, even while
you persist
in judging us:
maligning our ease,
our width, praising us
for being narrow, steep. Listen,
we do not care
for what you think,
believe. All

we require,
all you require,
is your weight,
your forward movement,
before something
comes and rips us
from under your feet.

On April 8th, 2012 there's an exceptionally low tide and the sea is
calm under an overcast sky, even if the wind bullies me a little as I
walk along Morfa Beach towards the harbour. I'm hoping to see the
remains of a Cromwell Tank[68] that took part in training operations
for the Allied invasion of Normandy in June 1944 when American
troops were based in the town. It became stuck in soft sand during
a simulated beach landing and was abandoned after the removal of
its gun turret and engine. To be honest, I'm not exactly sure what I
should be looking for. From a distance even the exposed dark peat
beds look like they could be tank parts so I keep on going towards
the next promising looking extrusion.

Maybe it's the deep pools around the peat beds, the brooding,
smoky steelworks on my right and being out here on my own,
combined with the knowledge that a low tide has to turn at some
point, but I start to feel uneasy. I could just turn around now; I'm
not that interested in tanks anyway. A healthy respect for the power
of the sea is turning into a gut-bound fear. But another voice tells
me to keep going; this could be the only opportunity for a long
time, and there's another wreck here to see, if the tide allows: the
wreck of the *Amazon*.

I don't find the tank but I do find the scattered remnants of a
Mulberry Harbour, another relic of the D-Day preparations, that
broke loose while being towed across Swansea Bay and was washed
up on Morfa Beach. Considered to be one of the greatest engineering feats of World War II, the artificial harbour was designed for
rapid off-loading of troops, vehicles and supplies to sustain
Operation Overlord, code name for the Battle of Normandy. One of
the Mulberry Harbours that was towed across the Channel and
constructed at Arromanches was used to land over 2.5 million men,
500,000 vehicles and 4 million tonnes of supplies over a ten month
period following D-Day[69].

The peat beds on Morfa Beach hark back to a time when you
could have walked from Margam to Mumbles on the other side of

Swansea Bay. The wreck of the *Amazon* belongs to a more recent era. The *Amazon* left Port Talbot docks and set off across Swansea Bay on Monday 31 August 1908, loaded with 2,000 tonnes of coal bound for Chile, but had to anchor in the lee of Mumbles Head because of bad weather. As the storm worsened both the ship's anchor cables snapped. It was swept back across the bay, past Aberafan Beach and ran aground near the dock entrance the next morning. Waves continued to batter the four mast ship and the 28 crew members tried to save themselves by jumping into the sea. The Mumbles Lifeboat attempted a rescue but heavy seas prevented it from getting closer than a mile to the ship. Nineteen men died, although not all the bodies were recovered, including the Captain Andrew Garrick. On Monday September 1st 2008, the hundredth anniversary of the disaster, a commemorative plaque was unveiled at the RNLI station on Aberafan Beach[70].

I make it all the way to the wreck, almost to the southern break-water of the tidal harbour, and I feel a mixture of ghoulishness and fascination as I walk around the encrusted ribs of a ship that had once been painted white and was known as the Ghost Ship.

Perhaps we're drawn to disaster. Perhaps it makes us feel lucky to be alive. Was that one of the reasons for hundreds of sightseers who arrived on special trains from the Valleys on the following Sunday in 1908 to see what was left of the *Amazon*?

There's a short animated film of the wreck of the *Amazon* on

YouTube[71], illustrated, animated and told by pupils from years 4 &
5 at St. Therese's Catholic Primary School on Sandfields Estate.
The focus is on rescue rather than on lost lives but the imagery is
atmospheric and the tension is effectively captured with music and
children's voices.

There could be a lot more under the sand. Treasure has been
found here. Bronze Age axe heads, a Roman bronze wheel-shaped
brooch, a brass sestertius coin of Titus Caesar, AD 77-78, a fourth
century bronze dress pin of Irish origin, a gold San Vincente piece
from 1556-57 probably from the wreck of a ship that foundered
here, a seventeenth century pewter spoon, seventeenth century
musket balls, two pairs of brass nautical dividers from the sixteenth
or seventeenth centuries, the lead cap of a seventeenth century gin
bottle, shoe buckles, and a whole pocketful of silver and copper
coins from the fifteenth to the eighteenth centuries.[72] I can already
hear the stampede for metal detectors heading down the West Mall
of the Aberafan Shopping Centre towards Argos.

The only people I've seen brandishing a metal detector along the
coast were a couple of guys on the tumps beyond the western end
of the Prom at Aberafan Beach.

"Any luck?" I asked.

He showed me his haul: some AA batteries, a tangled pair of iPod
headphones and 60p. "First time I've used it. And my mate found
the 50 pence," he said accusingly.

THE STEELWORKS

The steel industry has defined Port Talbot since the 1950s, the way
coal-mining defined the South Wales' valleys during the previous
hundred years. A black and white picture postcard from the early
1960s features the Steel Company of Wales' Margam Steelworks as
one of the town's attractions, dominating the land between the
mountains and the coast. I can understand the pride: it was
Europe's largest steelworks when it was completed in 1953 and the
largest single employer in Wales. High employment figures and high
wages contributed to the town's nickname of Treasure Island. The
industry's decline in subsequent decades, and brutal redundancies
in the 1980s[73] gave rise to the equally expressive, Giro City. The
once 18,000 strong workforce currently stands at around 3,000.

Iron-making in the Margam area, using locally mined iron ore,

can be traced back to the thirteenth century under the auspices of the monks at Margam Abbey[74]: small scale iron smelting and forging mainly for domestic and agricultural uses that continued for centuries. The first industrial forge in Port Talbot opened at the beginning of the eighteenth century[75] but it was towards the end of the nineteenth, with the expansion of the Port Talbot docks in 1898, that the concept of steelmaking, in its modern metallurgical sense, was fully embraced. In 1901 Messrs. Gilbertsons of Pontardawe built the first Port Talbot Steelworks at a cost of £250,000. There were a few hiccups in its early days but the intervention of Baldwins Ltd in 1906, and a rapidly expanding market for steel railway products, put the works on a fast track to success.

Between 1916 and 1922 the construction of a new Margam Works took place at the dockside with much of the heavy labouring work around the three blast furnaces carried out by German prisoners of war interned at the disused celluloid works at Goytre[76]. Given the high levels of post-war unemployment in the town local people were understandably resentful and, after protests in parliament in 1919, 430 of them were replaced by local men[77].

A strip mill project at the Margam Works, owned by Guest, Keen-Baldwins, that was conceived as early as 1939, became a reality in 1947 following the formation of the Steel Company of Wales. The works would cover nearly 600 acres of Margam Moors and stretch for four and a half miles. £60 million was the estimate for the initial development plan with over a £100 million more

invested by the end of the 1950s. And it was the S.C.O.W. who offered my dad a job at the Abbey Works in 1957 though it was decades before I realised why it was called that. I wonder how many of the thousands of people who poured in to work there – 18,000 by 1960 – knew of the iron-making link to the medieval abbey?

There's still a visible link to the abbey on the steelworks site today, now operated by the multinational, Tata Steel Europe[78]. A ragged stone wall is all that remains of New Grange, believed to have served as the abbey's Home Farm[79]. There was a second abbey grange on the reclaimed saltmarsh of Margam Moors, Theodoric's, first excavated by Thomas Gray[80] in 1898 and rediscovered, and subsequently levelled, during the construction of the works. A thirteenth century key found on site was presented to King George VI to mark the opening of the hot-strip mill in July 1951[81].

The wall is firmly buttressed and protected by a steel fence: local legend warns that should the wall ever collapse the steelworks will fail.

The cluttered flatlands of towers and sheds, grit, smoke and steam that accompany you for a good five minutes as you drive along the M4 have recently been quieter than their appearance suggests. The worldwide demand for steel has been low. At the end of 2012 there were 500 redundancies amongst management and administrative posts at the Port Talbot plant. But at the same time Tata have been making Croesus-like investments at the works. A new blast furnace costing £185 million was built in 2012, and fired up in February 2013, and they've spent another £53 million to reduce energy costs by recycling the gasses that are a by-product of steelmaking[82].

It was the 'blow down' or decommissioning of Blast Furnace 4, and the construction of a new one[83] intended to work alongside the existing BF5, that prevented my walkabout tour of the works. But given the size and sprawl of the site the windshield tour, offered by Robert Dangerfield, Public Affairs Manager at Port Talbot, was undoubtedly a better idea. You can clock up more than a dozen miles driving around the chaotic network of private roadways past coke ovens, towering furnaces, hot mills and cold mills, slab yards, over a web of railways, and through the moonscape stockpiles of iron ore, limestone, coke and coal intended for the iron making process. And the height and wheel size of the lumbering trucks you meet along the coastal Haul Road are guaranteed to make you feel like Gulliver in the Land of the Brobdingnag.

As a general purpose communications manager, Robert is often called upon to explain the technical processes of steelmaking. Not an easy job when your audience can be as diverse as new recruits to the industry, the media, and me, the girl who failed every single science O-level she took. And Welsh Assembly Government ministers. The only way I could begin to understand the process was to ask him to use my kind of language. So, feeling liberated from scientific incompetence, allow me to explain it to those of you who feel similarly challenged:

- Imagine a claret bottle. That's the furnace vessel into which the raw materials are charged at the top: iron ore, coke and limestone.
- Imagine that claret bottle slipped inside a ring doughnut. That's the plant that injects gas, air and granulated coal into the furnace to create the necessary chemical reactions.
- Imagine a tap opening towards the bottom of the bottle releasing a stream of golden liquid. That's the molten iron, the basic material from which steel is made.

As we drive past Blast Furnace 5 I'm lucky enough to see just that: all 370 tons of it pouring into a 'torp', a refractory-lined giant flask shaped like a torpedo sitting on its side.

The torps convey the hot metal to the BOS (Basic Oxygen Steelmaking) plant, where it's mixed with steel scrap and blasted with pure oxygen, at the rate of a Concorde jet engine. This molten steel is then cast into 22 tonne slabs which are rolled into the product the Port Talbot site is known for: hot rolled coil. The four final processes – roll, pickle (clean), anneal (toughen) and coat – depend on the final use and destination the steel's intended for.

The next time you pick up a tin of Heinz Tomato Soup think 'Port Talbot', because the steel for their canned products is made here (and processed into tinplate at the Trostre works in Llanelli). It puts a whole new spin on shopping locally around here.

And while you're rooting about in your loose change, again think 'Port Talbot' because Tata produce strip steel for the Royal Mint at Llantrisant. One and two pence coins have been made completely out of steel for years but soon the new five and ten pence pieces will also be made from steel and protected with an alloy coating.

And then there's strip steel for Jaguar Land Rover, BMW Mini, Honda and Nissan, who Tata Steel has supplied since they started UK production in Sunderland in the 1980s. The latest Nissan vehicle featuring steel produced in Port Talbot is the electric powered Nissan Leaf.

At the other end of the 'capability curve', as Robert describes it, Tata has developed Super Bainite, a lightweight steel that's incredibly hard and used as armour plating for military vehicles to replace the Snatch vehicles that have been so vulnerable to IEDs (improvised explosive devices, or roadside bombs) in Afghanistan and Iraq. And that's produced by the same blast furnace that gives us our soup cans.

There's a lot of R&D (research and development) in the steel industry. It can be painstaking and mundane but it has its eureka moments with discoveries that have the potential to change our world.

Photo-voltaic steel, which is at the prototype stage, is the result of one of those eureka moments: a technician testing steel for corrosion discovered that a tiny charge of electricity was created when he reversed the process. Eureka: what if you could retain that charge but prevent corrosion?

This particular type of steel has a coating which works like photosynthesis in a leaf and generates energy everywhere on its surface. In theory, a building made of this material could be its own power station. Imagine a hospital, complete with operating theatres, powering itself in the middle of a jungle.

This discovery has 'science fiction' written all over it[84]. In his short story, 'The Woman in Del Rey Crater'[85], author Larry Niven gives an account of a new solar electric paint:

> Black Power, they call it. It turns sunlight into electricity, just like any solar power converter, but you spray it on. Place your cables and then spray over them. All you need is sunlight and room.

The next step is experimenting to test for longevity and adherence but as Tata already have a 15 foot module, limited to tinplate for the moment, the future of PV steel is firmly grounded in science fact.

There are unavoidable noise and pollution problems with an industry that covers 20 square kilometres working 24/7. It's true that the works produces half the CO_2 it used to, but the general problem that has bugged people living around here is kish, small black particles released into the air from the iron making process. Imagine ground up graphite smeared across your clean laundry and you'll get the idea. Kish incidents have fallen over the years thanks to new technology and changes to working practices and Tata have a phone line for all complaints and send their people out to deal with problems or offer compensation.

The grey box you see on Talbot Road, by the old Plaza cinema, is one of about eight PM10 monitors dotted around the town, the highest density of monitors anywhere in the UK. No, they're not alarms to alert the populace of the imminent arrival of David Cameron, but monitoring stations for particulate matter in the air of a size less than 10 micrometres in diameter. That's dust to you and me: dust you can't see but that doesn't do your lungs any favours. There have been elevated levels of PM10 in Port Talbot since 1996[86], when they were first recorded, and while there's been a decline over the last ten years they still exceed the national recommended level from time to time.

NPTCBC has its own pollution monitoring and air quality website[87], not your usual tourist support feature, where you can check out what you're breathing on a Bulletins Map that's updated hourly. The 26th of July 2012 didn't look good for lungs in the Talbot

Road area with levels peaking at 120ug/m3[88]. Concern usually starts kicking in at 50ug/m3, the national air quality objective.

It's not the presence of industry per se that causes the dust but the handling of industrial material and vehicle movement, as well as wind and land configuration. Dry weather can also be problematic and Tata's not responsible for all the PM10. Sand from the Sahara is supposed to be an issue (as if we didn't have enough of it along our six mile stretch of coastline) and the construction of the new Peripheral Distributor Road[89] is also a suspect. Tata have attempted to minimise dust generation on their site by coating raw material piles, covering conveyors and spraying on-site roads with water. They've also greened up the works, re-soiling and turfing slag areas and planting indigenous fruit trees and shrubs which also helps to suppress the dust. In 2011, 60 members of the local Army Cadet Force planted 1,000 trees around the lagoon within the works that provides cooling water for the steelmaking process. The trees were the last of 150,000 planted in the UK as part of a woodland creation project to celebrate 150 years of the Cadet Forces[90].

From glancing through back issues of Tata's in-house newspaper, *The Journey*, the safety of its workforce does come across as a top priority and tragic accidents are a source of genuine grief. Kevin Downey lost his life in a horrific accident involving molten slag in April 2006 when the steelworks was controlled by Corus Strip Products UK Ltd. The thoroughness of Health & Safety Executive investigations inevitably takes time so it was down to Tata, as the current owner, to plead guilty to breaches of the Health & Safety at Work Act and pay the £500,000 fine imposed on them in July 2012.

The site was also part of Corus, in 2001, when a blast furnace explosion killed three men and left 12 more with horrific burns. In 2006 the HSE accused Corus of "systematic corporate management failure" at that time and encouraged "the iron and steel industry, worldwide [to] learn from Port Talbot."[91] Corus were fined £1.333 million and ordered to pay costs of £1.744 million.

The 2001 tragedy is respectfully and earnestly remembered each year. On the tenth anniversary of the fatal blast Tata unveiled a memorial garden, opposite the main offices, for these men and for others who have lost their lives at the works. "In memory of those who never went home."

There's another memorial at the steelworks to the 188 miners who lost their lives in six explosions at the Morfa colliery between

1849 and 1890. The sinking of the Morfa mine on Margam Moors, more or less where the memorial stands today, began in 1847 by Messrs. Vivian & Sons. There were difficulties at first with water – one of the seams ran out under the sea – but the first coal was brought up in 1849 to feed the Vivian's copper works in Taibach. The death rolls on the Welsh coal mines[92] site make for chilling reading: the amount of children left fatherless, the number of men who'd lived as neighbours in a single street, the local community of Taibach decimated.

The Times[93] newspaper covered the worst of the Morfa disasters, an explosion on March 10 1890, and the subsequent inquiry at Aberafan Town Hall:

> The full extent of the disaster at the Morfa Colliery is now known. After careful inquiry the officials put the number of lives lost at 87. Sixty-eight of the men were married, three were widowers, and the remaining 16 were single. The number of children left fatherless by the disaster is 178, of whom 121 are under 13 years of age.

Four days later, after several heroic attempts by rescue teams to recover the bodies of their friends and fellow-miners, despite roof collapses and temporary entombment, they discovered the Cribbwr seam in the pit was on fire and the only option was to flood it, leaving the bodies of 43 men below ground.

Four years later, when the mine was still being worked, the bodies of two more men were recovered: John Griffith of Gwarycaerau, Port Talbot and John David of Groeswen Row, Taibach.[94] The mine stopped production and closed in 1913.

Seams of coal are still here, in the ancient and highly complex geological structure under Mynydd Margam, but the difficulty, in the history of coalmining, has always been in knowing exactly where, and how much of it, and in what formation. Tata has found it, possibly three seams of up to 380 million tons[95], by using reflection seismology which creates a three dimensional subterranean picture of a target area up to a kilometre in depth. The exploration surveys took place in 2010 and 2011 on around 10 square kilometres to the north east of the steelworks although the entrance to the planned mine would be on Tata land.

The new deep drift mine would access seams much deeper than the old Morfa ones, between 800m and 1km below ground and running inland, to good coking coal. Currently, Tata import all their coking coal so the savings on raw material costs and freight, as well as CO_2 emissions, would be hugely significant. But they are still a long way off – around 5 years and £500 million of investment long way off – from bringing the first coal to the surface. They've already spent between £7 and £10 million and there's no firm commitment to the drift mine yet but Robert thinks they'll do it. The project would make Tata the only steelworks in the EU to access coal within its own site.

The mine would need to employ 500 people, above and below ground, and yes, it would still be a dangerous occupation, although new technology and the long-wall method of mining would eliminate a lot of the risks associated with traditional coalmining. But where do you find miners, under the age of 50, in our current society? Tata would need to inspire, recruit and train them and the carrot at the end of the stick would be a £60,000 salary. They've already done the maths.

The future isn't orange. It's black gold.

One of the Indian technicians responsible for setting the seismic charges in 10 metre deep holes on Mynydd Margam came back to the works one day and mentioned to Robert, "I didn't know you had panther here." Neither did he.

The technician had seen a black cat as big as a Labrador on the mountainside and assumed, as anyone might from the Indian continent, that it was a panther. There have been stories of large feral cats around Bryn[96] but the closest the steelworks has ever come to magical beasts is the Steel Company of Wales's dragon logo which used to be fixed to the side of one of the old mills.

Aficionados of the Welsh flag will notice that it differs from that particular red dragon which is *passant*, in heraldic terms. In old money that's waving with his front right foot. S.C.O.W.'s red dragon has all four feet grasping the rolled coils.

notes

1. Cadw record 23153
2. http://en.wikipedia.org/wiki/Plate_girder_bridge
3. Cadw record 14173
4. Traditional folk tale also known as Henny-Penny and Chicken Little. Chicken Licken believed the sky had fallen on her head.
5. Skempton, A.W., et al, eds. *Biographical Dictionary of Civil Engineers, Volume 1, 1500-1830.* London 2002, p.211-12
6. Cadw record 23250

7. Perhaps the choice is connected to British Steel whose original blue logo wasn't too far from the current Tata Steel blue.
8. Cadw record 15845
9. Fychan, p.60
10. Powell & Thomas, p.109
11. Lewis, p.xii
12. *The Encyclopaedia of Wales*, Edward Williams, p.952
13. http://www.afanvalleyangling.com/
14. Lewis, Ibid
15. Lewis, p.9
16. In 1989 the club came 11th out of 352 entries in *The Times* newspaper's nationwide competition for the most worthy environmental group.
17. http://www.thisissouthwales.co.uk/pound-200-000-pass-clears-path-River-Afan/story-16718413-detail/story.html
18. Glanville Vernon Williams 1929-1988
19. Fychan, p.44
20. Y Castell, Castell y Wiriones, and the barrow excavated by Sir Mortimer Wheeler in 1921, Evans, *Baglan*, pp. 14-17
21. See East: Margam Country Park
22. Evans, *Taibach*, p.20
23. Gray, p.177
24. Port Talbot Harbourside and Town Centre Development Framework SPG, April 2011
25. Protected under the Wildlife and Countryside Act.
26. NPTCBC http://tiny.cc/imfclw
27. NPTCBC Planning Portal P2012/0712
28. The *Lynx* was a twin funnel paddle steamer registered at Dumbarton in 1854. 213 feet in length with a registered tonnage of 499 tons. Evans, Leslie A., 'Ship Owners of the Port Talbot Area', *Transactions of the Port Talbot Historical Society*, No.3, Vol.III.
29. Hanson, *Profile* p.7
30. Parsons, *Dock Street* p.18
31. Deadweight tonnage: a measure of how much weight a ship is carrying or can safely carry.
32. *Royalty and Afan*, souvenir brochure published by the Borough of Afan Silver Jubilee Committee, 1977.
33. Cadw record 23155
34. Morgan, p.29
35. British Empire Medal
36. Slag: industrial waste product from blast furnaces that's recycled and used in the building industry.
37. http://www.riotinto.com/aboutus/history.asp The Rio Tinto Company has connections with the town as far back as 1884 when they purchased the Copper Works in Cwmafan. Rees W&C, p.48
38. Cadw record 23154
39. Now called The Mission to Seafarers, an Anglican charity.
40. Demolished in 1991.
41. Parsons, *Dock Street*, p.8
42. www.aboutmanutd.com
43. http://jetski-club.co.uk/
44. http://www.broscafe.co.uk/
45. Wales Online: http://tiny.cc/acu9qw
46. http://www.imdb.com/title/tt2125651/
47. http://www.imdb.com/title/tt1727300/

48. http://www.imdb.com/title/tt0038723/
49. Hanson, *Profile*, p.143
50. http://babylonwales.blogspot.co.uk/
51. http://www.imdb.com/title/tt0036204/
52. http://www.imdb.com/title/tt0064074/
53. http://www.imdb.com/title/tt0099740/
54. http://www.imdb.com/title/tt0102220/
55. http://www.imdb.com/title/tt0120394/
56. With 318 curses. *Nil by Mouth* (1998) got the number one slot with 428. http://www.love film.com/community/view_list.html?customer_list_id=25335
57. http://www.imdb.com/title/tt1029123/
58. http://www.walesonline.co.uk/news/wales-news/2012/03/15/port-talbot-a-magnificent-movie-location-says-director-of-new-film-the-darkest-day-91466-30533318/
59. http://www.imdb.com/title/tt0088846/
60. http://www.imdb.com/title/tt0076221/
61. http://babylonwales.blogspot.co.uk/search?q=port+talbot
62. http://www.walesonline.co.uk/news/wales-news/2008/07/24/message-in-a-bottle-sparked-a-40-year-friendship-91466-21393901/: and http://www.telegraph.co.uk/news/newstopics/howaboutthat/2455534/Penpals-meet-on-beach-where-message-in-a-bottle-was-found-40-years-ago.html
63. https://www.facebook.com/groups/SaveMorfaBeach/
64. http://www.walescoastpath.gov.uk
65. The new section of path from Kenfig to Margam, across the newly built river bridge, remained closed as at the end of February 2013 as Tata had still not signed the access agreement.
66. Control of Major Accident Hazards: Health & Safety Executive.
67. *Evening Post*, 13.10.2011
68. World War II tank, named after Oliver Cromwell, leader of the English Civil War, first deployed at the Battle for Normandy in 1944.
69. http://en.wikipedia.org/wiki/Mulberry_harbour
70. *Port Talbot Guardian* 11.9.2008
71. YouTube - http://tiny.cc/gdzyjw
72. Rees, David B., 'Interesting Finds at Morfa Beach 1970-1975', *Transactions of the Port Talbot Historical Society*, No. I, Vol. III, 1977 and Morgan, p.13
73. In early 1982, 20% of Port Talbot's potential workforce was unemployed. Evans, *Taibach*, 2nd ed., p.231
74. See East: Margam Park
75. See Central: Forge Road
76. See East: Goytre
77. Evans, *Taibach*. p.78
78. The Steel Company of Wales (1947) was nationalised and re-privatised then absorbed into the nationalised British Steel Company in 1967. It was privatised in 1988, as British Steel plc, and merged with a Dutch steel producer to form Corus Group in 1999. The Tata Group acquired Corus in 2007 and rebranded the company as Tata Steel Europe in 2010
79. Evans, *Margam Abbey*, p.44
80. Author of *The Buried City of Kenfig*, T. Fisher Unwin, (London 1909)
81. Evans, *Margam Abbey*, p.43
82. BOS = Basic Oxygen Steelmaking. A new cooling system will create steam that will allow the plant to generate up to 10MW of electricity. That's the equivalent of the energy to power 20,000 homes
83. A local photographic studio, Port Studio, http://www.portstudio.co.uk/ was contracted to

produce a time-lapse video and photographic record of the refurbishment.

84. http://www.technovelgy.com/ct/science-fiction-news.asp?newsnum=1907
85. From the short story collection, *Flatlander* (Del Rey Books 1995).
86. Understanding PM10 in Port Talbot, Air Quality Expert Group, Defra 2011http://uk-air.defra.gov.uk/documents/110322_AQEG_Port_Talbot_Advice_Note.pdf
87. http://pollution.npt.gov.uk/home.asp
88. Micrograms per cubic metre.
89. See South: The Docks
90. *Western Mail* 21.4.2011
91. http://www.hse.gov.uk/press/2006/e06116.htm
92. http://www.welshcoalmines.co.uk/deathrolls/Morfa.htm
93. http://www.mit.edu/~dfm/genealogy/morfa-times.html
94. *Western Mail*, 21.4.1894
95. The steelworks currently uses 2.5 million tons per year
96. See North: Bryn

EAST

NO-MAN'S LAND

Head east out of Port Talbot town centre, along the Talbot Road
stretch of the A48, and straight through the traffic lights at the
Abbey Road junction. Between this point and the River Ffrwdwyllt,
about 500 yards ahead, the Port Talbot Arts Centre, St. Theodore's
Church and Talbot Memorial Park are bundled along the left hand
side of the road. The river is the official boundary between Port
Talbot and the community of Taibach but for me the boundary falls
just after Abbey Road. And I'm sure that Dr Charles Dawe, a native
of Taibach, who emigrated to the United States in 1912 and
founded the Cleveland Orpheus Choir[1], and subsequently donated
a priest's prayer desk to St. Theodore's, his local church, would
agree.

PORT TALBOT ARTS CENTRE

The ivy wrapped house in its own grounds, on the corner of
Theodore Road, was built as the vicarage to St. Theodore's in 1900-
01. It became the Headquarters of a Barrage Balloon Detachment
of the RAF in 1940[2] and in 1959 the Church of Wales sold it with
an acre of land to the local authority for £6,500. It opened as the
Arts Centre in 1975, offering a range of courses from art to wood
carving and also catering for the dramatic arts. A separate theatre
was built in the grounds in 1985.

Port Talbot's home-grown contribution to stage and film is inter-
nationally recognised: Richard Burton, Anthony Hopkins, and
more recently, Michael Sheen. Less widely known are Di Botcher[3],
film and TV actress, and Robert Blythe[4], actor and voice-over artist.
Then there's Bernard Fox[5], an actor with 30 film credits to his name
between 1956 and 2004 who appeared in TV and film classics as
diverse as *Bewitched*, *The Man from U.N.C.L.E.* and *Titanic* (1997).
There are two theatrical companies in the town: the Port Talbot
Little Theatre[6], dating back to 1941, and the Port Talbot & District
Amateur Operatic Society[7] whose origins can be traced back to the
1920s[8]. Michael Sheen's Port Talbot born father, Meyrick, who lives
in Baglan, has performed with the latter for fifty-seven years. Since
1989 he's also had a successful career as a Jack Nicholson lookalike[9], a likeness that's so convincing you expect the witches of

Eastwick to pop up with a bowl of cherries at any moment. And then there are the town's choirs: Cymric Male Choir[10], Cor Serenata, Cor Afanedd[11] and Cantorian Afan.

Apart from Andrew Vicari[12], I can't think of a visual artist from Port Talbot with a national reputation, but there's a surprising amount of unsung talent for a small industrial town: artists, photographers and sculptors, professional, amateur and everything in between. Among them, Bert Evans[13], who I've already mentioned, and Ray Davies Snr,[14] a retired steelworker who recreates Port Talbot's past and present on canvas with astonishing vibrancy: anything from a ruined chapel to The Three Sisters, the cranes in the deep water harbour. Craig Jenkins is a graffiti artist who goes by the name of Rarebit. His street work has appeared, and disappeared, in Cardiff as well as Port Talbot: you can still see it on his website[15] and the back door of the Art & Soul Tatu Parlour[16] in Station Road.

There's photographic skill in abundance on Port Talbot Camera Club's website[17], and if you watch the opening scenes of *The Gospel of Us*, the film version of Michael Sheen's *Passion*, you'll see the intricate and beautiful coal, slate and glass sculptures by local roofer, Tony Pugh: miniature houses, their rooms carved with dressers, tables and the minutiae of daily life.

But there's no trace of any of these at the Arts Centre. The Victorian house was closed abruptly in 2004, followed by the theatre in 2009, when the council withdrew the budget. The economic argument was solid: the premises needed a significant amount of money spent on them for maintenance, repairs and modernisation to meet Health and Safety requirements, and there were other, underused adult education facilities in the town. The Port Talbot Society of Arts, responsible for the day to day administration of courses, was offered a lease but decided they couldn't take on the responsibility. The value of the creative arts in people's lives is difficult to measure for the purposes of financial accounting or, every local authority's favourite buzzword, sustainability. The value of land is easier to calculate: the plot was earmarked for housing. The amount of unused space around the buildings was always going to be a threat. But, as far as I can establish, the centre was run for decades under an umbrella of benevolence: all the building's overheads met by the council while the PTSA had a free rein to choose what courses they'd run and the fees they'd charge. I can understand students' and tutors' anger and disappointment over the closure but surely that comfy administrative set-up wasn't realistic in the economic climate of the twenty-first century?

In 2103 both buildings were saved from likely demolition when a Neath veterinarian obtained planning permission to open a new practice in the old vicarage. And there was good news for part of the centre's heritage too. Thanks to Les Sexton, a former ceramics and pottery tutor, the Swansea artist, Michael Freeman[18], who taught there for over thirty years and Dr Ceri Thomas, Curator of the Glamorgan Art Collections, some murals, painted on board by WEA art students in the late 1970s and early 1980s, were removed last year with the hope of finding them a permanent home. One of them, a naïve collage of needlewomen, ore carriers, terraced houses, mountains, working men and a prominently placed car scrapyard, has ended up on the wall of a diner, Starvin Jacks[19], in the Swansea Enterprise Zone.

ST. THEODORE'S CHURCH

The church[20] was built a few years before the vicarage in 1897. Emily Talbot, of Margam Castle, met the £25,000 building costs in memory of her brother, Theodore, and sister, Olivia who had died in 1876 and 1894, both of whom were particularly devout. Theodore had been a close friend of Father Arthur Stanton[21], one of the great figures in the Anglo-Catholic revival in Britain in the nineteenth century, and spent a lot of time working alongside him in the slums around Holborn, London. Olivia founded St Michael and All Angels Theological College in Aberdare (1892). The college later moved to Llandaff, one of its most famous alumni being the irascible Welsh poet/priest, R.S. Thomas[22].

The church's architect, John Loughborough Pearson[23], is best known for Truro Cathedral and refurbishment work at Westminster Abbey which might account for the grandiosity. Viewed from the west, it feels out of place opposite the row of terraced houses, an architecturally imposing critic. From the east, softened by the trees in the park, it's more approachable.

The single storey stone building on the roadside, within the church grounds, predates both vicarage and church. The Mission Room was built in 1882 and once thronged with dances, suppers and fund-raising activities. An account of a coffee supper in 1913 notes: "There we were stuffed together, like sardines, in the Mission Room, and everyone enjoying plenty of coffee and tea, with a good plate of meat"[24]. Those Anglo-Catholics really knew how to party. Though it's surprising they had any time for that, or even for prayers, given the range of groups and societies the church once boasted, many of them quaint products of their time: White Cross League of Purity for Men, A Children's Penny Bank. There was also a soccer team and a rugby team: St. Theodore's Temperance All Whites RFC. And after the game the publicans wept.

Well, maybe one or two did. The devout Anglo-Catholicism of the Talbot Family didn't encourage public houses in the parish but any thirst you worked up could be slaked and re-slaked in upwards of thirty-five free-flowing beer venues over the River Afan bridge in Aberafan.[25]

TALBOT MEMORIAL PARK

A window on the south side of the church commemorates Lieutenant Rupert Price Hallowes MC VC who was killed in Flanders in 1915, Port Talbot's only Victoria Cross. Hallowes, who was an assistant manager at the Mansel Tinplate Works in Aberafan, is remembered again in the gateway[26] to the Talbot Memorial Park next door. The gateway was built, along with its brace of lodges, in 1925 and the park, an open space of over twelve acres donated by Emily Talbot in 1902[27] and dedicated as a memorial to those who died in World War I in 1919[28], was formally laid out and officially opened to the public in June 1926.

The theme of remembering is reinforced by another war memorial[29] as you walk into the park; the bronze work is by Louis Frederick Roslyn[30], a British sculptor noted for his World War I memorials. Roslyn was born Roselieb in London in 1878 although by 1914 he had, understandably, changed his name to something less Germanic.

There's more remembrance in the park's right-hand corner: a drinking fountain[31] in honour of Dr John Hopkin Davies who came to Taibach at the request of Theodore Talbot in 1872 and practised there for 48 years. It was moved to the park in 1926 but had been erected in 1910, a decade before his death: a heartfelt tribute from the people of Taibach, paid for by public subscriptions. The mood of genuine veneration might have been somewhat marred at the original unveiling ceremony by an unscripted announcement from Sir A.P. Vivian, manager of the Taibach Copper Mill, that he would close the mill if men on strike at the time didn't return to work the following Monday. I don't know whether that event soured Dr Davies' appreciation of the fountain but there's a story in *Outline of a Welsh Town*[32] which records how he drew down the blind on his

coach every time he rode past. Although the fountain's similarity to
a tombstone couldn't have helped either.

There's a cracking octagonal bandstand[33] in the centre of the
park that Cadw have, fortunately, listed as, "an increasingly scarce
building type." It wouldn't be that scarce if two other bandstands in
Port Talbot hadn't already disappeared in puffs of demolition dust[34].

The latest addition to the theme of remembrance drapes itself
over the grass nearby. The Richard Burton Memorial Flower Bed
was unveiled on 9 November 2012, the day before what would have
been Burton's eighty-seventh birthday, by Dr Hywel Francis, MP
for Aberafan. A flower bed might not be most people's idea of a
permanent memorial, given the vagaries and moods of weather and
delinquents, but it's a relief to see a cheery, organic memorial rather
than another hunk of sculpted stone and brass. Kids from local
schools helped in its design and planting and the production of a
leaflet for a new section of the Richard Burton Trail[35], the
Childhood Trail, which circles Taibach and some of Burton's homes
and haunts.

TAIBACH

Turn left out of the park's main gates and Talbot Road relinquishes
control of the A48 to Commercial Road as it runs through
Taibach[36]: 'little houses' in Welsh and named for two pairs of
thatched semi-detached cottages that in the eighteenth century
would have stood where the end of St. Alban's Terrace is now[37].
They were demolished in 1936 but you can catch a glimpse of them
on Taibach Rugby Club's badge[38].

The boundaries of the young Burton's (or Jenkins' as he was
then) Taibach stomping ground are marked by the library he
frequented, just past the River Ffrwdwyllt, and the Eastern Primary
School he attended in Incline Row. The library[39] was completed in
1916, one of 660 Carnegie libraries built in Britain and Ireland
between 1883 and 1929 with funds donated by the Scottish-
American philanthropist, Andrew Carnegie. If it looks remarkably
similar to a building on the opposite side of the road it's because
they had the same architect, John Cox, the latter being built for the
old Margam Urban District Council in 1906/7 where Cox worked
as Surveyor. According to J. Ivor Hanson the initials M.U.D.C. gave
rise to the local nickname Mudcart[40]. If anyone can get any mileage

out of N.P.T.C.B.C. please let me know.

Burton lived in Caradoc Street but his second home was the cinema[41] and there were two in Taibach: The Picturedrome (locally known as The Cach[42]) in Alma Terrace and The Regent on Commercial Road.

The Picturedrome had been built as the Workers' Hall in 1872[43], a social and cultural meeting room for the people of Taibach. It also housed a small library and acted as the headquarters of the 2nd Volunteer Battalion of the Welsh Regiment until 1908 when the Royal Horse Artillery Territorials took it over for a few years. It was reborn as the Taibach Picture Palace in 1913, continued as a cinema until it closed in 1966 and re-opened as a bingo hall. It leads a quieter life these days as the Taibach Nursing Home.

You can conjure The Regent back into existence if you look up at the architecture above Warehouse gym on Commercial Road. The cinema opened in 1937, in plenty of time for Rich Bach[44] to watch James Cagney and Humphrey Bogart in *Oklahoma Kid*[45], and closed in 1956. The Co-operative Society bought the premises, extending their central stores a few doors along, now Filco's supermarket, where Burton worked for a short while in the early 1940s.

The small chapel opposite Warehouse squashed between houses

and derelict shop premises, originally called Noddfa (1939), was the chapel Burton attended with his sister and her husband after a fractious rift in the congregation at Gibeon Chapel[46] opposite Gallipoli Row. The triangle of grass in front of Gibeon, known as Gallipoli Field, used to be the marshalling point for Whitsun Marches for a hallelujah of chapels in Taibach – Gibeon, Smyrna, Noddfa, Dyffryn, Wesley. They're still all there in body but only two remain in spirit, Wesley and Gibeon, the other three having been sold for conversion.

Gallipoli and Smyrna: echoes of the Crimean War[47] (1854-1856) that identify streets and rows of houses built in its wake all over Great Britain. Alma's another, and Scutari and Varna. Balaclava, Inkerman, Pira and Stamboul were demolished over the years. But there was housing in Taibach at a much earlier date: accommodation for a rapidly increasing industrial workforce.

In 1774 Constantinople Row[48], a run of whitewashed cottages that acted as a landmark for incoming shipping, was built on the mountainside above Caradoc Street. And if you follow the road up from Incline Row, and head under the motorway, you'll come to a dead-end and a single bungalow, the site of Dormitory Row, or 'The Barracks', a large house built in 1850 for workers at the new Morfa pit[49].

More houses were built on the flat for employees at the Copper Works which began operation around 1777-80[50] across the site of today's fire station and Aldi's superstore. Five new rolling mills and furnaces and a new engine house appeared in 1800 to produce copper sheets and in 1839 the Copper Works changed ownership from the English Copper Company to Messrs. Vivian and Sons, the big Swansea industrialists. Malay coins were produced here, as well as Muntz's Yellow Metal[51], an alloy of copper, zinc and a trace of iron, a replacement for copper sheathing on the bottom of boats at two thirds of the price.

The demand for copper required more coal for the smelting process from local collieries and more workers' housing: there were a thousand people in Taibach employed by the Vivians in coal pits and the Copper Works in 1865.[52] There were also two Tinplate works chugging away in the area. All of which created a poisonous and smoky atmosphere for people, livestock and vegetation. And you can rely on a poet to make the most of that.

'Mwg Gwaith Taibach' was an englyn written by Rev. Richard Morgan, a lyrical composition about the mwg, or noxious fumes and choking gases, that kills "man and meadow" and it won him a prize at an eisteddfod in Gibeon Chapel in 1868[53]. But at least he told it as it was unlike one of the Vivians whose sparkling wit came up with, "The smoke in Taibach does not go up in volumes, it goes up in encyclopaedias."[54] Good for him.

Foreign competition forced the closure of the copper smelting works in 1898 but the Copper Mill remained operational into the twentieth century although by 1917 it had been largely demolished, the Vivians having concentrated their efforts on their Swansea premises. But before anyone could take a small gulp of slightly fresher air, the Margam Iron and Steel Works was built on the site in 1926[55] and started producing black plate, sheets of iron ready for the tin plate process.

The effects of industrialisation on Taibach didn't improve with the closure of the area's tinplate works and a shift into the production of steel between the late 1940s and early 1950s.[56] They just changed from mwg to grit: in September 1952 the *Western Mail* stated that grit was falling over Taibach at a "rate of 459 tons a square mile each month."[57]

Huge improvements have been made over the last sixty years but steelmaking is still a dirty business and problems arise, some more entertaining than others. A few years ago a woman in Connaught

Street[58] reckoned her cat was "a barometer for pollution": covered in glitter meant a fall of kish, shiny carbon flakes; if it turned pink there was a problem with sinter, or iron, dust[59].

There can't be any people alive with first-hand memories of the Copper Works but there might be a lot who don't realise their garden walls are part of its heritage. Copper slag, an incredibly hard, waste product of the copper smelting process, was used for coping stones and other building purposes. Take a walk around the back streets and see how many of the dark glossy blocks you can spot. While they're still there.

Richard Burton wrote *A Christmas Story* in 1964, a light-weight, pretty story set in Taibach in the 1930s. Three years earlier another local man, John Naish born in 1923, published *The Clean Breast, An Autobiography*[60] covering his childhood in Taibach to his migration to Australia in 1950. A lot of place and street names are masked: Taibach is Tailan, his home in Brook Street, next to the River Ffrwdwyllt, is Taibont Street Lane. But there's no mistaking the area in some of his descriptions: "From the beach and seaward stretches of the town the Welsh hills looked smooth and round, the quarries like neat apple-bites…". Since I read that, those old quarries, nibbled and mostly overgrown concavities in our mountain backdrop, seem to blink at me each time I look up at them.

Naish wrote and published a number of plays and two novels, *The Cruel Field* (1962) and *That Men Should Fear* (1963)[61] but a potentially prolific career as a writer was cut short when he died in Cooktown, Australia in 1963.

One event in *The Clean Breast* that's undisguised is a murder near Talbot Memorial Park in 1937: Vaughan Jones shot dead Arthur Richards, an ex-colliery manager, in Theodore Road, or Park Road[62] as Naish calls it. The *Daily Mirror* reported[63] that Jones was found guilty but insane: he claimed that Richards had taunted him with black magic and witchcraft. "Please don't hurt me. I'm under the Evil Eye," the murderer begs in Naish's account.

There's a more benevolent kind of madness in today's Taibach. Lunacy[64] is a boutique at 43 Commercial Road, in the centre of Taibach and its eclectic jumble of shops: haberdashery and hairdressing, pets and baguettes and a convenience store called Nooze and Booze, unquestionably more effective than News and Bews. Lunacy has a smell that no high street chain store can duplicate. It reminds me of a little dress shop, Lyn's in Forge Road[65], where in 1976 I bought a black crepe flared trouser suit, with a plunging neckline that raised my dad's eyebrows. What is that smell? Perfume, tissue paper, the scent of newness, the unexplored? Call me romantic, tell me it's probably the smell of the chemicals and machines involved in the manufacturing processes. Whatever it is, *Vogue* like it. In 2012 they included Lunacy in its list of top 100 shops outside London.[66]

It's not year-round madness at Taibach Rugby Club[67], on the corner of Commercial and Dyffryn Road, but you get a year's worth of it in December at the annual Christmas Panto. That's panto for adults, as 2012's show, *50 Shades of Peter Pan*, clearly suggests. And when the Lost Boys include Slasher, Basher and Crusher, Wendy has a moustache and Baby looks like Ernest Borgnine in a romper suit you know you're not quite in J.M. Barrie territory. In fact when J.M. Barrie said, "Fairies have to be one thing or the other, because being so small they unfortunately have room for one feeling only at a time[68]," he wasn't thinking of Nug (aka John Newman) as Tinkerbell who didn't just own the stage, he filled it. Along with a cute little number in lime green chiffon.

The club was founded in 1884 although they only scrummed down on their own ground in 1948 when the council allowed them to use the Plough field, at the back of Talbot Memorial Park.[69] They

continue to play at the Plough but their social club moved into its current premises, the former Talbot Arms Hotel[70] in 1968.

The annual panto raised its first curtain back in 1967, the inspiration of Hywel 'Mr Panto' David, along with Alan Davies and Ray Williams. Nearly fifty years later the upstairs function room is still packed with 200 people for each of its seven nights. The script is currently written by Colin 'Double' Deere and Mark 'Bush' Miles while The Druid (aka Aled Humphreys) directs. Quite a few of the Taibach guys appeared in *The Passion* and the experience has spilled over into the panto: in 2012 auditions were held for the first time rather than handing out the same kinds of roles to the same people. There was a distinct element of professionalism present at the first rehearsals because, for all the fun and antics, they acknowledge that people are paying to see them and they want to put on the best possible show. They rehearse three times a week in the three months before the show.

But like all shows not everything always runs smoothly. Someone stood too close to the pyrotechnics once and his socks burst into flames which set fire to the curtain; there's been the occasional fight back stage when creative tempers have flared (only plastic glasses are allowed now); and one year, Cinderella took off his wig, stepped off stage and ejected a drunken heckler.

Because of the panto's popularity and the demand for tickets they've been asked to perform at the Princess Royal Theatre in the Civic Centre instead but Aled says it wouldn't be the same. It's Taibach and it should stay Taibach.

I asked if there were ever any women in the show. Absolutely not. No 'flat-cocks' are allowed. Oh yes, I forgot to mention, if political correctness matters to you this isn't your kind of show. But you won't know what you're missing. Last year that would have been, among other hysterical performances, a naked pirate with a barrel strapped to his loins. Oh yes there was!

I can't leave Taibach without giving the last word to a Taibach boy who left school at 14 and who well might have insisted on having it. Clive Jenkins[71] (1926-1999), born at Maes-y-Cwrt Terrace, within my Taibach boundary, was a raconteur, an aficionado of fine wine and a shrewd manipulator of the property market. Not the kind of attributes you'd readily associate with a trade union leader but Jenkins managed to combine being General Secretary of the big white-collar union now known as MSF (Manufacturing, Science,

Finance) with being the original millionaire 'champagne socialist'.

In 1968 he declared himself an atheist but the skill and energy of rhetoric he'd acquired from attending Dyffryn Calvinistic Methodist Chapel[72], around the corner from his home, stayed with him for the rest of his life[73]. In *Who's Who* he listed his recreation as "organising the middle classes" while his skill at negotiating led his own members to describe him as, "a clever bastard, but at least he's our clever bastard."[74] He retired from trade unionism in 1988, published an autobiography, *All Against the Collar*, in 1990, and spent ten years living in Tasmania.

In his obituary in *The Independent*[75] he sounds like my kind of dinner companion: at TUC Blackpool conferences he'd eat in a local chip shop but take along his own fine, chilled white wine to accompany his fish and chips and bread and butter.

And talking about food... There's a hand-painted sign under the bridge at the end of Penrhyn Street, an old entrance into the steel-works at the back of Commercial Road: 'FOOD' it says with a big arrow. I expected to be disappointed; it leads to an abandoned scrap yard and the works' boundary fence but I wanted to make a pilgrimage to the former site of a portakabin café. I have it on good authority from several steelworkers that their "triple burger, sausage'n cheese was artery thickening good". If you're peckish in

Taibach today I recommend 12 Café at 37 Commercial Road, a social enterprise run by the West Glamorgan Council on Alcohol and Drug Abuse[76], where you can support people who are determined to turn their life around and also get a mean double-poached egg on toast.

GOYTRE

Turn up Dyffryn Road, past the rugby club on the corner, towards the concrete legs of the M4 flyover. Pass the Workies, or the Taibach Workingmen's' Club[77] sitting in its shadow, and head straight up the hill. Before you round the corner you can turn at any time and see the blast furnaces in the steelworks but then, suddenly, they're gone. On your right, the northern slope of Mynydd Brombil[78]; on your left the sound of the River Ffrwdwyllt in the valley below.

> leaf mulch, fresh rain
> the old stories we find
> along the banks of the wild brook

The unmarked lane on your left leads down to the riverbank and Dyffryn Mill[79] which dates to the fourteenth century and was grinding corn for local people until the end of the nineteenth. It was a flannel mill for a while in the 1920s and then left derelict. It's a private house now but I wouldn't recommend a curious unannounced wander down there because the owners have a couple of big, blubbery dogs that make Cujo look and sound like a wimp.

The cattle grid at the entrance of Goytre reinforces the rural nature although the muddle of housing styles announces a more motley past. Some of the earliest industrial housing here was Emroch Street and East Street, built around 1901-02 for workers at a Celluloid Factory in the valley. The popularity of celluloid, a material that launched the modern age of man-made plastics, should have led to a happier existence for the enterprise. It was an inexpensive substitute for ivory and tortoiseshell, flexible, transparent and cheap; everything from combs and jewellery, dolls and toys, and even detachable collars and cuffs were made from celluloid. One of its major drawbacks was its high flammability but that was more of a risk for the manufacturers than owners of the finished products.

With the luxury of hindsight I'd say the writing was on the wall for the company right from the start: its shareholders were British and French. Was it the triumph of hope over experience that convinced them they could achieve an 'entente cordiale'? Differences between them quickly led to litigation, Margam District Urban Council sued them for overdue rates and production came to an end within a few years of opening. The works was used as a prisoner of war factory between 1914 and 1918 and later demolished.

The only break from housing as you walk through Goytre is a little galvanised tin church on the corner of East Street. St. Peter's[80] was a former mission church, St. David's at Morfa on Margam Moors, and moved here in 1915 after the closure of the colliery. But the one thing that truly dominates the village is the cemetery at its furthest boundary: stretching downhill and uphill on both sides of the road.

Emily Talbot donated the original ten acres[81] in 1913 and, according to the groundsman I chatted with, the first person to be buried here in 1917 was an eleven-year-old girl; the oldest, at 109, spanned three centuries. 'In loving memory', 'treasured memories', 'cherished memories'… engraved on stones almost as far as you can see. Not words you would have chosen for an event in May 2002 when a team of forensic archaeologists and dentists, scientists, pathologists and policemen erected a blue tent to exhume the body of the killer known as the Saturday Night Strangler.[82]

I remember the Jersey Marine murders, as we called them, in 1973. The bodies of two 16 year old girls were found on a patch of land between the A483 – the main road towards Swansea – and Llandarcy. They'd been raped, beaten and strangled. It was the biggest murder inquiry in Welsh history and the investigation linked these deaths to the murder of another 16 year-old girl three months earlier. The police were sure the murderer was a local man but by 1974 they still didn't have a suspect and the inquiry wound down. All the files were moved to the police station on Sandfields Estate, Port Talbot; the most valuable forensic material was sent to a science lab in Chepstow.

By 2000 DNA testing had advanced to a point where results could be obtained from tiny specks of material. With a full genetic profile of the killer's DNA the police opened a reinvestigation, Operation Magnum and began the Sisyphean task of narrowing down 35,000 names on file to a list of 500 top suspects they could afford to DNA test. They made links to other unsolved rape cases in the area and produced a psychological profile for the killer, another investigative tool that wasn't around in 1973.

In 2001 DNA specialist Jonathan Whitaker came up with the idea, given the gap of thirty years, of searching for the murderer through any children he might have had. We inherit our DNA from our parents and pass 50% of that onto our own children. Whitaker had the killer's full profile so he also had a 50% profile for the killer's children. He checked the national DNA database for profiles added by South Wales' police and produced a list of 100 with close connections to the killer's. One name stood out: a young car thief with the surname Kappen, the son of one of the top suspects. Joseph Kappen grew up in Port Talbot and was living on Sandfields Estate at the time of the murders; his background and character closely mirrored the psychological profile.

Kappen had died in 1990 and made history for being the first serial killer to be exhumed in order to establish his guilt. It was also one of the first cases to use familial DNA searching to identify a murderer.

I was going to ask the groundsman, who was present at the exhumation, for the location of the grave, but I decided against it. Even standing at the graveside would be an act of remembrance, an act Kappen is entirely unworthy of.

Some of the graves in the older part of the cemetery have started to collapse, the ground around them giving way, the stones toppling. Old coal levels riddle the mountains and valleys: the land shifts and settles over time. The first old Goytre levels opened in the late 18th century and were re-opened as the Glenhafod Colliery in 1921. The last coal was dug in 1958 and the colliery closed by the National Coal Board.

No more collieries. No more factories. There are a couple of businesses on your left as you continue along the Goytre Road although no-one locally seems to know too much about them, perhaps put off by the plethora of 'No Entry/Private Keep Out' signs dotted around. One of them, Malpeet K9[83], is a dog training academy, more Schwarzenegger than Mary Whitehouse, that train handlers and dogs to detect explosives, drugs, and for anti-piracy maritime protection. I did contemplate, in the name of research, asking them if I could take part in one of their training exercises. And then I imagined a German Shepherd trying to gnaw through my inadequately padded arm. The other business has the unfortunate name – perhaps only to my salacious imagination – of Liquid Friction[84]. It's actually an adventure activity provider: gorge walking, white water rafting and abseiling in the South Wales area, all of which is bound to get your mojo working.

You'll have a far friendlier welcome at Hafod Grange[85], if you turn right up a Forestry Commission track just outside Goytre, from Gareth Needham and Alan Thomas who make exquisite paperweights with flowers and seed heads encased in resin. Barry Needham, Gareth's uncle, made the first paperweights in 1968 as a form of therapy for his muscular dystrophy. Someone challenged him to encapsulate a full dandelion head in a globe of clear resin, an ostensibly impossible task that he accomplished. After his death his brother, Alan, continued to develop and improve the design ideas and began producing the paperweights commercially in 1975.

You can choose from cultivated and wild flowers but my favourites are the seed heads: dandelions, thistles, teasels. Most of the plants grow naturally on the mountainside or in the Grange's gardens and no two paperweights are identical. Gareth and Alan also offer a bespoke service. And what do people want to preserve in resin? Baby teeth are common. And lucky golf balls. And the strangest? A kneecap. Bullets. And there was some rhino dung once. I'll just take the dandelion head and the teasel, thank you.

This luxury item business has managed to survive three recessions. But they're in a place with a reputation for longevity: Hafod Farm was the summer grazing area for livestock belonging to the monks at medieval Margam Abbey. 'Hafod' means summer dwelling[86], a place near to a mountain's summit. The winter dwelling would have been lower down towards the valley: *gaea tre* or Goytre.

The Port Talbot & Goytre to Bryn cycle path, the route of the old Dyffryn Valley railway line, abuts the main road about a third of a mile out of the village. You can head north here and take a spur path right into the forest towards the wonderfully meditative Cwmwernderi Reservoir[87]. It opened in 1902 to supply water to Port Talbot but abstraction stopped in 1972 with the building of the Llyn Brianne Reservoir[88] near Llanwrtyd Wells in Mid Wales. Cwmwernderi covers an area of about 7 acres and is around 15 metres deep, something to keep in mind if you decide to trek down the steep grassy dam towards the water's edge. It's hard to believe in the proximity of industry while you're sitting here, watching the

wind ripple the water, surrounded by trees, and you understand
why this area is known as Little Switzerland.

> wrapped
> by the forest canopy
> an eyeful of sky

Heading south on the cycle path takes you back towards Taibach,
across the river footbridge and into the Wildbrook Estate. Mowed
lawns, replacement windows, and block paved drives have replaced
coal dust, the belch of steam and the clank and screech of engines
and wagons: this used to be the Dyffryn Railway yard built in 1896
by the Port Talbot Railway and Docks Company. It closed in 1964
and the site was used for a concrete batching plant for the construction of the M4 before Wimpey's started on the new estate in 1972,
named for its watery neighbour – *y ffrwd/wyllt* – the wild brook.

MARGAM

I can't get a handle on Margam. It feels like a place of parts rather
than a cohesive whole: a club and playing fields, a park and a run of
shops, a hotel, a college and schools, and the A48, Margam Road,
running straight through the middle of it all, an artery hell bent on
taking you somewhere else. The topography presses in on you too:
a narrow strip of land between the flanks of Mynydd Margam and
the steelworks with suburban streets, from the nineteenth to the
twenty-first centuries, sprouting off two or three deep on either side
of the main road. Then add the terminal aspects of its eastern and
western boundaries: Margam Crematorium and Condon Funeral
Services.

    Any mention of Margam in history books generally refers to the
old parish, rather than this area or old Margam village near the
medieval abbey[89], land that stretched from the river Kenfig in the
east to the river Afan in the west. Until the early nineteenth century
there was a tradition of beating the parish boundary. A group of
men and boys accompanied by the parish priest walked the entire
boundary, stopping at notable points, like Twmpath Diwlith,[90] a
Bronze Age barrow up on Mynydd Margam, for a few priestly
words. Then they'd beat the children to ensure these sites would not
be forgotten.[91] Well, as long as it was in a good cause.

To see if Margam would grow on me I booked into The Twelve Knights Hotel. The hotel is named after the legendary Norman knights who galloped here with Sir Robert Fitzhammon, in about 1093, to help him conquer the old kingdom of Morgannwg (Glamorgan). They ousted Iestyn, who'd succeeded his father Gwrgan, and Fitzhammon divvyed up the land between the thirteen of them, keeping a fat chunk for himself which included Margam as part of Tir Iarll, the Earl's Land. There's an Earl Road in Margam, as well as a couple of Gwrgans: Heol y Gwrgan and Cefn Gwrgan Road. No Iestyns though: loser.

There was more revelry than chivalry at the Knights when I arrived. The scene of Paul Potts'[92] 1980s wedding reception was being filmed for *One Chance*[93] in the restaurant, the route to my upstairs bedroom, and the place was packed with shoulder pads, flower print frocks and hundreds of extras chowing down on takeaway meals. It was like ploughing through *My Big Fat Gypsy Wedding* with salt and vinegar.

This is the point on Margam Road where the Rhanallt stream tumbles down from the mountain, under the A48 and the hotel's car park, and eventually trickles out on Morfa Beach. Between this point and the Ffrwdwyllt river in Taibach there used to be six farmsteads. Brombil Farm is the only one still going, with much of its land and the land belonging to the others long since sold and built upon. One of the most recent housing developments is Parc Groeswen on the site of an old hospital. I'd prefer to think it was Hallowe'en celebrations rather than any mortuary hankerings that prompted one resident to embed a skeleton in their front lawn last year.

According to Les Evans, in his 1963 edition of *The Story of Taibach and District*, a last desperate measure, and 'curative process', of placing the liver and hot entrails of a freshly slaughtered sheep on the chest of a pneumonia sufferer was still being practiced up until 'a few decades ago'. So I guess it was a relief for many people, and not a few sheep, when Groeswen Hospital was built in 1932. It replaced the old Isolation Hospital, 600 yards up the side of Mynydd Emroch at the top of a steep lane called Pant-y-Moch, which had opened in 1896 in an attempt to tackle the infectious diseases of the day: diphtheria and scarlet fever. Not that infectious diseases and the need for isolation were eradicated that quickly. Groeswen featured in the national press in 1962 when a diphtheria scare meant 53 children were quarantined there from May until 5th June.[94]

Groeswen, although literally 'white cross', translates as holy, or blessed, cross, and takes its name from the wayside crosses that would have been carved in stone; familiar sights and stopping places of reverence for pilgrims in medieval times. The land the hospital was built on formed part of Groeswen Farm, and the site of Whitecross, one of the many agricultural granges attached to medieval Margam Abbey.

My stay at the Knights, the ease of walking out of the door each morning to explore Margam on foot, did pay off. I discovered Tambini's Express Café, near the Tollgate Park, where the coffee is frothy and Ron Evans pies are served all day. For the uninitiated a Ron Evans pie is a local legend and the stuff dreams are made of. The bakery and shop are currently at Commercial Road, Taibach[95] but Ron Evans pies have been made in Port Talbot since 1926. The classic, gravy-rich mince and onion is my favourite despite its local moniker of 'a runny Ron'.[96]

Marco Tambini, and his wife Sonia, have run the café for over twenty years, one of the last Italian cafés in Port Talbot that once boasted more than a dozen buzzing and steamy little centres of community. Marco took over from his dad, who passed away in 2010, but it's highly unlikely that Marco's children will continue in

Castle, is popular as a film-set location: episodes of *Dr Who*, *Torchwood* and *Da Vinci's Demons*, an American Cable TV series which premiered in the UK in April 2013, have been filmed here. Ghost-hunters are also impressed. During a 2006 episode of the UK paranormal TV series, *Most Haunted*[106], medium David Wells described feeling, "an odd mix of Catholicism to bare-knuckle animal-ripping part-paganism". Ah, that'll be the 1999 Catatonia concert in the park then?

In 2010 *Ghost Hunters International* flew in from Los Angeles and recorded the spectral chills for an episode of their show that aired to a million American viewers. When I was at the castle in October last year for a ghost walk organised by Wales History and Hauntings[107] the only chills I felt were the ones creeping through my jeans after shivering in the night air for nearly two hours. But to be fair to our guide, Jim Cowan, the focus was as much on history as ghost stories and untainted by the shrieking melodrama associated with *Most Haunted*. One person in the group claimed she saw a dark figure drifting behind the ruins of the medieval chapter house but

the great hall in the castle, where we finished the tour, remained free
of the uninvited so I had my fair share of the mulled wine, short-
bread and welshcakes.

If you do believe in ghosts, spirits or impressions of the past
manifesting, in some way, in the present then the history of the park
is brimming with potential: warfare, plague, revolt, family tragedy,
murder and illegitimacy.

Bronze Age tumuli, cairns and barrows and Iron Age hill forts are
sprinkled on the escarpments and higher slopes of Mynydd
Margam that rise behind the castle. In the first century AD the
area's inhabitants, the Esyllwyr or the Silures, battled against
Roman legions. And lost. Their battles and defeat are enshrined in
local place names: Cwm Lladdfa (Valley of Slaughter) above
Goytre, Cil y Gofid (Retreat of Affliction) in the Ffrwdwyllt Valley
and Rhiw Tor y Cymry or Cymerau (Mount of Conflicts) in north
Margam.[108] Romano Celtic memorial stones and cross slabs[109], from
the sixth to the eleventh centuries, have been rescued from fields,
farms and roadsides, in this area and elsewhere around Port Talbot,
and preserved in the Stones Museum[110], previously a nineteenth
century church school next to Margam Abbey Parish Church[111]. It's
ostensibly one of the most important collections in Britain.

The most popular spectral appearances are white-robed monks,
often identified as women in white dresses, adherents of the austere
Cistercian Order[112] who wore unbleached woollen habits. A
Cistercian Abbey was founded here in 1147, although only the
above mentioned parish church (the nave of the original abbey), the
walls of a rare twelve-sided Chapter House[113] and some fringes of
ruined stone arches remain, and the monks happily got on with
their daily lives for a couple of centuries. Apart from occasionally
beating off some of the locals who were cranky at being dispos-
sessed of their farmland or hostile towards the Norman presence.
The stone arched doorway of the Parish Church has a hollow on
either side where the monks could have slatted a robust timber
beam and barricaded the abbey's doors.

As a self-sufficient community they were heavily engaged with
farming in a dozen or more granges dotted around the Abbey's
lands. The pine end wall belonging to Cryke Mill, the ruin of a grist
or corn mill, on the western bank of the abbey fishpond, could
easily be mistaken for a chapel wall but the nearest surviving chapel
ruin is Yr Hen Gapel, or Capel Mair[114]. The monks weren't keen on
sharing their prayer space so this was built in the fourteenth or

fifteenth century, on the hillside north of the park, to accommodate the local people. It's still accommodating them, but in a very different way, if the rapidly disappearing stones are anything to go by.

The monks also pioneered the export of wool to Ghent, in Belgium, a nice little earner for the Abbey that owned over 5,000 sheep in 1291[115], and they dug their own coal. You can see the entrance to their mine in the north east corner of the park.

They also tinkered in more traditional devotions: the scribing of books. A twelfth century copy of the *Domesday Book* from Margam Abbey is preserved at the British Museum in London.[116] *The Annals of Margan* [Margam],[117] one of the most valuable surviving Welsh monastic chronicles covering the period 1065 to 1232, is at Trinity College library, Cambridge.

The fourteenth and fifteenth centuries weren't so benevolent. A downturn in donations from the pious, the pandemic Black Death, and the rise of Owain Glyndwr and the spread of Welsh revolt against the English crown into South Wales, all contributed to the Abbey's misfortunes. By the time Henry VIII decided that the Roman Catholic Church was being too uppity about his requested divorce, appointed himself the Supreme Head of the Church in

England and ordered the dissolution of the monasteries in 1536, there were only three monks left at Margam.[118]

> chapel ruins
> the bleating of sheep
> on a high ridge

MARGAM HOUSE

Between 1540 and 1546 the land and assets belonging to Margam Abbey were bought up by Sir Rice Mansel, owner of the Gower estates of Penrice and Oxwich, who created a Tudor mansion around the Abbey's domestic buildings, a house that was remodelled and extended over the following 200 years. Two early eighteenth century paintings, bought by Amgueddfa Cymru/National Museum Wales[119] in 2012 for £218,500, are the only substantial records of the house, one of Wales' great Tudor homes, and, by this time, the seat of the most important gentry family in Glamorgan. Important enough to have a separate Italianate banqueting house, making use of the stone from the abbey buildings, built on a rise of ground to the east of the house.

Thomas Mansel Talbot (1747-1813), who had inherited the Penrice and Margam estates in trust when he was eleven years old, returned home in 1772 from a Grand Tour of Europe with great plans for Margam as a pleasure garden. He introduced English pheasant to Margam and developed the herd of deer[120] but given he was a keen huntsman the pleasure would have been rather one-sided.

Between 1787 and 1793 he demolished the rambling mansion and the banqueting house. Perhaps the classical and romantic influences of his European trip persuaded him to let the ruined medieval Chapter House remain standing. Or maybe there was nowhere else to keep the coal. A plan of the house and abbey from 1736 shows it being used as a coal house[121]. He also preserved the façade of the banqueting house, attributed to Inigo Jones[122], which today buttresses the wall of Ivy Cottage[123] in the grounds of the park, once the gardener's house. The statues are nineteenth century additions and give it its popular name of the Four Seasons Façade. The opportunity to sleep with your head against a piece of Inigo Jones might become more than a dream if the local authority's plan to refurbish the cottage to a five-star holiday let go ahead[124]. A plan that looks more likely since grants of £1.6 million from the Heritage Lottery Fund and another £200,000 from the European Regional Development Fund were confirmed at the end of 2012[125].

THE ORANGERY AND CITRUS HOUSE

Mansel Talbot then got stuck into his big project: a 327 feet long Orangery[126] (built between 1786 and 1790) designed by the Neoclassical architect, Anthony Keck, to house the estate's collection of citrus trees that were only protected by dilapidated greenhouses. The trees are mentioned in a 1711 Margam House record but their origin lies in the worn threads of different stories told and retold to seventeenth century travellers about gifts between European royalty that were rescued from shipwrecks off the coast. The story of their loss is more exact: they were ousted from the building when American troops were billeted there during World War II and, unsurprisingly, failed to survive the winter.

A new collection was formed post-war and a restored Orangery was opened by Queen Elizabeth II in 1977 as a venue for swishy corporate events and weddings. In 1981 a spray of Margam orange blossom was fixed to Prince Charles and Lady Diana's wedding carriage.[127]

The Citrus House, a Georgian glasshouse originally called the Orange Wall when it was built in 1800, is also looking snappy after a recent £900,000 makeover[128]. The re-opening promises a new citrus collection and a learning resource centre for the local community. I'm not sure what we're going to learn – the description is ripe with the language of funding requirements rather than any practical information.

MARGAM CASTLE

The castle dominates the park and bustles with turrets, towers, pinnacles, cupolas, gargoyles and battlements. It was built between 1827 and 1835 by Mansel Talbot's son, C.R.M. Talbot (1803-1890), known as Kit, and designed by the architect, Thomas Hopper.[129] It's much prettier than the impression gained from Cadw's pages of weighty architectural detail,[130] the broadwalk stone

steps leading up to it[131], the rise of its octagonal tower, the backdrop of Mynydd Margam and the occasional herd of deer scampering past all contributing to a fairy tale atmosphere.

Talbot was called 'the wealthiest commoner' when he died in 1890 (his estate, inherited by his daughter Emily Talbot, was valued at £6 million), riches he'd amassed from considerable investment in the railways and local industry. It was Kit Talbot who made the speeches at every stop when the first train travelled through South Wales, from Chepstow to Swansea, in June 1850. He became one of the directors when the South Wales Railway merged with Great Western in 1863 and was the principal proprietor of the GWR Hotel at Paddington Station, London. Industrialist, MP for Glamorgan for a continuous 59 years, passionate interests in fine art and the development of photography[132] and a man of vision. In 1874, at a banquet for the opening of the Aberavon Public Hall he respectfully taunted the honourable member from Swansea: "He must know in his heart... that the ports of Swansea and Cardiff will have a great deal to do to hold their own with us [Port Talbot]".[133]

Talbot also dallied in a venture not readily associated with South Wales: tobacco growing. In 1886 he produced a successful crop that was processed in a tobacco factory in Water Street, Aberafan but any dreams of Port Talbot having its very own tobacco baron dissolved when the unwanted attention of the Inland Revenue Commission led to the project being abandoned.[134]

He was also known to be thrifty: he dressed plainly, wore no jewellery and personally monitored the estate's running costs. I bet he whooped when Window Tax[135] was abolished in 1851 although that still didn't prevent him from building a castle fit for a king.

A dairy, a brew house, a wine cellar, a bake house, a laundry, a boot room, a still room, kitchens, a larder, a scullery, a coach house and stables (with its own game larder, gun room, harness room and saddle room) and a whole posse of servants' rooms and quarters to look after the occupants of the drawing room, the dining room, the morning room, the business room, the library, the muniment room and the strong room. And that was only when they were awake. There were 25 principal and guest bedrooms. And one bathroom.[136] Now I understand that tight-lipped, stony look on people's faces in Victorian photographs.

Money has never protected people from tragedy though. In 1835 Kit Talbot married Lady Charlotte Butler, daughter of the Earl of Glengall. Eleven years later she was dead, probably from tuberculosis, leaving him with four children, Theodore, Emily, Bertha and Olivia, aged between seven and four.

Lady Charlotte's funeral took place at the Abbey church. There's

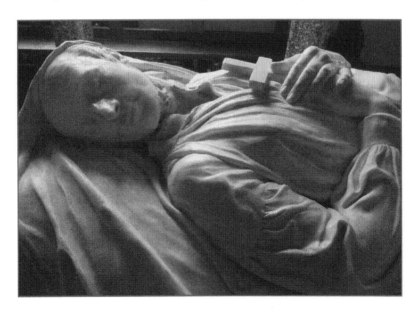

a memorial plaque to her, and her husband, on the south wall of the Talbot Chapel[137] but the chapel is dominated by the Gothic eight columned tomb and marble effigy[138] erected to the memory of their son, Theodore, who died in 1876 from chest and spinal injuries incurred in a riding accident a year earlier. When C.R.M. writes, following his son's death, "The necessity of living on is what most affects me,"[139] I hear the grieving collective voice of parents who have lost children.

A 'lost' child is the theme of another story connected to the castle. After the death of the unmarried Emily Talbot in 1918 the Margam Estate was left in trust to her great-nephew, John Theodore Talbot Fletcher (b. 1903), the grandson of her sister Bertha who'd married into the Fletcher family of Saltoun Hall near East Lothian, Scotland. It's a matter of record that the family frequently visited Margam. In the years before the outbreak of World War II they created a new pond in the grounds, converted the old stable block into a squash court and garage. It's also a matter of record that Ivy Pinn, who was born in Margam in 1910, worked at the castle as a maid.

According to an article in *The Independent* in 1996[140] Ken Matthews, who was adopted in the neighbouring town of Neath in 1938, discovered that an unmarried Ivy Pinn, his biological mother, had left the Castle in 1937 when she became pregnant with him. On his birth certificate his paternity was listed as 'unknown' and he imagined that a groundsman or a stable hand might emerge as his biological father. But former workers on the Margam Estate gave him details about his mother's long-term intimate relationship with John Theodore (Jock) Talbot Fletcher.

The extent of Ken's investigations and the numerous newspaper articles tracking his campaign can be read on a website he and his wife, Penny, set up.[141] He visited Jock Talbot Fletcher, the man he believed to be his father, in Epping in 1994 but the mention of Ivy Pinn's name brought their meeting to an abrupt closure. Ken put in a request to the family and their solicitors for DNA tests but these were refused. Jock Talbot Fletcher died in 1995; his body was cremated but the whereabouts of his ashes are unknown. By 2001 technology had advanced to a point where it might have been possible to obtain DNA results from them. Adoption papers? Nope. Neath Magistrates had already confirmed they couldn't find any papers or any reference to him by name in the adoption register for 1938.

In 2003, Andrew Fletcher, Jock Talbot Fletcher's nephew, claimed that his uncle could not have sired any children due to a medical problem. His allegedly unconsummated marriage had been annulled back in 1937[142] coincidentally close to the time that Ivy Pinn fell pregnant.

Ivy Pinn died in 1986. Ken never met her but his half-sisters gave him photographs of her, at Sker Beach near Porthcawl, about six months pregnant and in the company of a man who appears to be Jock Talbot Fletcher. Ken died in 2007 convinced of the truth of his mother's affair and in possession of sworn witness affidavits and a letter from the Talbot Fletchers' family solicitor disputing that Ken was a blood relative but offering to look into the matter if he irrevocably withdrew all claims to the estate.

So that's warfare, plague, revolt, family tragedy, illegitimacy. And murder.

The ghost story most intimately associated with the grounds of Margam Park is that of Robert Scott, Emily Talbot's head gamekeeper. In June 1898 Scott gave chase to a poacher but when he caught up with him, after clambering over a wall and armed only with a stick, the poacher shot him in the chest with a double-barrelled shotgun. Then shot him again. Joseph Lewis might have got away with the murder if he hadn't drunkenly boasted about it in a local pub. Scott is buried in Margam Abbey Parish Churchyard. Joseph Lewis was hung at Swansea Prison on 30th August 1898 in front of a crowd of around three thousand.[143] It was the last public execution held there.

What possessed the Trustees to dispose of Margam Estate during wartime?[144] A higher demand for antiquities and works of art? The crippling overheads of running an estate of this size? Whatever the reasons, Christie's led a four day sale in October 1941 and the castle's contents disappeared. Sevres, Dresden, Worcester, Chippendale, Adam, Rubens, Canaletto, Rembrandt, Titian: a catalogue of names to make any auction house's heart beat faster.

In 1942 the estate was bought by David Evans-Bevan, a colliery and brewery owner from Neath, although he lived at Twyn-yr-Hydd, a mini-estate within the castle grounds built by Emily Talbot in the 1890s for her land agent, Edward Knox. Evans-Bevan continued to live there after the castle was derequisitioned at the end of the war, leaving it not just empty but unguarded, a beacon for thieves and vandals. Evans-Bevan himself wasn't above a bit of authorised vandalism: he removed timbers from the library and bedrooms to create an antique atmosphere in a Vale of Neath pub[145].

He did undertake work at Twyn-yr-Hydd, employing the Welsh landscape designer, Ralph Hancock[146] to redesign the gardens and construct a ha-ha[147], the last garden Hancock worked on before he died in 1950, but the castle, with its lead-stripped roofs and broken windows gradually became a derelict liability. A seminary, a convalescent home, a country club: plans that trickled through the decades and dried up. The local authority, the Glamorgan County Council, stepped in in 1973 and bought it for £400,000.

Restoration has been understandably slow: we're talking about an on-going multi-million pound project of repair and maintenance. There was a major setback in 1977 when a fire, caused by workmen burning debris in one of the open fireplaces, took hold for days and almost gutted the castle to a shell. Plans for converting it into a luxury hotel fell through in 1989. A suggestion in the late 1990s that it would make a suitable home for the Welsh Assembly was also rejected. And I'm really pleased it's stayed in the local authority's possession. The only parts of the building's interior that are regularly open to the public are the entrance hall, the great hall and staircase within the octagonal tower and a couple of downstairs rooms but at least we still get to see and share this important facet of Port Talbot's history.

We can also strap ourselves in a harness and lurch along rope bridges, Tarzan swings and zip slides at Go-Ape[148], a tree-top adventure experience, or tootle around the grounds on a narrow gauge railway. The train doesn't run during the winter which gives people of a certain age, like me, the opportunity to regress and wander along a quiet railway track.

    winter sun
    me and a crow walking
    our shadows

MARGAM DISCOVERY CENTRE

This Field Studies Council Centre[149] was built at the eastern end of the park in 2009 with a clear view of the industrial terrain of Tata Steel, a view that was deliberately exploited as a part of the historical and social landscape. The building won a Royal Institute of British Architects award in 2010[150] and nothing could be architecturally further from the castle: state of the art, low carbon, sustainable building that responds to its environment rather than imposing itself upon it. The building is partially on stilts to minimise its impact on the natural lie of the land. Its main structural supports are made from recycled oil-rig. The chestnut cladding comes from sustainable UK plantations. It's energy efficient too: heat and hot water are supplied by a mini-biomass plant and there are harvesting tanks for rainwater on the roofs. But all these admirable twenty-first century design and ecological tick-boxes aside, the real success of the centre, for me, arises from its engagement with kids who come here on day and residential courses.

Everyone agrees that formative influences are important to how our lives develop. The courses are educational but they're also much more: there's social bonding, personal development, life building skills as simple as helping someone carry their suitcase upstairs (judging by the group I bumped into nine-year-old girls pack a lot of gear!) or putting the pillowcase and duvet cover on your own bed.

Then there's the effect of a rural environment on urban kids. Last year a group from a school in Stratford, East London spent a

week here. A boy lying in his bed one morning heard a regular tapping on the window, got up, opened the curtain, and saw a deer feeding on the grass outside, his antlers knocking against the glass. Local primary school kids get to stay too. The Centre's partnership with Neath Port Talbot Council provides for 1,100 subsidised residential places every year.

The Margam Centre is the newest and one of the largest Field Studies Centres out of seventeen in the UK, one of four in Wales. There were 7,500 visitors on day and residential courses in 2012; add people calling into the visitors' centre and Fair Trade café to that figure. When I commented on the racks of what looked like hundreds of pairs of gloves, for shelter building and gardening, Simon Ward, the Centre Manager, told me they also have 450 pairs of wellies. No excuse not to get down and dirty if you stay here.

If you don't fit the schoolchild category, take a look at the leisure learning courses on offer. History, photography, river safaris, beetles and bats, to name a few. You might bump into me there coming to grips with the pros and cons of keeping chickens. Failing that I'll be in the café.

ABERBAIDEN

I visited three working farms to the east of Margam Country Park – Graig Goch, Ton Mawr and Aberbaiden – and each one brought back childhood memories of my great aunt's farm near Llanelli: the smell of hay and livestock, spitting farm cats, a mud and stone yard. An environment so alien to urban/industrial Sandfields Estate I never felt at ease.

I now appreciate these rural histories and traditions but I'll never truly know what it's like to live off the land, attached to a place by generations who've lived and worked there before me. Gwyn and Edna David live at Aberbaiden, a farm that nudges the unitary boundary between Neath Port Talbot and Bridgend. This is the second Aberbaiden farmhouse[151] built around 1810 to replace one that had fallen into disrepair. Gwyn is the eleventh generation in his family to farm here. The earliest record he has is an ancestor's application to re-rent in 1630 which indicates the farm was already being worked by them.

Worked. Not owned[152]. The land, part of the old Margam Estate that once stretched from the River Kenfig to the River Afan, was

owned by the Mansel and Talbot families from the sixteenth century until 1947 when it became the property of the National Coal Board after the nationalisation of the coal mining industry in the UK. At one time the farm had 240 acres but the NCB appropriated land for coaling over the years, reducing it to about 100. In 1998, Gwyn, who's now in his eighties, managed to buy the farm. His family's home was finally his home, an emotional event difficult to articulate, but the joy still radiates from him when he speaks of it, despite the menacing 500 acre opencast coal mine that's gradually blasted its way to the end of his garden.

The original Aberbaiden colliery was sunk in 1906 and closed in 1959. The opencast Margam mine started up in 2001, an extension of the Parc Slip West colliery near Bridgend[153]. In 2007 site owners, Celtic Energy, submitted a planning application to extend coaling operations for another five and a half years. It was refused by the planning authorities, rejected by Assembly Members at a public inquiry in 2009, and, to the relief of people living in the area, an appeal to the High Court was dismissed in 2010. The argument that the extension would create jobs and boost the economy failed to outweigh the continuing harm to the countryside, the negative effects on health and the inevitable delay in restoring the site[154].

Three years later, Celtic Energy's obligation to restore the land appears to be on hold: the site has been cleared of machinery, and secured, but the apocalyptic scar across the countryside is as notice-able as ever. Oak Regeneration acquired the Margam site in 2010[155] and employed the big environmental guns of the international firm[156], SLR Consultancy Ltd[157]. In 2012 SLR issued a press release, with the view of submitting a planning application, for "one of the most ambitious regeneration projects ever seen in Wales"[158] at the Margam mine: 2,500 homes, new schools, neighbourhood services, the restoration of a river corridor and the creation of two lakes whose geo-thermal heat sources would provide renewable energy for the whole development. Anything else? They'd need to complete coal recovery from the area: about 1.5 million tonnes. Even the most innocent of minds couldn't help feeling a tad cynical.

The public's capacity to trust the word of any company associated with the site was further tested when, in January 2013, two former directors of Celtic Energy were charged with conspiracy to defraud, in relation to the transfer of the freehold for the Margam mine and for two other mines in Glyn Neath and the Upper Swansea Valley[159]. A Serious Fraud Office investigation has been on-going since January 2011.

I visited the mine at the end of 2012. One minute I was driving along a narrow country lane; the next I was in a scraped and shattered landscape. It's registered as a film set and I'm surprised there haven't been any takers yet: its monumental water filled void and bleak overburden mounds, from the waste removed from previous mining operations, are classic *Dr Who* territory. It did appeal to a musician from Kenfig Hill, Jayce Lewis[160], who filmed a video for his last single in the abandoned engineering shed.

The mine does have a desolate industrial fascination to it but that's more to do with the silence and the absence of heavy machinery as well as the encroachments nature has already made: patches of ground covering plants and deer tracks in the old truck lanes. And I remind myself that I didn't have to live alongside the mine while coal was being blasted out of the ground for seven years.

The river corridor in SLR's proposal is the Nant Craig yr Aber which was diverted through another part of the site to enable excavation to take place. Its bed is coated with ochre from mine water, not from the recent excavations, but from the old Aberbaiden colliery which flooded after closure. That's more than fifty years ago and still, on average, the mine waters discharge 10 tonnes of iron into the river every year[161]. This is the kind of lasting damage heavy industry can inflict on the landscape.

Port Talbot "has in general endured far, far more than its share of industrial pollution and visual blight, supposedly in the interests of the British economy".[162] And the economic argument card continues to be played. "The Proposed Development will bring committed financial investment to the local area," promised a report, prepared by Pegasus Planning Group on behalf of REG WindPower, for a 2012 planning application[163] for 5 wind turbines on Mynydd Brombil, the lower south western slope of Mynydd Margam. The local authority has asked for more information on the environmental impact, holding off any decision before the summer of 2013.

Port Talbot has paid, and paid dearly, for the loss of our natural landscapes, "land turned over and built on for hundreds of years in the interests of profit, profit deriving from some of the most unkind industrial processes".[164] It's time to value what we still possess, what has been so slowly recovered, what still needs time to heal.

> again this year
> the wind-sown welsh poppies
> flower between stones

notes

1. Evans, *Taibach*, p.216
2. Hanson, *Outline* p.61
3. http://www.historicalporttalbot.com/di-botcher.html
4. http://www.historicalporttalbot.com/robert-blythe.html
5. http://en.wikipedia.org/wiki/Bernard_Fox_(actor)
6. http://www.ptlt.org.uk/
7. Their rehearsal rooms can be found behind Taibach library.
8. Hanson, *Outline*, p.148
9. http://www.jacknicholsonlookalike.co.uk/
10. http://www.porttalbotcymricchoir.co.uk
11. http://www.corafanedd.co.uk
12. See West: Sandfields Estate
13. Central: Aberafan Shopping Centre http://www.bertevansartist.co.uk
14. http://www.historicalporttalbot.com/ray-davies.html
15. http://rarebit.weebly.com/
16. http://www.artandsoultatu.com
17. http://www.porttalbotcameraclub.org
18. http://www.fountainfineart.com/artists/thumbnails/artist_thumbs.php?supplier_id=31
19. http://www.starvinjacks.co.uk
20. Cadw record 14160
21. http://anglicanhistory.org/england/stanton_clayton.html

22.http://en.wikipedia.org/wiki/R._S._Thomas

23. http://en.wikipedia.org/wiki/John_Loughborough_Pearson

24.George, p.39

25. See Roberts Jones, *Welcome to Town*

26. Cadw record 23255

27. Minutes of the Margam District Urban Council 9.2.1902/3?

28. *Ibid* 16.7.1919

29. Cadw record 23256

30. http://en.wikipedia.org/wiki/Louis_Frederick_Roslyn

31. Cadw record 23257

32. Hanson, *Outline* p.91

33. Cadw record 23258

34. A bandstand on Aberafan Beach was removed for the construction of the first promenade c.1900. The bandstand in Vivian Park, Sandfields Estate, was dismantled in the late 1960s.

35. NPT CBC - http://tiny.cc/gh8dqw

36. The name Taibach supplanted Crosswen, or Groeswen, towards the end of 18th century, Evans, *Taibach*, p.22

37. Evans, *Taibach*, p.21, pp.25-7

38. Evans, *Taibach* RFC, p.24

39. Cadw record 22807

40. Hanson, *Profile*, p.38

41. Williams, *Richard Burton Diaries*, Introduction. His first diary for 1939/40 records 42 cinema visits.

42. Cach is Welsh for shit, rather more visceral than the English 'fleapit'.

43. Evans, *Taibach* p.182

44. Williams, *Richard Burton Diaries*, 1.1.1940

45. http://uk.imdb.com/title/tt0033090/

46. Cadw record 22806

47. http://en.wikipedia.org/wiki/Crimean_War

48. Demolished in 1912 because of subsidence. Evans, *Taibach*, p.45

49. For Morfa Pit see South: Steelworks

50. Coflein: http://tiny.cc/ljedrw

51. http://en.wikipedia.org/wiki/Muntz_metal

52. Evans, *Taibach* p.70

53. *Ibid*, p.71

54. *Ibid*

55. Coflein: http://tiny.cc/21edrw

56. See South: The Steelworks

57. Evans, *Taibach* p.70

58. Richard Jenkins moved to a lodging house in Connaught Street in 1943, the home of his mentor, P.H. Burton, whose name he subsequently adopted.

59. *Western Mail*, 14.7. 2010

60. Hutchinson, London, New Authors Ltd.

61. *Oxford Companion to Australian Literature*: http://www.answers.com/topic/john-naish

62. Naish, p.30/31

63. 25.5.1937 and 21.7.1937

64. http://www.lunacyboutique.co.uk/

65. See Central: Port Talbot town centre

66. *Vogue* UK, November 2012, No.71 in Gallery: http://tiny.cc/560hqw

67. www.taibachrfc.co.uk

68. Barrie, J.M., *Peter and Wendy*, C. Scribner's Sons, New York (1911), Chapter 4

69. Evans, *Taibach RFC*, p.23/4

70. Built in 1894

71. http://www.historicalporttalbot.com/clive-jenkins.html

72. Cadw record 23253. There's a plaque on a house at the corner of Tan y Groes Place and Dyffryn Road that commemorates the site of the *hen dŷ cwrdd*, the old meeting house, a farm building the Dyffryn congregation used, 1780-1841, before the chapel was built.

73. Coady, Matthew, 'The Man in Half Moon Street', *Daily Mirror*, 4.9.1968

74. *Ibid*

75. Pattinson, Terry, 'Obituary: Clive Jenkins', *The Independent* 23.9.1999

76. http://www.wgcada.org/peer_mentoring_social_enterprise.php

77. Built in 1966 to replace Tir Caradoc, an eighteenth century house and former home of Dr John Hopkin Davies, acquired by the Taibach & Port Talbot Workingmen's club in 1920 and demolished in 1964.

78. Part of Mynydd Margam: an historic patchwork quilt full of 'cymoedd' (valleys) and 'tonnau' (surfaces/slopes) and 'creigiau' (rocks). Glamorgan-Gwent Archaeological Trust: http://tiny.cc/y0vgrw

79. Evans, *Taibach*, p.36/7

80. http://www.st-theodore.org/saint-peters-church/

81. *Transactions of Port Talbot Historical Society* No.3, Vol III, 1984, 'Minutes of MUDC', p.20

82. Toolis, Kevin, 'The Hunt for the Saturday Night Strangler', *Guardian* 18.1.2003 – http://tinyurl.com/b9qq83x

83. http://www.malpeetk9security.com/#

84. http://www.liquidfriction.com/

85. http://www.hafodgrange.co.uk/

86. Ha/f is summer in Welsh.

87. Evans, *Taibach* p.104

88. http://en.wikipedia.org/wiki/Llyn_Brianne

89. See North: M4 for the story about old Margam.

90. Excavated by Sir Mortimer Wheeler in 1921 who uncovered a stone chamber containing fragments of charred human bones. Evans, *Taibach* p.11

91. Evans, *Taibach* p.165

92. See Central: Aberafan

93. Movie of Paul Potts' life shot around Port Talbot in 2012: http://uk.imdb.com/title/tt1196956/

94. *Daily Mirror* 5.6.1962

95. http://www.ronevanspies.com/

96. Peter Finch, the series editor for the Real books, suggested I make a comparison with Cardiff's Clark's pies – http://www.clarkspies.co.uk. I don't think so.

97. Hughes, Colin, *Lime, Lemon & Sarsaparilla, The Italian Community in South Wales 1881-1945*

98. There's a small chapel in Bardi cemetery dedicated to the victims of the *Arandora Star*.

99. Evans, *Taibach* pp. 93-95

100. See North: M4

101. To be relocated once the new peripheral road, Harbour Way, opens in 2013

102. http://www.corussailing.org.uk

103. http://www.museumwales.ac.uk/en/rhagor/article/bando/

104. *Ibid*

105. http://www.margamcountrypark.co.uk

106. You Tube: http://www.youtube.com/watch?v=sRDM1AQVcfo

107. www.waleshistory.co.uk

108. Evans, *Taibach* pp.12/13

109. Their discovery in the area suggests the presence of a flourishing Celtic monastery.

110. http://www.margamabbey.co.uk/page6.html
111. http://www.margamabbey.co.uk/
112. A French order that had spread rapidly through Great Britain by the end of the twelfth century.
113. Cadw record 14149
114. Cadw record 14155
115. Evans, *Margam Abbey*, p.51.
116. *Ibid*, p.53
117. http://www.monasticwales.org/source/549
118. Evans, *Margam Abbey*, p.99
119. http://www.museumwales.ac.uk/en/margam_house/
120. Hughes, 'Thomas Mansel Talbot of Margam & Penrice', pp. 75/6
121. Evans, *Margam Abbey* p.36
122. http://en.wikipedia.org/wiki/Inigo_Jones
123. Cadw record 14153
124. *Evening Post* 5.10.2012
125. *Evening Post* 17.12.2012
126. Moore, p.22
127. Hughes, *Margam Castle* p.78
128. *Evening Post* 29.10.2011
129. http://en.wikipedia.org/wiki/Thomas_Hopper_(architect)
130. Cadw record 14170
131. Cadw record 23275
132. His cousin, Henry Fox Talbot, the inventor of photography, was a regular visitor at Margam. A daguerreotype of Margam Castle, taken in 1841 by Revd. Calvert Jones and held at the National Library of Wales, is reputedly the first photograph taken in Wales. Coppock, pp.17/18
133. Hughes, *C.R.M. Talbot*, p.26
134. Evans, *Taibach* p.87
135. http://en.wikipedia.org/wiki/Window_tax
136. By the beginning of the twentieth century, under Emily Talbot's directions, there were 8 bathrooms.
137. The elaborate marble and alabaster Mansel family tombs, dating from the early seventeenth century, are in the south aisle of the church. See Cadw record 14148 for St Mary's Abbey Church.
138. Completed in 1881 by H.H. Armstead, best known for his sculptures for the podium of the Albert Memorial.
139. Hughes, *C.R.M. Talbot,*, p.32
140. *The Independent,* 30.1.1996
141. www.smokescreen.org.uk
142. *Western Mail* 24.3.2003
143. Goodall, p.51
144. Hughes, *Margam Castle*, pps.70-71. The two Margam House paintings were withdrawn and sent to the Talbot Fletchers at Saltoun.
145. Hughes, John Vivian, *Margam Castle*, p.71
146. http://en.wikipedia.org/wiki/Ralph_Hancock
147. A feature of landscape design, usually a ditch, designed to separate areas of land without interrupting the view.
148. http://goape.co.uk/days-out/margam
149. http://www.field-studies-council.org/centres/margamdiscoverycentre.aspx
150. RIBA: http://tiny.cc/ci2gpw

151. Cadw record 23261
152. One of the later barns has a stone inset – ECT 1911– under the eaves: the initials of Emily Talbot. Evidence of her ownership and financial aid to the farm.
153. http://en.wikipedia.org/wiki/Tondu
154. *Evening Post*, 21/11/2009: http://tinyurl.com/aj4aumk and 2/8/2010: http://tinyurl.com /av579ab
155. http://www.oakregenerationgroup.com/margam/index.html
156. http://www.slrconsulting.com/
157. http://www.slrconsulting.com/
158. Oak Regeneration: http://tinyurl.com/b3o43pd
159. *Evening Post* 25.1.2013
160. http://www.jaycelewis.com
161. Environment Agency Wales Newsletter July 2010
162. Coppock, p.12,
163. NPTCBC Planning Portal: P2012/0638 – 'Non Technical Summary'
164. Coppock, p.16

AFTERWORD

On 23 March 2012 I posted on the Port Talbot Old and New Facebook page[1] asking people for their memories about Port Talbot, big and little things they missed, from pick'n'mix in Woolworths to the Miami Beach Amusement Park. I underestimated the enthusiasm of the group's members: over 100 people[2], 677 posts and nearly 8,000 words later it was looking more like a book of its own and I was panicking over a rash promise to use the list in *Real Port Talbot*!

Food was a prominent theme, as was the loss of some wonderful architecture and popular landmarks. It seemed that people were literally and metaphorically hungry for their past and that gave me the framework to select and shape some of the material into the poem below. Gill Roberts at the *Evening Post* ran with the story and published the poem on 4th February 2013. It's a tribute to the people of the town, a record of their generosity and warmth. Thank you.

HUNGER

You'd think us starved by the way we mourn
a steamed pie, Len's rissoles, an Eynon's custard slice,
a pasty in the fat from the chippie by the Burgess Green.
But we're talking more than food. Yes, we remember

the cafes: Moruzzi's, Viazzani's, The Continental.
Yes, we remember when you couldn't get a table
at the weekend in The Grand. And the pop delivery vans
that mapped the streets of our town. Yes: the streets

of our town. Beach Hill, Hospital Road with only
its hospital wall, Llewellyn Street facing its own ghost,
Green Park, High Street, The Causeway, Cwmafan Square.
And framed within the memory of their names:

New Hall, The Walnut Tree, The Mountain School,
The Vivian Park and Dock and Jersey Beach Hotels,
the indoor market, the Jubilee Shopping Hall,
the imposing stone of the Post Office in Station Road.

Remember the Boating Pool along the Prom,
Miami Beach Amusement Fair, the putting green
in Tollgate Park? And the latest names added
to the litany of what is lost: Royal Buildings,

Port Talbot Railway & Dock Offices, Custom House.
The Afan Lido. Times change, we're told.
You're just nostalgic for a past that keeps you young.
But there's more to it than that: these are the stories

of our lives, the threads of history that make us
who we are: people from a town of copper, coal,
iron, steel and sand, a town that's more than the view
glimpsed by cars passing on the M4. We're hungry

for our past because what remains is slowly going,
going, gone. Enough now. And with enough of us
tides can change. Storms have slapped
across the bay for centuries. And still we're standing.

Notes

1. https://www.facebook.com/groups/55937132080/permalink/10150639650747081/
2. Gary Andrews, Gary Antolin, Rachel Baltes, Kim Banham, Gareth Bates, Steven Beavis, Marianne Bright, Vance Broad, John Cardy, Paul Clement, Catherine Collins, Frazer Collins, Jan Cositore, Denise Crews, Christopher Daniel, Shirley Crago Was Davies, Williams Desmond, Jamie Discos, Alison Dodd, Kerry Doyle, Christine Duggan, Nigel Eley, Julie Ellis, Annette Evans, Gareth Evans, Kelvyn Evans, Sian Evans, Ceri Davies Fletcher, Rhian Gadd, Samantha Fluffy Hill Gallagher, Linda Garvey, Andrea Garvey, Michelle Jovigirl Hartley, Tom Harwood, John Honest, Roderick Hughes, Carl Kirby, Barry Captain Beany Kirk, Paul James, Phil James, Jamie Discos, David Jenkins, Anthony Jones, Georgia Jones, Gerald G Jones, Lianne Jones, Lisa Jones, Margaret Buckingham Jones, TC Jones, Adrian Lewis, Ann Lewis, Darren Lewis, Jamie Lewis, Jen Lewis, Lorna Lewis, Simon Lewis, Cathy Llewellyn, Lisa Loveday, Helen Lund, Martin Mccarthy, Julie Mctague, Linda Martin, Jan Mason, Mike Matthews, Karen Morgan, Colin Charles Morris, Roger Needs, Debbie Newman, Gwyn Nichols, Shaun O'Brien, Jenny O'Kane, Craig Owen, Gary Owen, Chris Painter, Paula Paisley, Gwyneth Mary Parry, Meryl Partridge, Robbie Phillips, Lisa Rinaldi, Arfon Roberts, Anthony Rose, Peter Ross, Sian Rosser, Gareth Swanter Sandbrook, Linda Sharp, Christopher Wayne Sheehy, Bryan Smith, Joanne Southcott, Sue Sullivan, Lorraine Suter Stevenson, Sync Speed, Marc Tanner, Amanda Taylor, Brian Thomas, Diane Thomas, Julian Thomas, Myra Thomas, Terry Townend, Brenda Turner, Janine Underwood, Andrea Walters, Dorothy Williams, Hugh Raymond Philip Williams, Lisa Williams, Martyn Williams, Susan Bamsey Williams.

ADDENDUM 2021

"Change is the only constant in life." What was true for Heraclitus in the sixth century has been manifestly accurate for Port Talbot from the eighteenth until the twenty-first. Change for the good and the bad, by natural and industrial catalysts, and in the name of greed, progress, improvement and indifference. But I'm happy that key changes to the town, since the book's publication in 2013, fall into the improvement category.

CENTRAL: ABERAFAN SHOPPING CENTRE pp.28-31

Well done, Hacer Developments! Aberafan House, sitting alongside the shopping centre, has been an architectural carbuncle, or 'one of the M4 corridor's most prominent buildings' as their website preferred to call it, since it was built in the early 1970s. But now it's had a £4.7 million makeover, courtesy of the Welsh government's Vibrant and Viable Places funding, I'm more inclined to agree. The redundant offices were converted into forty-one energy efficient and affordable housing association flats in 2018 and the refurb also extended to the riverside area around the building. It makes my heart glad that Hacer supported the local economy by using local tradespeople for their project.[1]

CENTRAL: PLAZA & STATION ROAD, pp.41-54

It's glory days again for the old Plaza cinema as its conversion into a community venue, to include a café, gym, conference area, recording studio and shops, nears completion. The project is funded jointly by the European Regional Development Fund, the Welsh Government and Neath Port Talbot Council and should be open by the end of 2021. BAM Construction[2], the company behind many iconic buildings in Wales, have preserved the fabulous Grade II listed art-deco frontage, with cream faience tiles, and added a new-build at the rear with a giant skylight over a main atrium. You can follow its progress on the Facebook page, 'The New Plaza Project – YMCA Port Talbot'.

Just west of the Plaza, Port Talbot's Banksy is on display in Ty'r Orsaf, a residential/retail new-build on the site of the former police station, and opposite the new Transport Hub for buses, taxis and cycles. The Hub's pedestrianised area also hosts the Port Talbot Farmers' Market that re-opened in June 2021 following the easing of Covid restrictions. Banksy's 'Season's Greetings' appeared on two walls of a Taibach garage just before Christmas in 2018. From one angle, it shows a kid in a bobble hat trying to catch what look like snowflakes on his tongue but the painting around the corner reveals the flakes as ash rising from a bonfire in a metal skip. Art dealer John Brandler bought the painting from the garage owner and in May 2019 all 4.5 tonnes of it were transported to its present location. Everyone hopes it'll stay in the town and that some kind of art space can be created around it.[3]

The Banksy is already part of ARTwalk Port Talbot, an art trail and free app launched in June 2021 which aims to identify the town with world class street art. It's a Heritage Lottery Wales-funded project, led by Cardiff-based theatre director Paul Jenkins, and includes work by renowned British graffiti artist Ame72 as well as local street artists, Rarebit, Bims and Mongo Gushi, plus a string of newly-commissioned, site-specific work.[4] You can download the app by scanning the QR code on posters around the town or from Theatr3's website.[5]

Meanwhile, at the other pedestrianized end of Station Road, Glanafan School, which opened in 1896 as Port Talbot's County Grammar School, has been demolished and the site redeveloped mostly for housing. The iconic nineteenth century red brick façade has been preserved behind contemporary glass fronted units that will soon be a community hub for BID[6], Port Talbot's Business Improvement District. It'll offer bookable meeting and work-spaces, a business advice service, pop-ups, market stalls and a range of other support for the town's businesses and retailers. The closure of the school led to a predictable drop in retail traffic at a Gregg's, opposite. So now, if you want one of their humungous custard slices or a golden, flaky, corned beef bake, you have to walk to their store in the Aberafan Shopping Centre. Let's be honest, the extra exercise isn't a bad thing.

NORTH: BRYN pp.93-98

The Welsh village that could be surrounded by 'monster' 750ft turbines[7] was a local headline in October 2020. Energy firms, Coriolis Energy Ltd and ESB, are in a pre-application consultation to erect twenty-six turbines on Margam mountain, from Brombil to Bryn, the village in the headline, and over towards Maesteg. These really are monsters, the biggest turbines you can get, and will have significant visual and environmental impacts on the landscape, but we are asked to offset that with enough renewable energy to power over 125,000 homes. There were several public exhibitions in June 2021 and there's also a website to persuade people about the benefits.[8] Neath Port Talbot Council has given permission to erect a mast to measure wind speeds and velocities and, after further consultations between now and Spring 2022, an application will be submitted to the Welsh Government.

Progress and opinion have always clashed. In the 1930s Rudyard Kipling and John Maynard Keynes complained to *The Times* about the first electricity pylons disfiguring the landscape. In the opposite camp a group of poets led by Stephen Spender were so inspired by the metal pylons they called themselves The Pylon Poets.[9] The extra dimension to the arguments these days is, of course, climate change and the need for renewable energy sources.

WEST: BAGLAN BAY pp.104-108

How could I have missed this huge building, The Quays, the administrative headquarters of Neath Port Talbot Council, on the banks of the River Nedd at the western end of the Baglan Energy Park back in 2013? Although, in my defence, the new road and bridge to access that half of the Park weren't completed until 2015[10]. And it was a long walk around. The Quays opened in 2007 to help centralise services within the borough and by around 2014 staff from council offices at Aberafan House also moved there. The site's latest addition, currently under construction, is a three-storey 'net-positive' office building[11]. Think of it as a small power station: excess energy from the building, provided by solar and other renewable technologies, will be converted into hydrogen, at the nearby Hydrogen Centre run by the University of South Wales, and used to fuel hydrogen vehicles. This is the kind of carbon footprint-speak I understand. And there's more.... To the south, St. Modwen completed the largest photovoltaic park on a brownfield site in Wales in 2014: 20,000 panels producing enough electricity for 1.200 homes every year[12].

Plans for a new school on the site shifted to the playing fields at its eastern boundary, so, strictly speaking, a part of Sandfields Estate. Ysgol Bae Baglan replaced four schools in the borough, including Glanafan in the centre of Port Talbot and Sandfields Comprehensive School (p.124) both of which closed in 2016. Ysgol Bae Baglan was selected by Microsoft as a 'Microsoft Showcase School'[13] for the academic year 2016-17. In 2017 it was the winner of the National Eisteddfod of Wales Gold Medal for Architecture and a finalist or winner for a whole clutch of other awards.[14] And, in 2019, a team of girls from the school that included, (proud aunt shout-out) my great-niece, Ffion, were the Winners of Young Business Dragons.[15] But you don't have to wear socks and carry a book bag to enjoy the school: all their innovative arts and sporting facilities can be hired by the community outside of school hours.

A second school, Ysgol Gymraeg Ystalyfera Bro Dur, a Welsh language Comprehensive, opened in 2018, on the opposite side of the road on the site previously occupied by Sandfields Comp. *Da iawn, Cyngor Castell-nedd Port Talbot.*

WEST: ABERAFAN BEACH, THE PROM, PRINCESS MARGARET WAY pp.108-124

2020 saw more foreshore defence work along Aberafan Beach to protect the 1950s sea wall[16], part of the Welsh Government's £150 million Coastal Risk Management Programme. The existing structure was repaired and 30,000 tonnes of rock were laid at the foot of the concrete steps like a small army preparing to face one of the biggest bullies in the world: the sea.

Very different kinds of coastal support are now available at the western end of the Prom after decades of wilderness status. Toilets. Yay! And coffee and ice-cream. Double Yay! The coffee shop, Memo Beach, is owned and managed by Mehmet and Suat who strengthen local ties by selling Argie's Coffee (Bridgend) and Joe's Ice-Cream (Swansea). Mix both of those together and you get a cracking *affogato*. And soon, even the bay's bruising winds won't stop you from enjoying it: the cabin is getting an indoor seating extension.

It is so refreshing to see independent businesses run by local people flourishing along The Prom rather than the ubiquitous chains, and Richard Hibbard, Dragons and former Wales international rugby player, is responsible for the most recent addition. The Front, a snappy looking drive-through and eat-in Bar & Kitchen gratefully replaces the ill-fated burger bar on the previously forlorn Hollywood Park site. In fact, this whole area has been transformed since I last wrote about it. The old Chinese restaurant was taken over by award-winning Cinnamon Kitchen, and the spanking new leisure centre opened in 2016. The site of the demolished Afan Lido is still empty but there's serious interest from Persimmons Homes for upmarket housing. Add to all this a refurbished Aqua Splash for the kids, a new outdoor gym, and colourful hub and decking for the Welsh Surf School and you'll understand why Aberafan Beach deserves, in buckets (did you see what I did there?), the 2021 Seaside Award.

But there is a little niggle in all this the novelty: Associated British Ports are restricting access to the breakwater pier for safety reasons[17]. They're erecting a guardrail along the first 150 metres then a fence to close off the remaining 250, denying access to fishing enthusiasts who favour the end of the pier. And the rest of us, who treat it and the sea with respect and don't head out there at night, or in a storm, or while drunk. But it's impossible to keep the box of idiots permanently closed, so I do understand ABP's dilemma. Neath Port Talbot Council are trying to negotiate some kind of safe public access to the seaward end in the future.

SOUTH: THE STEELWORKS pp.174-183

It's still here. And that's a huge relief to the town, and for the local and national economy, after a media headline in 2015 roared, *British Steel Industry Goes Into Meltdown*[18] and when, in March 2016, Tata Steel announced an intention to sell off its UK plants.[19] But the Leave result in the EU referendum had an unexpected effect. Tata confirmed a commitment to their UK operation with a view to making it self-sustaining and not relying on funding from its Indian parent company. But they remain in talks with Westminster as to what long term support the UK government can provide for a foundational industry disadvantaged by energy costs and cheap imports in a post-Brexit climate.

You can get a more up-close view of the Tata plant since Harbour Way opened in October 2013, funded by £54 million of European money. This major link road from the M4 and the A48 at Margam to the docklands area will allow for the development of two sites into waterfront business and industry centres: Harborside and the Port Talbot Waterfront Enterprise Zone. It sliced though the Tata Steel golf course, reducing the 1970s 14 hole course to 9, and now runs directly alongside Tata Stores, The Academy (training centre) and the Visitor Centre.

Tata, Tata, Tata, the edges of the blue Stores announce as you drive past. *Helo, Helo, Helo*, feels equally appropriate as regeneration works get underway.

all of us are holding out our hands sometimes empty sometimes full

THE BIGGER PICTURE

More universal events in the intervening years have also had an impact on the town.

In June 2016, Neath Port Talbot voted to leave Europe by 56.8% to 43.2%[20] despite the indefatigable Remain campaign of one Port Talbot man, Steven Bray. From September 2017, on every day parliament was sitting, 'Mr Stop Brexit' began seven hour shifts on the pavement at Westminster's Old Palace Yard warning people the UK was heading for disaster. He regularly interrupted media broadcasts with loudhailers and five metre flag poles over a period of 847 days.[21] NPT weren't alone in their Brexit support: Wales voted to leave by 53% to 47% despite the country, and NPT in particular, being major beneficiaries of EU funding. But perhaps feeling ignored by a Westminster Conservative government, on top of the insidiously misleading Leave campaign about the NHS, immigration and sovereignty, tipped the balance.

A triptych of general elections saw the Labour party's hold on the constituency of Aberavon remain adequately tight. Stephen Kinnock won the nomination to fight the Aberavon seat for Labour after Hywel Francis MP[22] stood down, and retained a majority vote in 2015, 2017 and 2019. Kinnock is political Marmite – people tend to either love him or hate him, the latter not necessarily for logical reasons. An ex-miner complained, after discovering Kinnock had written the foreword to my latest book, 'The name Kinnock tends to leave a nasty taste in the mouth of many miners. We will never forget his father Lord Kinnock.' But ask Port Talbot's steelworkers, who Kinnock has worked tirelessly for in connection with the British Steel pension scheme, and you'll get a completely different response. I can't say I love Marmite to the exclusion of all else, but I absolutely don't hate it.

And then the pandemic in 2020. Up to July 2021 there'd been 12,028 confirmed cases of Covid in the Neath Port Talbot administrative area and 475 deaths.[23] My Dad was one of them. He arrived here from Llanelli in 1957, with my mother and older sister, on a tsunami of expansion at the Steelworks and into a new council house on Sandfields Estate which he bought when he retired in 1986. Sadly, Mam also died in March 2021, in that same house where I was born. And now I live there. So many memories. And so many children's, grandchildren's and great-grandchildren's pets buried in the garden over sixty years to bamboozle archaeologists in future centuries!

Heraclitus also said, "Character is destiny", that our fate or future is determined by our own inner character. Mam and Dad created their future in Port Talbot, my future, with fortitude and generosity, the same characteristics I associate most with the people of the town. We face challenges. We move forward. We see the light. And how could we not with all those magnificent sunsets we marvel at from Aberafan Beach.

beach sunset
a woman kisses the light
on her baby's face

Notes

1. https://www.poblgroup.co.uk/about-us/pobl-story/pobl-story-feb-2018/deputy-leader-visits-aberafan-house-redevelopment/
2. https://www.bam.co.uk/media-centre/news-details/bam-to-remodel-historic-cinema-in-port-talbot
3. *The Guardian* 18th December 2019
4. *Nation Cymru* 3rd July 2021
5. https://theatr3.com/artwalk.html
6. https://www.walesonline.co.uk/news/wales-news/whats-happening-old-glan-afan-20251954
7. https://www.walesonline.co.uk/news/local-news/welsh-village-could-surrounded-monster-19017727
8. https://www.ybryn-windfarm.cymru/
9. https://www.nationalgrid.com/stories/energy-explained/everything-you-ever-wanted-know-about-electricity-pylons
10. https://www.walesonline.co.uk/business/business-news/20m-projects-transforming-baglan-energy-8208089
11. https://businessnewswales.com/7-9-million-technology-centre-for-baglan-energy-park-moves-forward/
12. https://www.stmodwen.co.uk/largest-browfield-solar-park-in-wales-close-to-completion/
13. https://www.fgould.com/uk-europe/projects/ysgol-bae-baglan/
14. https://stridetreglown.com/projects/ysgol-bae-baglan-neath-port-talbot/
15. https://www.young-dragons.co.uk/index-whatwedo
16. https://www.jbaconsulting.com/knowledge-hub/coastal-protection-scheme-to-future-proof-aberavons-promenade/
17. http://thebeach.cymru/abp-to-restrict-access-to-north-pier
18. *The Guardian*, 19th October 2015
19. *The Guardian*, 30th March 2016
20. https://www.bbc.co.uk/news/politics/eu_referendum/results/local/n
21. https://en.wikipedia.org/wiki/Steve_Bray
22. Hywel Francis 1946-2021, Obituary, *The Guardian* 1st March 2021
23. https://www.bbc.co.uk/news/uk-wales-52380643

Other Sources
Welsh Government https://gov.wales/
Neath Port Talbot Council https://www.npt.gov.uk/

WORKS CONSULTED

Local History

Adam, D. John, *Margam Abbey, The Mansel-Talbots & their Tombs*, n.d.

Campbell, Thomas Methuen, 'CRM Talbot: A Welsh Landowner in Politics and History', *Morgannwg* vol 44, 2000

Coppock, Christopher & Ingham, Karen, *HaHa – Margam Revisited*, FFotogallery, Cardiff & Seren, Bridgend 2002

Dumbleton, Bob, *The Second Blitz, The Demolition & Rebuilding of Town Centres in South Wales*, privately published, Cardiff 1977/8?

Evans, A. Leslie, *Margam Abbey*, Port Talbot Historical Society 1996

Evans, A. Leslie, *The Story of Baglan* (Port Talbot), privately published 1970

Evans, A. Leslie, *The Story of Taibach & District*, privately published, Port Talbot 1963 & 2nd edition Alun Books, Port Talbot 1982

Evans, A. Leslie, *Taibach RFC 1884-1984*, Taibach 1985

Fychan, Madog, (Daniel Evans), *Hanes ac Ystyr Enwau Lleoedd as Amaethdai yn Nyffryn Afan, 1889*, translated and edited by Graham Hughes as *Place Names of the Afan Valley*, Corlannau Press, West Nyack, NY 2004

Goodall Peter J.R., *For Whom the Bell Tolls, A Century of Executions*, Gomer, Llandysul 2001

Gray, Thomas, 'Notes on the Granges of Margam Abbey', *Journal of the British Archaeological Association* 1903, reprinted as a pamphlet

Hanson, Ivor, *Profile of a Welsh Town*, privately published Port Talbot 1968

Hanson, Ivor, *Outline of a Welsh Town*, Daffodil Publications, Port Talbot 1971

Howells, Bill, *Antiquities of Margam Mountain*, Llynfi Valley Historical Society 2010

Hughes, Colin, *Lime, Lemon & Sarsaparilla, The Italian Community in South Wales 1881-1945*, Seren 1991 & 2003

Hughes, John Vivian, *C.R.M. Talbot MP FRS, The Wealthiest Commoner* (1803-1890), privately published, Port Talbot 1977

Hughes, John Vivian, *Margam Castle*, West Glamorgan Archive Service 1998

Hughes, John Vivian, 'Thomas Mansel Talbot of Margam &

Penrice', *Gower, Journal of the Gower Society,* Vol 26, 1975, pp. 75/6

Ifan, Will, Afan, *A Welsh Music Maker,* Western Mail and Echo Ltd, Cardiff 1944, reprinted The Afan Glee Society & Elwyn Evans 1980

Jones, Brian, *Port Talbot, A Gallery of Past Personalities,* Vols 1, 2 & 3, privately published 1989, 1990 & 1992

Jones, Eben, *Bryn, The Village in the Hills,* privately published 1989

Jones, Colin Spong, *Percy Hunt, The Great Mavello, Life & Times of a Health & Strength League Athlete,* One Off Publishing, Port Talbot 1999

Lawrence, Ray, *The Collieries of the Afan Valley and the Port Talbot Areas,* privately published, Newport 2008

Lewis, Ivor, *The Afan Fisheries,* Afan Valley Angling Club 1999

Morgan, Keith E, *Around Port Talbot and Aberavon,* Chalford Publishing Company, Gloucester 1997

Moore, Patricia, *Margam Orangery,* Glamorgan Archive Service Publication 1986

Moore, Patricia & Donald, *A Vanished House, Two Topographical Paintings of the Old House at Margam,* Glamorgan, reprinted from *Archaeologia Cambrensis* Vol CXXIII (1974), privately published 1980

Parsons, Denys, *In War and Peace, Port Talbot 1939-1999,* Goldleaf Publishing, Port Talbot 2000

Parsons, Denys, *The Dock Street Story,* Goldleaf Publishing, Port Talbot 1995

Perry, Walter T, *Shifting Sands, Turning Tide & High Tide,* privately published, Port Talbot 2000, 2001 & 2002

Powell, Afan & Thomas, Glyn, *The Rise and Fall of the South Wales Coal Industry with a View of Port Talbot and The Afan Valley,* privately published for the South Wales Miners' Museum, Afan Argoed Country Park, Afan Valley, Port Talbot 1999

Reed, Dennis, *Port Talbot and Aberavon, Past and Present Scenes* Vol 1 & 2, privately published 2012 & 2013

Rees, Arthur, *Some Street and Place Names of the Port Talbot District,* Port Talbot Historical Society, Port Talbot 2004

Rees, William & Cyril, *Brief Historical Surveys of Taibach and Cwmavon,* privately published 1972

Roberts Jones, Sally, *The History of Port Talbot,* Goldleaf Publishing, Port Talbot 1991

Roberts Jones, Sally, *Welcome to Town, A brief account of Port Talbot's Inns,* Alun Books, Port Talbot 1980

Rowlands, John, *Dechreuad a Chynnydd Gweithiau Cwmafan* (1853) translated as *In the Valley Long Ago* by Graham Hughes, privately published, New York 1985

Smith, Clive, *Bygone Railways of the Afan Valley*, Alun Books, Port Talbot 1982

Strawbridge, Don & Thomas, Peter, *Baglan Bay, past, present and future*, BP Chemicals Ltd, Baglan Bay 2001

Thomas, William, *Gleanings from the Fields of Past Years*, privately published 1913

Biography & Autobiography

Burton, Richard, *A Christmas Story*, WW Norton & Co, New York 1991

Davies, Melanie & Barrett-Lee, Lynne, *Never Say Die*, Harper Collins, London 2009

Jenkins, Clive, *All Against the Collar, Struggles of a White-Collar Union Leader*, Methuen, London 1990

Naish, John, *The Clean Breast*, Hutchinson, London 1961

Needs, Chris, *like it is* and *And There's More*, Y Lolfa, Talybont, Ceredigion 2009 & 2011

Voyle-Morgan, Brian, *Bryn and Tonic, Odyssey of a 'Homer'*, Now Look Who's Talking Ltd, Cardiff 1996

Williams Chris, ed., *The Richard Burton Diaries*, Yale University Press 2012

General

Cooper, Tim, *How to Read Industrial Britain*, Ebury Press, London 2011

Davies, John, Jenkins, Nigel, Baines, Menna & Lynch, Peredur I, eds., *The Welsh Academy Encyclopaedia of Wales*, University of Wales Press, Cardiff 2008

Drabble, Margaret, ed., *Oxford Companion to English Literature*, OUP, London 1985

Farley, Paul & Symmons Roberts, Michael, *Edgelands, Journeys into England's True Wilderness*, Vintage Books, London 2012

Isaac, Ian, *When We Were Miners*, Ken Smith Press 2010

Jarvis, Matthew, *Ruth Bidgood*, Writers of Wales, University of Wales Press, Cardiff 2012

Sheers, Owen, *The Gospel of Us*, Seren, Bridgend 2012, text originally published in three volumes, National Theatre of Wales 2011

Williams D.H., *Atlas of Cistercian Lands in Wales*, University of Wales Press, Cardiff 1990

THE PHOTOGRAPHS

THE AUTHOR

Lynne Rees is a poet, novelist, editor and award-winning tutor who was born and grew up on Sandfields Estate, Port Talbot. lynnerees.com and on Twitter @hungrywriting.

ACKNOWLEDGEMENTS

Thanks to Nigel Jenkins, author of *Real Swansea One & Two*, whose encouragement led me towards the real Port Talbot.

Big thanks to all the people I met on walks, in cafés and at meetings, who spoke with me in person and via the numerous Port Talbot Facebook groups. These boundless resources that the book couldn't contain have granted iceberg properties to *Real Port Talbot*: only the peak is visible here. Specific thanks, for their stories and company, for tea and cake, and the devil in the details, go to Gary Antolin, Captain Beany, Lorna Beckett, Wendy Cross, Gwyn & Edna David at Aberbaiden, Richard Derrick, Bernard Donovan, Joan Edwards, Anne Evans of Graig Goch, Graham Hughes, Karen Hughes, Roderick Hughes, Aled Humphries, Ian Isaac, Alex Jones, Georgia Jones, Sally Roberts Jones, Marian & Eric Lewis, Margam Marchers, Chris Needs, C.W. Nicol, Chris Noblett, Bill Matthews, Penny Matthews, Hugh Nicholas, Dennis Reed, Les Sexton, Ian Shakeshaft, Meyrick Sheen, Marco Tambini, Andrew Vicari and John Victor.

Thanks to Ray Davies Snr. for allowing the reproduction of his painting, 'The Viv', to Keith Suter and Damian Owen for their generous lending of books and photographs, and to Sean Pursey for his inspirational photographs that I haven't been able to emulate.

For expanding my horizons: Sebastien Boyeson, sculptor, Robert Dangerfield at Tata Steel, Julia Griffiths at Ysgol Gyfun Rhosafan, Kelvin Hood at the GE Baglan Bay Power Station, Gareth Needham & Alan Thomas at Hafod Grange, Jon Price at the Forestry Commission, Kay Rees and Lee Rogers at Aberafan Shopping Centre, John Smith of St. Modwen, Jonathan Thomas, Site Manager at Margam Mine, Simon Ward at Margam Discovery Centre and Ralph Windeatt of Associated British Ports.

Thank you to staff at NPTCBC who responded patiently to my steady trickle of enquiries and requests; particular thanks to Gill at the Mayor's Parlour and Leader of the Council, Ali Thomas.

And finally, Allen Blethyn, aka The Groes Scholar, The Taibach/Margam Lone Reporter and The History Man. Thank you for your company, generosity and for being my careful reader.

INDEX